T0131803

Fighting Immigration Anarchy

by
Daniel Sheehy

iUniverse Star
New York Bloomington

Fighting Immigration Anarchy

First published by Rooftop Publishing 6/23/06

iUniverse Star
an iUniverse, Inc. imprint

iUniverse books may be ordered through booksellers or by contacting:

iUniverse
1663 Liberty Drive
Bloomington, IN 47403
www.iuniverse.com
1-800-Authors (1-800-288-4677)

ISBN: 978-1-935278-34-4 (pbk)
ISBN: 978-1-935278-35-1 (ebk)

Printed in the United States of America

iUniverse rev. date: 3/11/09

Contents

Barbara Coe

Forced to resign from the police department for reporting crimes committed by illegal aliens, this patriot founded the California Coalition for Immigration Reform, has been a leading organizer to resist the invasion of America, and played a key role in the state's historic Proposition 187.

Joe Guzzardi

Teaching English to immigrants and writing hundreds of columns about open borders helped convince the former Wall Street banker to run for governor of California in the 2003 recall election to bring attention to the illegal immigration crisis.

Tom Tancredo

A one-time schoolteacher, this Colorado congressman has become the leader of the immigration reform movement on Capitol Hill for putting America ahead of party and politics.

Jim Gilchrist, Chris Simcox, and the Minutemen

Retired CPA Jim Gilchrist and former schoolteacher Chris Simcox co-founded the Minuteman Project, bringing the crisis of illegal immigration to the national stage in 2005.

Introduction

When the U.S. House of Representatives in a historic 239-182 vote passed what is arguably the strongest immigration enforcement bill to date at the end of 2005, it was responding to the unrelenting pressure generated by years of efforts from the many individuals whose stories fill this book.

After four decades of mostly ignoring the consequences of increasingly permissive immigration policies, the House suddenly found its backbone. The House bill included at least four of the half-dozen or so most important missing tools needed to slow the flow of new illegal immigration and to encourage the current illegal population in America to return to their home countries, according to Roy Beck, head of NumbersUSA, a national immigration reduction organization.

"The victories that were won both behind the scenes and on the House floor are a testament to the strength and resolve of those members who have heard the will of the American people in their desire to curb illegal immigration and return the United States to the rule of law," Beck said.

The legislation requires businesses to use an electronic system to ensure that employers are not hiring illegal aliens. It authorizes the building of a security fence and other physical infrastructure along 700 miles of the U.S.-Mexico border. The bill calls for the federal government to end its interior catch-and-release program in which it tells local governments to release most of the illegal aliens that they catch. The legislation mandates federal cooperation with local authorities in picking up all illegals they detain. The bill also ends the visa lottery program that annually awards 50,000 green cards to randomly selected winners, marking the first time since 1924 that a chamber of Congress voted to reduce legal immigration. However, Republican leaders would not allow a vote on a proposal to deny citizenship to the hundreds of thousands of babies born in the U.S. each year to illegal aliens.

The House bill infuriated the Mexican government. President Vicente Fox denounced the legislation as "shameful." Foreign Secretary Luis Ernesto Derbez called the border fence "stupid." Mexican workers were urged to denounce "rights violations" in the U.S. Fox hired Texas PR man Rob Allyn, who helped George W. Bush win elections, to influence public opinion in the U.S.

The press in both countries attacked the legislation, as did the U.S. Chamber of Commerce, Hispanic separatist organizations, and other open-borders advocates.

As this book was going to press in early 2006, U.S. Senate leaders were preparing to pass their own immigration legislation that included massive guest-worker programs and some form of amnesty.

Meanwhile, the border war was intensifying. Heavily armed Mexican soldiers were invading Texas, in so-called "incursions," forcing outgunned and outmanned sheriffs' deputies to retreat. Homeland Security Secretary Michael Chertoff called concern over the issue "overblown." President Bush and Defense Secretary Donald Rumsfeld said nothing.

The *Inland Valley Daily Bulletin* in Southern California reported that Mexican alien smugglers were planning to pay violent gang members known as the Mara Salvatrucha and smuggle them into the U.S. to murder Border Patrol agents.

Federal authorities discovered several tunnels in the San Diego area, including "a massive, spectacular tunnel," used for smuggling drugs and people.

In his State of the Union address on January 31, 2006, Bush referred to illegal aliens as "immigrants" and claimed that the U.S. economy "could not function without them."

In response to Bush's speech, Congressman Tom Tancredo called the border crisis "anarchy."

Later, the president also called for more visas for foreign workers to replace America's skilled workers.

(Just weeks before, the Center for Immigration Studies reported that the period between January 2000 and March 2005 marked the highest five-year period of illegal and legal immigration in American history.)

In early February, chaos was spreading. The Mexican Mafia "greenlighted" Hispanic inmates to attack outnumbered black Americans in the Los Angeles County jail system. Two blacks were murdered, and dozens were injured. County Supervisor Gloria Molina predicted the warfare will "absolutely spill out. I hope that's not the case. It will be very dangerous for L.A."

Protests, counter-protests, and other activities were quickly growing across America.

Outside the U.S. Capitol, Minutemen and other patriotic Americans protested Bush's proposed guest-worker amnesty program and urged the government to send military troops to secure the U.S.-Mexico border. Minuteman founder Jim Gilchrist declared that lawmakers who support the president's illegal immigration agenda would be replaced on Election Day in November.

A diverse group of pro-borders candidates were running for Congress: former state representative Randy Graf in Arizona, County Commissioner Robert Vasquez in Idaho, and businessman Sonny Sardo in Southern California, among others. Said candidate Vasquez: "It is easier to cross the border than it is to board an airplane."

Pro-borders candidates also were running on the state and local levels. Arizona gubernatorial candidate Don Goldwater, nephew of the late Senator Barry Goldwater, promised to bring a halt to the illegal-alien invasion by putting National Guard, the Minutemen, the Arizona Rangers, and other volunteer groups on the border.

Concerned Americans were holding a candlelight vigil at Senator Dianne Feinstein's Los Angeles office urging her to support American workers by using her power to stop Senate passage of a guest-worker amnesty program.

University of California professor and open-borders activist Armando Navarro was holding an "Immigration Summit" in

Riverside to plan protests, boycotts, and marches against the House bill.

Los Angeles-area city councils representing large illegal-alien populations were passing ordinances prohibiting police from cooperating with federal authorities and enforcing immigration laws.

In Las Vegas, organizers for the group Secured Borders U.S.A. were continuing two years of work collecting notarized signatures from fed-up Americans across the country and making plans to deliver the petitions in trucks to the U.S. Capitol.

Latino Americans for Immigration Reform and the Texas Minutemen were planning a demonstration at Bush's ranch in Crawford because the president has refused to direct federal authorities to "round up illegal aliens in our cities and willfully failed to put our military on the border."

In Indianapolis, the Indiana Federation for Immigration Reform and Enforcement and the Indiana Minuteman chapter were planning a protest at the Mexican Consulate. "We want the Mexican government to stop interfering with the will of the American people when it comes to securing our borders and enforcing our immigration laws!" they announced.

On the steps of the state capitol building in Atlanta, a group calling itself "Coalition for a New Georgia" derided state legislative efforts seeking to crack down on illegal aliens and those who hire them. Across the street, activist D.A. King staged an opposing rally. "We are here because we demand that the United States secure its borders as is required by the Constitution," King told the press. "I'm very encouraged. What you see here is the beginning of a citizen uprising."

And while all of this was happening, U.S. government leaders were working to end 230 years of American independence by merging the U.S. with Mexico and Canada, unbeknownst to most Americans, as you will read in chapter twelve.

Today's activism to save America as a sovereign nation is the result of years of work by the visionary patriots who are the subjects of this book. The pro-borders political movement stands on the shoulders of individuals who saw the immigration crisis coming and warned of the looming danger.

This book profiles some of the courageous men and women who have been willing to put their reputations, resources, and even their lives on the line for what they believe. These extraordinary people refused to surrender to the propaganda and the powerful forces pushing massive immigration and open borders. Working in their own distinctive ways, these heroes have contributed greatly to energizing today's rising opposition to open borders. Now, read about America's immigration anarchy and the people who are battling to save the nation.

Part One

The Crisis
and the Victims

1 | A Stranger in My Own Country

In 1964, Southern California was paradise for many people, including me. That was the year I moved to the Golden State from Maryland with my parents and brother. I was twelve years old. It also was the year before Congress decided to open its door to mass immigration.

My dad had been transferred to a new aerospace company in Canoga Park, which is located at the western end of the sprawling San Fernando Valley in Los Angeles County. The Valley consisted of mostly middle-class Americans at that time.

We bought a house in a new development in Canoga Park near the rocky Santa Susanna Mountains and just a few miles from the pass leading into the Simi Valley. Many Hollywood westerns were shot on those locations. Our small development was nearly surrounded by orange groves, open spaces, and movie ranches, where TV series such as *Lassie* were filmed.

Canoga Park was so peaceful that we didn't lock our house or car doors. California schools, including my junior high, were the envy of the nation. I remember learning to ride horses with my dad at a ranch in nearby Chatsworth, a mostly rural area back then. I remember our family driving on surface streets and freeways, where there was no gridlock, to Hollywood to see movies at famous Grauman's Chinese Theatre. And I remember us driving up to central California to vacation at one of our nation's natural wonders, the Sequoia National Park. Those are some of my memories.

But my dad lost his job in layoffs at his company, and we ended up moving back to our birthplace, Binghamton, New York, in 1968. I was heartbroken and dreamed of returning to sunny Southern California.

That day finally came twenty years later in 1988 when I left my position as media relations manager for United Airlines in Chicago and moved to the Los Angeles area to manage corporate communications for United's Mileage Plus subsidiary. I was thrilled to be returning to the Golden State.

A Flood of Immigrants

However, Southern California was not the place I remembered fondly. Because of massive legal and illegal immigration, the population was exploding. The immigration boom was also occurring in other states, but California was impacted the most.

Millions of poor and uneducated people from south of the border, mostly Mexicans, had flooded into California and other states to seek jobs and take advantage of free social services. The nearly three million illegal aliens amnestied by Congress and President Reagan in 1986 encouraged millions more to come illegally. People also were pouring in from other parts of the world.

I remember half joking with my buddies that Americans seemed to be disappearing. In fact, they were disappearing. Thousands of native-born Americans were leaving the Golden State because the California they grew up in was becoming another country, and the quality of life was deteriorating.[1]

Initially I did not comprehend all of the consequences. But as the years passed, those consequences were becoming clearer as the Los Angeles area increasingly resembled a Third-World city.

I was especially angry about illegal immigration because it wasn't fair to native-born American citizens or legal immigrants—not to mention the fact that illegal immigration is simply illegal. I sometimes asked friends, some of whom disagreed with my views, "Suppose the roles were reversed and millions of poor Americans invaded Mexico;

how would Mexicans feel, and what would they do?" However, I rarely expressed these common-sense thoughts outside of my social circle for fear of being called a racist, even though my concerns were about the rule of law, the effects of overpopulation, and the American way of life. "Political correctness," a nice term for censorship, silenced many Americans then as it does today.

In 1994, millions of Californians voted in favor of ballot measure Proposition 187. The initiative would have denied most social services to illegal aliens and eliminated a magnet for people to enter the state unlawfully. The measure passed overwhelmingly. Then pro-illegal-alien groups set out to overturn the will of the voters through lawsuits and legal delays. Several years later, Governor Gray Davis killed the proposition in a backroom deal with open-borders politicians and organizations, angering Californians. The proposition was never enacted, and the invasion and quality of life continued to worsen.

By the late 1990s, Californians were increasingly fed up with the immigrant tidal wave. In the worst affected areas, some stayed home to escape the constant traffic gridlock or to avoid communication barriers as foreign languages, mostly Spanish, were becoming more prevalent than English. And, shockingly, many foreigners were arrogant toward Americans, with no regard for American interests or culture.

Awakening After 9/11

However, it took the terrorist attacks of September 11, 2001, to fully awaken Americans to an immigration crisis and our federal government's failure to protect us. Since the 9/11 hijackers broke U.S. immigration laws, the effects of rising immigration and porous borders begged for our attention.[2] Web sites, talk radio, cable TV shows, and books discussed the issues. Community meetings focused on the problems. Here, this writer came to know the people featured in this book, as well as many others in the growing movement fighting to end illegal immigration, re-establish national borders, and bring common sense back to immigration.

These knowledgeable and patriotic Americans exposed the root cause of symptoms addressed in newspapers and news broadcasts:

mass immigration. For years Congress has been deliberately importing millions of foreigners legally and illegally to drive down wages in America and gain new voters. Well-funded and politically powerful pro-illegal-alien organizations in America gained political influences. The Mexican activists' agenda, led in part by U.S. elected officials, sought to re-conquer the Southwestern United States for Mexico through uncontrolled immigration. And, multinational corporations aided the immigrant flood to achieve the globalists' goal of a new world order of erased borders, increased corporate power, and decreased individual rights.

Our elected officials created this disaster, voted to provide numerous incentives that encourage more immigration, favored aliens over American citizens, and taxed citizens to pay for all of it. The media deceived Americans about immigration and pushed the open-borders agenda. We were collectively duped and betrayed.

From Paradise to Third World

And what about the California I remember from my youth? It no longer exists. The once-golden state is many billions of dollars in debt. Most of the Los Angeles region has gone from paradise to Third World and become a Mexican colony surrounded by affluent gated communities. Much of this cultural transformation has occurred since 1988, two years after the federal government's ill-advised amnesty triggered a nonstop flood of people mostly from Mexico.

In the 1960s, there were six million residents in Los Angeles County. Today that number has climbed to a staggering and unmanageable 10 million. Between 1994 and 2004, California's population jumped by more than five million people, bringing the total to more than 36 million. Virtually 100 percent of the population growth for both California and L.A. is from illegal aliens, legal immigrants, and children born to them.[3]

While local TV news anchors eagerly report on the latest celebrity trial, cosmetic surgery procedure, or movie blockbuster, the Los Angeles area is crumbling under the immigration-driven population explosion and importation of massive poverty. The region has officially become America's poverty capital[4] and has the worst traffic in the nation.[5] Housing costs are the least affordable in the U.S.[6] The area has officially become the gang capital of the world, with at least 80,000 members.[7] Illegal-alien gangsters terrorize neighborhoods and commit virtually all of the murders in the region. Up to two-thirds of all fugitive felony warrants are for illegal aliens.[8] Public schools, hospitals, and jails are overwhelmed, thus draining taxpayer resources. Schools have gone from best to worst in the nation, with more than 60 percent of Hispanic students dropping out of high school, the highest of any group.[9] Nevertheless, dozens of schools are being built, at a cost of billions of dollars to taxpayers, to accommodate illegal aliens and their children.[10] Violence between Hispanics and American citizens occurs regularly in the schools.[11] Hospitals become bankrupt and close every few months because countless uninsured illegals use emergency rooms for everything from primary care to birthing services and actual emergencies.[12] More than two-thirds of the births are to illegal aliens, mostly Mexicans.[13] Fifty-three percent of the workers in Los Angeles County aged sixteen and older can barely read, write, or speak English.[14] Thousands of aliens loiter on street corners and in parking lots every day hoping for employers to pick them up and take them to work sites.

Dozens of languages are spoken in the L.A. region,[15] but Spanish is the predominant foreign language. Signs in stores, gas stations, restaurants, hospitals, and government offices are printed in Spanish as well as English. Many highway billboards and ads on mass transit buses are completely in Spanish. Voter ballots and state driving manuals are printed in multiple languages at the taxpayers' expense. It is becoming difficult to find English-speaking stations on the radio among the many foreign-language stations, mostly Spanish. Employers increasingly require job applicants to speak Spanish in addition to English.

Los Angeles looks more like Mexico every day. In many areas of the region, discarded furniture and trash are piled up in front of houses and apartment buildings. Mexicans push carts on sidewalks selling food. Teenage Mexican mothers push baby carriages, sometimes with one or more toddlers trotting alongside. Houses and storefronts look like the ramshackle ones in Tijuana. Dozens of aliens are crammed into single-family homes and apartments. The Mexican flag hangs from the front porches of many properties. Canoga Park, where I lived safely as a teenager, is now home to some of the San Fernando Valley's most notorious Mexican gangs. My junior high has mostly Hispanic students. Chatsworth, the rural area where I learned to ride horses with my dad, is now swallowed by the Los Angeles sprawl, like the rest of the region. Hollywood is no longer an American city. In the once-pristine Sequoia National Park, where I vacationed in the 1960s, international drug cartels have taken over large remote areas. The criminal gangs grow marijuana and protect their fields with AK-47s, handguns, and machetes, using illegal aliens from Mexico.[16]

As a result of these cataclysmic changes, I feel like a stranger in my own country. California has become Mexifornia, and Los Angeles has become its capital.

Marxist Revolutionaries Rally

On September 20, 2003, the "Immigrant Workers Freedom Ride" rally started a trek across the nation from Los Angeles City Hall. The event marked the send-off for "activists taking part in a campaign based on the civil rights bus rides of the 1960s," the *Los Angeles Times* reported.[17] L.A. was one of nine cities sending buses filled with "immigrants" to Washington. "Supporters are calling for legalization for the nation's estimated 10 million illegal immigrants, a clear path for them to become U.S. citizens and quicker procedures to reunify families," the *Times* said. In truth, organizers demanded much more, including drivers' licenses, in-state tuition benefits, general public assistance, and open borders.

Organizers said the campaign was supported by a coalition of labor unions, religious groups, and civil rights activists. In fact, the campaign was organized by many radical groups such as the Communist Party USA, the Center for Marxist Education, the National Lawyers Guild, the National Council of La Raza (a leftist Hispanic lobby for "the race"), and MEChA (a group active on university and high-school campuses calling for a Hispanic homeland—"Aztlan"— made up of our Southwestern states).[18]

The *Los Angeles Times* called the spectacle a "boisterous crowd waving orange balloons, American flags, and union banners." But what I saw and heard that morning at city hall was alarming. On the lawn of our government building were hundreds of illegal aliens angrily demanding all the rights of American citizens. Demonstrators were carrying flags of Mexico, banners calling for open borders, and publications advocating socialism and communism.

The rally featured a parade of opportunistic labor organizers, religious leaders, and elected officials, including Los Angeles Mayor James Hahn and city council members.

After Mayor Hahn and other city officials spoke, Hispanic organizers screamed into the microphone in Spanish, calling for "rights" for the "immigrants" and open borders. The hundreds of invaders fervently chanted back in Spanish while pumping their fists in the air. The noise was thunderous. It resembled a Hollywood portrayal of a South American revolution. But this pro-communist revolutionary activity was real and happening in the United States.

2 | Wake Up, America; Time Is Running Out

*"The more we become a nation of illegal immigrants,
the deeper we fall into anarchy."*

—Congressman Elton Gallegly

On December 4, 2004, T.J. Bonner, president of the National Border Patrol Council, representing 10,000 U.S. border agents, made an alarming statement at a national conference of immigration experts near Washington, D.C.:

> "Today, as we sit here, and every other day, 10,000—that's thousand—10,000 illegal aliens will cross our border. The United States Border Patrol will catch about 3,000 of those people.... We are in the midst of an unprecedented crisis."[1]

Just four weeks later, in January 2005, Wall Street investment firm Bear Stearns published an equally startling report by business analysts Robert Justich and Betty Ng, titled *The Underground Labor Force Is Rising To The Surface*. Justich and Ng state that there are about 20 million illegal aliens in the U.S. today and estimate that illegal aliens hold between 12 million and 15 million jobs in the U.S., representing about 8 percent of the current labor force. Since 1990, according to the report, between four million and six million

U.S. jobs have shifted from the legal work force to the underground economy as employers have methodically replaced American workers with lower-wage illegal labor subsidized by taxpayers.[2]

Those numbers from the National Border Patrol Council and Bear Stearns differ sharply from the figures routinely trotted out by many of our government officials in Washington and the mainstream news media, who repeatedly tell the American people there are eight million to ten million "undocumented immigrants" in the U.S.[3] It is the same number they have been using for years, even though millions of illegals invade the United States each year across our border with Mexico. In California alone there are approximately six million illegal aliens, a figure that has more than tripled during the past decade.[4]

Our government leaders and media proudly tell us the Border Patrol catches one million people illegally crossing the border each year, but for some reason they don't tell us that several million elude the Border Patrol and make it into our country.[5]

President Bush repeatedly tells us that these "good-hearted" and "hardworking" people are just coming to the U.S. to do "the jobs Americans will not do."[6] What exactly are those jobs citizens won't do? Apparently those are the jobs millions of Americans used to do in construction, meatpacking, janitorial services, restaurant and hotel work, landscaping, and other trades. In 2005, some 14 million Americans were either unemployed, underemployed in part-time jobs out of economic necessity, or had become so discouraged that they gave up searching for work.[7] Yet many in our government want a "guest-worker" program, and the use of visas to bring overseas workers to America continues. Our elected representatives and media tell us that if we just make the illegal aliens legal then everything will be okay.[8]

Our government leaders continually tell us we are in a "war on terror." They create a bureaucracy called the Department of Homeland Security and order Americans at airports to present picture IDs several times, open their bags, remove clothing, and even submit to intimate body pat-downs.[9] But they leave our borders unsecured while borrowing hundreds of billions of dollars and using hundreds of thousands of U.S. troops to secure the borders of other countries to "spread democracy."

Invasion Across America

While California has suffered the longest and the most from unrestrained immigration, the crisis is no longer limited to California and the other states bordering Mexico, particularly Arizona and Texas. The invasion of the U.S.—10,000 per day and several million a year—by aliens of extremely different national and cultural identities has spread across America. If it hasn't reached your neighborhood yet, it will.

Americans from Oregon to Georgia are seeing their local communities transformed by mass immigration from Third-World countries. We are seeing our children forced into crowded and often bilingual classrooms. Our hospitals are bankrupted and closing because illegals can't pay their bills yet receive "free" medical care. Previously eradicated diseases are returning. Foreign gangs growing into large and dangerous armies terrorize citizens. Trash and foreign-language graffiti accumulate in our once-beautiful neighborhoods. "Undocumented workers" urinate in public and harass Americans while they wait for employers to take them to jobs formerly held by Americans. Further, we often feel like strangers in our country when we walk into a fast-food restaurant or turn on the radio and are barraged with foreign languages.

Let's take a quick tour across America.

The vicious gang Mara Salvatrucha (MS-13) has spread from El Salvador to Los Angeles and across the United States. Thousands of MS-13 members are operating in thirty-four states, and they are increasingly well organized. Members are tied to numerous killings, rapes, robberies, and home invasions. They are involved in narcotics trafficking and human smuggling. Machetes are often their weapon of choice to hack up their victims.[10]

In the upper-middle-class suburbs of Long Island, New York, there were no MS-13 members a few years ago. Today there are hundreds. And their growing numbers and violence, including murder, are frightening citizens.[11]

In the northern Virginia and southern Maryland communities around Washington, D.C., there are between 5,000 and 6,000 MS-13 members. Police have been warned that the gang is plotting to ambush and kill them when they respond to service calls.[12]

Further south, in Charlotte, North Carolina, MS-13 has been involved in at least eleven murders since 2000. It is by far Charlotte's largest gang.[13]

This violent gang also has been linked to efforts to help al-Qaeda infiltrate the U.S.-Mexico border.[14]

But it's not just the MS-13 criminals that are wreaking havoc on our nation and costing taxpayers. Shockingly, about 30 percent of federal and state prisoners are criminal aliens, non-citizens who commit crimes.[15] There are 40,000 illegal-alien prisoners in California alone.[16] In the Cameron County Jail in Olmito, Texas, one in three prisoners entered the U.S. illegally. They are awaiting trial for burglary, assault, drunken driving, and other crimes. They cost taxpayers in the nation's poorest county $460,000 per year.[17]

Cities across the U.S., plus the state of Maine, are havens for illegal-alien criminals. They rely on so-called "sanctuary" policies. These rules prevent local law enforcement from cooperating with federal officials on immigration matters, despite federal law explicitly prohibiting such policies.[18]

In Loudoun County, Virginia, recently a rural area, explosive population growth through uncontrolled immigration has made housing impossibly expensive for first-time homebuyers and causes terrible traffic jams. Citizens in the county complain that neighboring homes contain scores of renters—overwhelmingly Hispanic—who sleep on floors in townhouses, urinate in yards due to overcrowded conditions inside, and park more than a dozen cars on the street and in the yard.[19]

In New Jersey, doctors and hospital administrators are complaining that the hundreds of millions of dollars spent treating the growing illegal-alien population in their state has forced them to delay the purchase of life-saving technology and the addition of needed staff.[20]

In California, the healthcare system is on life support because of the millions of uninsured illegal aliens overwhelming hospitals and emergency rooms.[21] Four ERs have closed in San Diego in the last five years.[22] The situation is even worse in Los Angeles, where six ERs shut down in just eighteen months between 2003 and 2004.[23]

Of the 43 million people without health insurance in the nation, at least 25 percent, and possibly as many as 50 percent, are illegal aliens.[24] Hospitals and emergency rooms across the country are subsidizing illegals, even as the illegals send billions of dollars home to Mexico and elsewhere each year. Federal law requires states to provide free emergency health care to illegals, and many states also provide them with non-emergency care. Illegals use emergency rooms and hospitals for their primary care and to give birth to hundreds of thousands of babies annually—"anchor babies"—who are granted instant U.S. citizenship plus generous welfare benefits. For example, in Stockton, California, 70 percent of the 2,300 babies born in San Joaquin General Hospital's maternity ward in 2003 were anchor babies.[25] The ease by which illegals can receive medical treatment has reduced prospects for Americans to receive decent and timely coverage. Americans who can still afford coverage are paying ever-higher premiums and co-pays.

Up and down the West Coast in 2004, illegal alien Feliciano Morelos from Mexico infected scores of people with tuberculosis. (Illegal aliens, of course, enter the U.S. without being screened for disease.) That example is only the tip of the iceberg. About 53 percent of the people diagnosed in the U.S. each year with TB are foreign born. In the Los Angeles area, this number jumps to 80 percent, with Mexico the leading source, followed by the Philippines, Vietnam, India, and China. By 1983, Americans had essentially eliminated tuberculosis within our borders. But TB increased again after 1986, when Congress amnestied several million illegal aliens, mostly from Mexico.[26]

We are experiencing outbreaks of tuberculosis in schools and businesses. Illegal aliens are also spreading diseases such as HIV/AIDS, hepatitis, malaria, polio, and even leprosy.[27] This danger exists even without physical contact, since illegal aliens often take jobs as food service workers in restaurants, hospitals, and schools. Public restrooms are another place vulnerable to indirect contact.

Because some diseases such as TB are difficult to detect even in the best circumstances, legal immigrants are introducing unfamiliar or once-conquered diseases. For example, in January 2005, state health department officials in Minnesota began finding tuberculosis among the thousands of recent Hmong refugees from Thailand.[28]

Illegal-alien children and non-English-speaking children are overwhelming public schools and forcing American kids into overcrowded and bilingual classrooms. Georgia taxpayers are shelling out more than $230 million per year to educate illegal-alien children in K-12 schools. The cost is more than $484 million in Illinois and tops $140 million in Colorado.[29]

At high schools in big cities such as Los Angeles,[30] Chicago,[31] and Dallas,[32] and in small cities such as Reno, Nevada,[33] violent confrontations are on the rise between "Latino immigrants" and American students.

In Schuyler, Nebraska, Americans are in shock because illegal aliens, mostly from Mexico, have invaded their town. On Main Street, the former Ben Franklin True Value dime store is now La Chiquita, a shop filled with Mexican foodstuffs and crafts. What was once Hardee's has become the Dos Americas liquor shop. The old Didier's Grocery is now The Latino Club.[34] Small Midwestern towns such as Schuyler, where Americans once made good livings before being forced out of work, are evolving into Mexican villages.

In Colorado, illegal aliens use phony Social Security numbers to obtain Federal Housing Administration loans, while American citizens are finding it harder to purchase affordable homes.[35]

In Canyon County, Idaho, county commissioners led by Robert Vasquez passed a resolution declaring their region a disaster area because of illegal immigration. They said their county needs relief from an "invasion" that is costing taxpayers millions of dollars.[36]

That's just a glimpse at what's happening across the U.S. today. Immigration is out of control and destroying the quality of life—and America itself—before our very eyes. But how did this happen? How did the U.S. become a nation of 20 million illegal aliens and counting?

Government-Forced Mass Immigration

Between 1925 and 1965, America was a low-immigration country, basically living under immigration laws written in 1924. Immigration into the U.S. averaged 178,000 per year during that forty-year period. In the resulting tight labor market, wages rose and America essentially became a middle-class society. Our many ethnic groups— mainly European—assimilated into the common national culture and English language.[37]

But a 1965 statute opened the immigration floodgates. That's when Congress amended the Immigration and Nationality Act, eliminating quotas based on national origin and introducing family reunification. Also called "chain migration," this policy allows immigration by relatives, including spouses, minor children, parents, siblings, and adult children. The newcomers can later extend the chain to their spouses and relatives in the same way. The bill, signed into law by President Lyndon Johnson, discriminated against low-fertility nations in favor of the more overpopulated high-fertility Third-World countries.[38]

Senator Ted Kennedy, as Immigration Subcommittee chairman, managed the bill through the Senate. On February 10, 1965, he reassured his colleagues and the nation:

> The bill will not flood our cities with immigrants. It will not upset the ethnic mix of our society. It will not relax the standards of admission. It will not cause American workers to lose their jobs.[39]

Americans can now see that Kennedy was wrong on all counts. Was this simply a matter of congressional ignorance? Or, now that we have forty years of experience, was Congress lying to cover a carefully orchestrated long-term scheme designed to dismantle the American middle-class, lower wages, and divide our national culture?

Three years later, in 1968, the Ford Foundation created the Mexican American Legal Defense and Educational Fund (MALDEF) and the National Council of La Raza (The Race, meaning those of Mexican descent) to strengthen the "ethnic identity" of newly arrived immigrants, legal and illegal, from south of the border rather than aid their assimilation into the American mainstream.[40] La Raza's president at that time was Maclovio Barraza, a life-long labor activist.[41] The Ford Foundation, American corporations, even federal government agencies have contributed hundreds of millions of dollars over the years to these and other Hispanic advocacy groups such as the Southwest Voter Registration Education Project.[42]

As legal immigration climbed during the '70s and '80s, so did the opportunities and motives for illegal immigration.[43] Communities of new legal immigrants helped create support networks, providing jobs, housing, legal aid, and social services for illegal aliens.

By the early 1980s, Americans were beginning to notice. During a news conference on June 14, 1984, President Ronald Reagan sounded a dire warning:

> But the simple truth is that we've lost control of our own borders, and no nation can do that and survive. [44]

However, instead of deporting people illegally in our country and protecting our states from further invasion, as our elected officials are sworn to do under Article IV, Section 4 of the U.S. Constitution, Congress and Reagan passed the Immigration Reform and Control Act (IRCA) in 1986. For the first time ever, our government rewarded about three million illegal aliens, mostly from Mexico, with amnesty and a path to U.S. citizenship. To discourage more illegal immigration, IRCA also included employer sanctions, making it against the law to knowingly hire illegal aliens. The sanctions were never enforced.[45]

Today, Atlanta-based Home Depot is one of many corporations aiding and abetting illegal immigration. The company, with sales of $73 billion in 2004, funds illegal-alien day laborer centers and has a special "partnership" with the National Council of La Raza to give hiring preference to Spanish-speaking employees.[46] Interestingly, Home Depot appointed former Homeland Security director Tom Ridge to its board of directors after Ridge resigned his government job in early 2005.[47]

The IRCA amnesty, sold to the American people as a never-to-be-repeated action, only encouraged millions of additional foreigners— mostly Mexicans—to stream across our southern border, in the hope and anticipation of further amnesties.[48]

But our politicians wanted still more immigration. In 1990, Congress and President George H.W. Bush passed another immigration act, increasing the level of legal immigration by several hundred thousand to an overall "flexible cap" of 675,000 annually.[49]

Since IRCA in 1986, Congress has passed seven amnesties, rewarding several million additional illegal aliens with legal residence and putting them and their relatives on the path to citizenship. Amnesty makes a mockery of law-abiding foreigners waiting their legal turn to enter. Newly legalized aliens from the various amnesties have imported their relatives, wave after wave, through the process of chain migration.[50]

In 2004, nine more amnesty bills were pending in Congress, waiting for approval.[51] Those bills are in addition to President George W. Bush's January 2004 proposal for a guest-worker program to amnesty the millions of illegals in America today. His administration also proposes allowing unlimited numbers of the world's six billion foreigners to move to America to work at whatever wages employers determine.[52] Just imagine what this tidal wave of people would do to our quality of life.

Today, approximately one million legal immigrants arrive in America each year, far more than accepted by all other nations combined.[53] That number is in addition to the millions of illegal aliens pouring in, including an estimated three million in 2004 alone.[54]

In 1970, five years after Congress decided to open the door to mass immigration, America's population stood at 203 million. By 2005 it had soared to almost 300 million. Only Communist China and India have bigger populations. In just thirty-five years, nearly 100 million people were added to the U.S. population, with most of the increase coming from immigrants, illegal aliens, and their U.S.-born children. This population explosion is a direct result of post-1965 legal U.S. immigration policies and our government's refusal to enforce laws against illegal immigration.[55] If immigration into the U.S. is not dramatically reduced, our population is projected to climb to 360 million in 2020, 405 million in 2030, 460 million in 2040, and more than half a billion in 2050.[56] So if you think our roads, schools, hospitals, employment lines, prisons, communities, landfills, national parks (you name it) are crowded today, just wait.

Thousands of Illegal Aliens Every Day

On the day you're reading this, thousands of illegal aliens from many countries and cultures are pouring across our border with Mexico. Most of these invaders will avoid capture by our 10,000-outnumbered Border Patrol agents.

As this lawless migrating mass of people crosses our southern border, they leave behind mountains of trash, destroy property, kill livestock, and attack Americans.

The invaders are mostly the unskilled, uneducated, and poor from Mexico.

The flow of President Bush's "good-hearted" and "hardworking" folks also includes murderers, rapists, pedophiles, drug smugglers, thieves, and gang members. For example, between September and November 2004, the Border Patrol identified 23,502 criminals trying to sneak into the U.S., mainly across our southern border. The Border Patrol identified 84 foreigners suspected of murder, 37 for kidnapping, 151 wanted for sexual assault, 212 for robbery, 1,238 for other assaults, and 2,630 for dangerous narcotics-related charges. And those are just the ones authorities were able to catch during that three-month period.[57]

Our unguarded borders are gateways for terrorists. "People are coming here with bad intentions. I know of ten that have been detained at my station alone," said one Border Patrol agent on the southern border in November 2004, adding that this is something agents have been told not to talk about. "We know for a fact that people from the Middle East are now coming into Mexico and spending a year, even two years in Mexico, to learn how to speak Spanish."[58]

"In 2004," said Congressman Tom Tancredo, a Republican from Colorado, "1.15 million illegal aliens were apprehended crossing our borders, and more than 76,000 of them were non-Mexicans from countries with terrorist cells such as the Philippines, Indonesia, Morocco, Iran, Syria, Pakistan, and Iraq. *Time* magazine estimates that another three million made it past the Border Patrol successfully. More than 95 percent of them came through Mexico, not Canada."[59]

Republican Congressman Dana Rohrabacher from California, a long-time opponent of illegal immigration, stated, "Any American that thinks we have security on our southern border is mistaken."[60]

Mexicans apprehended by the Border Patrol are routinely deported to Mexico, but many return again and again until they succeed in reaching America's heartland. Non-Mexicans are checked against U.S. government watch lists for security or criminal threats. If their names do not appear, many are released on their own recognizance and told to appear at a deportation hearing, often months in the future. Naturally, most manage to evade the hearing and settle in the U.S.

While many illegal aliens sneak across our southern border, some come across our border with Canada or ride ships and planes. In January 2005, for example, border agents arrested a man they said was trying to smuggle seventeen Chinese and an Albanian into the U.S. through a train tunnel under a waterway linking Canada and Detroit.[61] Also that month, thirty-two Chinese were found in two cargo containers on a Panamanian-flagged ship at the Port of Los Angeles. A crane operator spotted them, not Homeland Security or law enforcement.[62] Three months later, a nearly identical scenario played out at the L.A. port when federal authorities arrested twenty-nine Chinese smuggled inside two shipping containers. They were spotted by private security guards and smuggled aboard a Panamanian-registered ship.[63] This begs the question: Just like the millions of people who sneak across our southern border undetected each year, how many smuggled into our nation's ports avoid capture?

However, most illegal aliens come across our border with Mexico, and most are Mexican. The Mexican ruling class is using the U.S. as a safety valve for millions of Mexico's poorest people and criminals so the elites and ultra-rich can continue avoiding economic, social, and political reform.

In fact, Mexico is an "immensely wealthy nation," according to Professor George W. Grayson of The College of William & Mary. Mexico is the wealthiest nation in Latin America in terms of Gross National Product and GNP per capita. Mexico is home to nearly half of the billionaires in Latin America, and Grayson has said that the Mexican ruling class "lives like maharajas."[64]

The Mexican government enjoys the added benefit of billions of dollars in remittances sent back to Mexico from its citizens working in the U.S. In 2004, $17 billion in remittances flowed to Mexico, becoming that country's largest source of foreign income for the first time, surpassing even oil.[65]

Most invaders are coming to America to take the so-called "jobs Americans won't do." Employers in labor-intensive industries illegally replace Americans with gatecrashers from the Third World, who—because of their illegal status and consequent fear of deportation if they make a fuss—will accept low wages and deplorable working conditions. Illegal aliens can be paid off the books to save the employer taxes and insurance costs. Illegal workers receive welfare benefits paid by the very American taxpayer whose job the illegal is stealing.

In March 2005, for example, the U.S. Labor Department's Household Survey of employment, which reports ethnicity, showed a dramatic displacement of American workers. It reported 357,000 new American jobs for the month. Hispanics received 60 percent of the new jobs, even though they account for just 13.1 percent of the total employment.[66]

Simultaneously, U.S. corporations replace American professionals with low-wage guest workers who come primarily from Asia and Eastern Europe on non-immigrant visas. These visa holders take jobs in areas such as high-tech, education, health care, accounting, and manufacturing. A large percentage of such "temporary" workers have become illegal aliens in the U.S. because they didn't leave when their visas expired.[67]

But illegal aliens are pouring into the U.S. for more than jobs and an easy life of crime. They may "come to work," but they take welfare, free medical care, free K-12 education for their children, and possible future amnesty.

In addition, since the children born to illegal aliens on U.S. soil become instant citizens, they also qualify for the full range of public benefits furnished by American taxpayers. When those children turn twenty-one, they can sponsor the immigration of other relatives.

Mexico's Colonization of America

In past generations, immigrants assimilated into the American culture. However, so many foreigners are arriving legally and illegally each year that there now is little or no pressure on them to assimilate. They can often lead entire lives within autonomous ethnic enclaves.

Americans in California and other border states have witnessed this for many distressing years. Today, Americans in other states also are seeing their communities invaded.

Thanks to pandering U.S. politicians, greedy employers, and others disloyal to America, the Mexican government and the invaders are creating a Mexican nation within our nation. Those sworn to protect us are allowing our nation to be colonized by a foreign power.

At the opening of a new Mexican Consulate in Chicago in June 2004, President Vicente Fox made his country's intentions clear in a speech before U.S. politicians and people waving Mexican flags. "We are Mexicans that live in our territories, and we are Mexicans that live in other territories," proclaimed Fox. "In reality, we are 120 million people that live together and are working to construct a nation."[68]

The Mexican Consulate in Chicago is just one of dozens across the U.S. pressuring local and state governments to ensure that illegal aliens who are here from Mexico continue to have their jobs and full access to American benefits.[69]

On July 27, 1997, Mexican President Ernesto Zedillo, also in Chicago, made a similar declaration before a meeting of the National Council of La Raza: "I have proudly affirmed that the Mexican nation extends beyond the territory enclosed by its borders and that Mexican migrants are an important, a very important, part of it."[70] Today Zedillo is director of Yale University's Center for the Study of Globalization.

Many Hispanic U.S. elected officials, appointed officials, university professors, and well-financed organizations such as La Raza are actively working to take over America, as you will read later in this book. Henry Cisneros, Secretary of Housing and Urban Development under President Clinton, stated: "As goes the Latino population will go California, and as goes California will go the United States of America.... We should stand for the proud Latino future. We must stand for the people, now more than ever, and then be prepared to fight."[71] A U.S. Cabinet secretary said that. Astounding, isn't it?

Many patriotic Hispanic Americans with affection for America do not align with this radical movement. Some are quoted in this book. However, the takeover is moving along at a rapid pace.

Schools in many states are practically Mexican schools. With the approval of administrators and teachers, large Mexican flags are displayed in the lobby and classrooms of a Denver high school that is 84 percent Hispanic.[72]

A junior high school in Gadsden, Arizona, celebrates Mexican Independence Day with students marching through the school carrying Mexican flags, the school's mariachi band performing songs, and teachers from Mexico performing traditional dances.[73]

At a high school in Reno, Nevada, a growing number of fights between Hispanic and American students matches the climbing Hispanic population. Said the school's former principal, "One student mentioned to me last year that the school is now being taken over by Hispanics."[74]

Crowds of Mexicans and other illegal-alien Hispanics aren't just in the streets of Los Angeles asserting arrogant demands while waving foreign flags. Such scenes are repeated in cities across America. On September 16, 2004, about one thousand mostly Mexican illegal aliens were screaming in Spanish on the steps of the capitol building in Atlanta. They demanded the state of Georgia grant drivers' licenses to illegals.[75]

The Hispanic invasion and colonization of America is coming in loud and clear when one scans the radio dial, as more broadcasters replace English-language-format stations with Spanish formats nearly every week.

On October 28, 2004, for example, Clear Channel Communications shut down San Jose, California's oldest rock station, KSJO-FM, and began programming in Spanish. "It's an emotional format that brings back memories from the listener's homeland," said the station's general manager. "People will hear a song they haven't heard since they were in Mexico watching their mothers make tamales."[76]

Two weeks later, KLOL-FM in Houston, Texas, switched from a rock format to Latino music.[77]

Clear Channel Communications, the largest U.S. radio broadcaster, planned to convert as many as twenty-five stations to a Spanish-language format in 2005.[78]

There are approximately eighty Spanish-format radio stations in California alone and hundreds in the U.S.[79]

In addition, there are numerous Spanish-language television stations in the U.S. and hundreds of Spanish-language newspapers.[80]

In April 2005, Clear Channel put up seventy-five billboards across the Los Angeles region advertising a Spanish-language newscast on KRCA-TV Channel 62, owned by Liberman Broadcasting. The provocative posters showed two newscasters sitting in front of the Los Angeles skyline, with "Los Angeles, CA" printed above. The "CA" was crossed out, and "Mexico" was printed alongside in red letters. Only a public outcry caused the posters to be pulled.[81]

Many of these media are Mexican propaganda outlets that advise illegals how to avoid deportation, participate in pro-illegal-alien demonstrations, and obtain IDs and welfare.[82]

A growing number of colleges and universities across the U.S. are offering courses to train students to work in the Spanish-language media.[83]

In late 2004 and early 2005, two actions by the Mexican government were extreme acts against the sovereignty of the United States.

A particularly egregious act occurred in December 2004: The Mexican government published and distributed 1.5 million copies of a thirty-two-page book titled *The Guide for the Mexican Migrant*. It gives advice on how its citizens can illegally invade the U.S. The guide offers information on safety for border crossers, legal rights, and living inconspicuously in the U.S. Drawings show illegals wading into a river, running from the U.S. Border Patrol, and crouching near a hole in a border fence.[84] (Another outrageous example of a guide for illegal aliens was produced by the Colorado state government. In January 2005, Denver resident Terry Graham discovered Colorado's fifty-page online pamphlet in Spanish, with an introductory welcome from Republican Governor Bill Owens. The guide provides tips on how to seek employment at companies that will not try to verify their documents, obtain medical care, open a bank account, earn university scholarships, and deal with police and other authorities.[85])

Another egregious act by the Mexican government occurred on January 28, 2005. During a radio interview, Foreign Secretary Luis Ernesto Derbez threatened the state of Arizona with legal action through international courts if attempts to reverse Arizona's Proposition 200 fail.[86] (In November 2004, Arizonans voted decisively for the measure to prohibit illegal aliens from receiving non-federally mandated taxpayer benefits and from voting in elections. The historic measure went into effect in January 2005 and is discussed in detail in chapter four.)

There was no comment from the Bush administration about the Mexican government's guidebook for invaders or their threat to overturn the vote in a sovereign U.S. state.

Outright violence is also used to aid the invasion. In January 2005, snipers working as lookouts for drug traffickers and illegal-alien smugglers targeted U.S. Border Patrol agents from vantage points across the U.S.-Mexico border. In just one week, agents assigned to the Douglas station in Arizona's southeastern corner were fired on at least six times.[87]

Government Ignores Americans and Immigration Laws

The vast majority of Americans want illegal immigration stopped, illegal aliens sent home, no amnesty, borders secured, a significant reduction in legal immigration (a growing number want a moratorium), and visa laws enforced.[88]

But President Bush and Congress—and presidents and Congresses before them—refuse to perform their constitutional duty to defend the states of the Union from a foreign invasion. Instead, elected officials propose amnesty and further relaxation of borders. Many in our government, Democrat and Republican, on local to federal levels, arrogantly ignore the American people and laws while taking security risks. Here are a few examples:

- Two years after thousands of Americans were murdered in New York on 9/11 by illegal-alien terrorists, Republican

Mayor Michael Bloomberg revived the city's sanctuary policy for illegal aliens. "People who are undocumented do not have to worry about city government going to the federal government," he proclaimed.[89]

- In response to a caller on a Los Angeles talk-radio program who was opposed to L.A. Police Chief William Bratton's endorsement of the city's sanctuary policy protecting illegal aliens and illegal-alien gangsters, Bratton said, "If you don't like it, leave the state."[90]

- Democratic House leader Nancy Pelosi verbally attacked law enforcement officers for applying our immigration laws and arresting a couple hundred illegal aliens working at Wal-Mart stores. She said the arrests amounted to "terrorizing" workers and demonstrated the need to legalize "undocumented workers." Pelosi made the comments in Mexico, where she was courting President Fox.[91]

- Pennsylvania Judge Leonard Zito complimented twenty-seven Hispanic illegal aliens and set them free. The illegals were arrested for using false or stolen Social Security numbers to procure employment. The judge acknowledged it was wrong for them to use false Social Security numbers but said their crimes warranted no punishment because they broke the law to earn a living.[92]

- Commenting on illegal aliens receiving tax-funded rent subsidies, Barbara Favola, Democrat and chairman of the Arlington County Board in Virginia, pandered, "We really work at developing a trust level with all our residents in Arlington. I want to be a friendly and welcoming place, period—to anyone who comes within our borders."[93]

- Republican Asa Hutchinson, while undersecretary of Homeland Security, admitted that the immigrant enforcement agency is not doing its job at the border or in the interior of the country. He believes that enforcing our immigration laws is "unrealistic."[94]

- The Bush administration removed critical immigration policy reforms from a national security bill that would have implemented the recommendations of the 9/11 Commission in 2004. The bill cracked down on illegal aliens obtaining drivers' licenses, allowed easier deportation, and limited the use of foreign consular ID cards. The provisions were excluded in the final bill.[95]

- President Bush professes we must fix the Social Security system to protect the retirement years of American citizens. But in 2004 his administration quietly signed an agreement with Mexico allowing Mexicans working illegally in the U.S. to receive Social Security payments after working only eighteen months. The agreement is projected to drain $350 billion from the Social Security Trust Fund during the next decade.[96]

- At a White House press conference on December 20, 2004, President Bush revealed his compassion with the sweatshop lobby by announcing: "We want our Border Patrol agents chasing, you know, crooks and thieves and drug-runners and terrorists, not good-hearted people who are coming here to work."[97]

- Attorney General Alberto Gonzales is a member of the National Council of La Raza, the militant subversive organization with which he has been affiliated for many years. During his Senate confirmation hearings in January 2005, he paradoxically observed that illegal aliens are U.S. citizens.[98] On March 8, 2005, Gonzales revealed in his address at an awards ceremony of La Raza, "I ... have this organization to thank for support of my nomination for attorney general."[99]

Millions of Americans are out of work, underemployed, or have given up searching for jobs altogether. Our cities are bursting with people, and our nation is trillions of dollars in debt and engaged in a "war on terror." So why would so many in our government violate their oaths of office and allow America to be invaded by millions of people from Third-World countries?

There are many aspects to this crisis. There are different motives for massive illegal and legal immigration. Open borders are about politicians pandering to business demands for a never-ending stream of cheap labor, to ethnic advocacy groups, and to their hoped-for alien votes.

Americans are increasingly realizing that years of unrestrained immigration and intentionally unprotected borders are part of the long-term internationalist agenda to slowly take down America's middle-class, erase sovereignty, and integrate the U.S. with Mexico and other countries in the Western Hemisphere, similar to the European Union. This is the path to world government. Of course, the American citizens who work to abolish our borders and merge the United States with other nations are engaged in subversion and treason.[100] With the exception of CNN's Lou Dobbs, you haven't heard news anchors tell you and their millions of viewers about our globalized future when they're reading scripts on the nightly national newscasts.

Although it is hard for many Americans to accept such a fundamental reversal, the U.S. is becoming a lawless country. Government refuses to enforce our immigration laws and uphold our Constitution by protecting each state against invasion. Corporations knowingly hire illegal aliens at the expense of American workers and their families—and our government turns a blind eye. Millions of foreigners break our laws by sneaking into our country. And the media refuse to report the truth.

California Republican Congressman Elton Gallegly, who has fought illegal immigration for years, cautions: "Our nation's foundation is undermined if we fail to enforce our laws. Law gives liberty order. Without it, we have anarchy. Nowhere is this more obvious than in the intentional failure over the years to enforce our immigration laws. That failure has thrown into disarray our healthcare system, our economy, our education system, and our security…. When we were a nation of legal immigrants, we were a nation of laws. The more we become a nation of illegal immigrants, the deeper we fall into anarchy."[101]

3 | The Real Victims of Mass Immigration

*"I know illegal aliens want a better life,
but what in hell about mine?"*

—Ray W., Phoenix, Arizona

Mass immigration is harming countless American citizens and America itself. Sounds like a big story for the news media, one they should be covering regularly. But do you see many stories about this in newspapers or on the local or network broadcast news? With a few notable exceptions, the mainstream media ignore the momentous changes inflicted by open borders.

Where are the stories about the incalculable number of Americans having lost jobs to illegal aliens and legal immigrants?

Where are the stories about the Americans injured, raped, and killed by illegal aliens, or citizens suffering from the diseases illegals bring with them?

Where are the stories showing the spiraling healthcare costs illegal aliens are imposing upon U.S. taxpayers?

Where are the stories about American children stuffed into crowded schools with illegal aliens and legal immigrants and forced into "bilingual" classrooms?

Where are the stories about the millions of illegal aliens and legal immigrants causing home prices to skyrocket, creating massive sprawl and congestion, and straining precious natural resources?

After President Bush and Democratic Party leaders announced in January 2004 their respective "guest-worker" proposals that would open the door to an unlimited number of foreign workers, where were the stories in the mainstream media about how these plans would impact Americans? Where were the stories about any of these serious immigration issues in the months leading up to the 2004 general election?

In the three presidential debates between Bush and Senator John Kerry in the weeks prior to the election, only one question was about illegal immigration. Moderator Bob Schieffer, a veteran CBS newsman, asked it during the final debate on October 13 in Tempe, Arizona. Schieffer said he received more e-mails about this issue from concerned citizens in the days prior to the debate than about any other subject. After Bush and Kerry said they wanted "guest-worker" programs as their solution to illegal immigration, Schieffer didn't ask why the U.S. needs guest workers when millions of Americans are out of work. Nor did Schieffer challenge the president—whose oath of office includes the promise to protect the U.S. from invasion—when he invited foreigners to violate the border. Said Bush: "You're going to come here if you're worth your salt, if you want to put food on the table for your families." Nor did Schieffer challenge Kerry, who said the borders weren't secure enough but then called for an illegal-alien amnesty.[1]

Living in the Los Angeles area for many years has given me a front-row seat to uncontrolled immigration. Most of the Los Angeles region has become a Third-World Mexican colony.

But day after day the *Los Angeles Times* carries sad stories and op-eds on "undocumented immigrants," where lawbreakers are sympathetically portrayed as victims.

While the *L.A. Times* is possibly the most pro-open borders newspaper in America, it is not the only mainstream media organization ignoring the immigration disaster. Virtually all of the print and broadcast media routinely report on "struggling immigrants" while disregarding mass immigration's impact on American citizens.

Surprisingly, *Time* magazine, an admired voice of the establishment press, crossed over to the other side with its September 20, 2004 cover story, "Who Left the Door Open?"[2] It's an in-depth investigation by Pulitzer Prize-winning reporters Donald Barlett and James Steele on our porous southern border and the havoc caused by illegal aliens. The popular media, however, remain cheerleaders for unrestrained immigration.

It's particularly irritating and blatantly dishonest that the media refer to illegal aliens simply as "immigrants" or "undocumented workers," or some other euphemism. The word "illegal" has mostly disappeared for these corporate journalists and even many elected officials.

[These reporters have] "average intelligence with a below average work ethic and are uninterested in getting to the facts that would lead to a fair and balanced story," reports Joe Guzzardi, a long-time writer for www.Vdare.com, which covers immigration's impact on our society. "The reality is that newspapers are a hopeless cause. They most likely will never report professionally on immigration. And, in general, enlightened readers now discount the establishment media completely."[3]

Out of all the major metropolitan area newspapers, the *Washington Times* always provides neutral reporting and informed commentary on the issue of illegal immigration.

There are a few nationally known journalists and news commentators who talk openly and truthfully about immigration. Virtually all are on talk radio, cable television, and the Internet. *Lou Dobbs Tonight* on CNN is the top news show for telling America the facts about open borders, illegal immigration, trade, and outsourcing. The Center for Immigration Studies chose Dobbs as the 2004 winner of the prestigious Eugene Katz Award for Excellence in the Coverage of Immigration. "Lou Dobbs stands out for his success in airing all sides of a complicated issue," said Congressman Tom Tancredo, who presented the award to the CNN anchor. "Lou is performing a service to our country."[4]

Commentator Bill O'Reilly on Fox News and talk radio has discussed illegal immigration for several years, but his blind spots are troubling. Wanting Bush to secure our borders, he nevertheless supports the president's guest-worker proposal, which is an amnesty for millions of illegal aliens. O'Reilly says "the country needs new blood," even though millions of Americans are out of work.[5] For a man who wrote a book titled *Who's Looking Out for You?* his inattention to the harm done to Americans by flooded labor markets is disappointing. On the other hand, O'Reilly has been a strong voice against the outrageous "sanctuary" policy of some cities that actually protects criminal foreigners.

Radio talk-show host and best-selling author Michael Savage has been preaching "borders, language and culture" to millions of listeners for years.

Pat Buchanan, best-selling author and former presidential candidate, writes and talks about the dangers of mass immigration in many mediums.

In local markets across the country more talk-radio hosts are talking about illegal immigration. For example, the *John and Ken* show in Southern California, with more than one million listeners, began making illegal immigration its top issue in mid-2004. In September, the duo, John Kobylt and Ken Chiampou of KFI-AM, held a poll on their Web site to decide which pro-illegal-immigration GOP congressman from the Los Angeles area should be defeated in the general election in November. At the same time, they made it fun by calling it the "Political Human Sacrifice." Their listeners overwhelmingly chose Congressman David Dreier, a twenty-four-year incumbent and chairman of the powerful House Rules Committee. From the Democratic Party, the radio team selected local Congressman Joe Baca as their sacrifice because he persuaded the Department of Homeland Security to end the U.S. Border Patrol round-ups of illegal aliens in Southern California in the summer of 2004.[6] (As you will read in chapter seven, Baca once told a large Hispanic audience that the "agenda is about ensuring that we increase our numbers" of Latinos.)

But John and Ken focused most of their attention on Dreier and his pro-illegal-immigration voting record because they expect the

Republican Party to be tougher on the problem than the Democratic Party. Thanks to the duo's Political Human Sacrifice campaign and subsequent "Fire Dreier" campaign, the Republican congressman was forced to spend an estimated $1 million on fliers and radio ads and struggled to beat Democrat Cynthia Matthews, a first-time candidate who had little campaign money.[7] Dreier's victory margin—51 percent to 45 percent—was the smallest of the dozens of congressional incumbents in California, sending a message to Washington that voters are becoming increasingly fed up with illegal immigration.[8] Baca easily won reelection, but his challenger, Republican Ed Laning, received more than twice the votes of Baca's 2002 challenger.[9]

In another example, Los Angeles talk-show host Doug McIntyre provides daily news and commentary on KABC-AM on the disastrous effects of illegal immigration. In early 2005, he repeatedly exposed the media and various organizations for deliberately excluding Republican candidate Walter Moore, a business trial lawyer, from the L.A. mayoral debates because Moore vowed to do everything possible to fight illegal immigration if elected mayor.

Sad Stories About 'Immigrants'

There are hundreds of articles on immigration from newspapers across the country. Mostly, the stories are about "poor immigrants" seeking work in America, without medical insurance, or dying in the desert to do "the jobs Americans won't do." Here is a news bulletin: Americans did do those jobs until the government stopped enforcing the law against unscrupulous employers illegally hiring aliens at wages offering no dignity to labor. In fact, Americans still do those unglamorous jobs in regions where there is little immigration.

It is not just illegal aliens who are taking jobs from Americans. Legal immigrants also are taking jobs away from Americans, as you will read later in this chapter and in other chapters of this book. At the same time, U.S. companies are shipping hundreds of thousands of American jobs, from telemarketing to software design, to cheap-labor havens overseas.

Today's news organizations have betrayed their most fundamental role: to be honest watchdogs exposing government waste, fraud, corruption, and abuse of power. They have refused to tell the American people about government-forced mass immigration and its effects on us. Most of today's reporters, editors, producers, and anchors are nothing more than politically correct contortionists. Their self-serving news is incomplete and deceptive.

In 1983, fifty corporations controlled most major media outlets in the U.S. By 2004, only twenty-one years later, that number had dwindled to just five mega corporations dominating the mass media: Time Warner, Disney, Murdoch's News Corporation, Bertelsmann of Germany, and Viacom.[10] All are dedicated to open borders and globalism.

Here are the opening paragraphs of typical newspaper stories on "undocumented immigrants," in which lawbreakers are portrayed as victims:

Los Angeles Times
"'Dream Act' Offers Hope for Immigrant Students"
(September 19, 2004)

On a good day, 20-year-old Elvia Flores feels she's making her family proud, studying in college to become a nurse while working nearly full-time to help her pay her family's bills. But in darker moments, Flores wonders if all the work and sacrifice is worth it. Flores is an undocumented immigrant. And despite the nation's shortage of bilingual nurses, Flores will likely end up after graduation with little more than a low-paying restaurant job, because she lacks a Social Security number and legal residency card.[11]

Houston Chronicle
"Immigrants Flee Disastrous Economies"
(October 18, 2003)

Fed up with the extreme poverty in Honduras, Oscar Trochez, 31, left with his wife, three children, sister, niece and nephew and headed to Houston. The 31-year-old father led his family on a grueling six-week exodus across Central America and Mexico because the Honduran economy has worsened since the last time he made the journey alone, back in 1998. With the help of a smuggler, the Trochez family crossed the Rio Grande near Matamoros and went directly to U.S. immigration offices, where members received temporary visas...[12]

Seattle Post-Intelligencer Reporter
"Immigrants' Safety Net Unravels"
(October 13, 2003)

Aurelia Baltazar Loza slipped over the Mexican border into the United States with three of her children not long after her husband of 25 years was killed in a traffic accident. At the time of his death, the mother of nine had never worked outside her home in a poor pueblo in Jalisco. Two years later, though, she was making $6 an hour packing fish in a cannery in South Bend—barely enough to keep her 9-year-old twins, Pedro and Nelida, and 14-year-old son, Alex, fed and to send money to a sister caring for the children she had to leave behind.[13]

"The press is full of stories about the struggling immigrant, often here illegally, who has come to America 'in search of a better life,'" reports Brenda Walker, project director for ImmigrationsHumanCost. org, which is dedicated to telling the stories of Americans harmed by open-borders policies. "These stories are easy to write for lazy journalists. They can knock one of these out in a few hours then take the rest of the day off.

"The media fail to note," explains Walker, who has written about unrestrained immigration for years, "that this same foreigner will achieve his better life at the cost of some American who makes less money in a flooded labor market or will directly lose his job to an alien willing to work for peanuts.

"While legal immigrants and illegal aliens come to America for an improved standard of living, those millions of foreigners are harming the quality of life for many in this nation—from those who have been displaced in their jobs by cheap immigrant workers to taxpayers paying for endless infrastructure and services, students getting a worse education in radically 'diverse' classrooms, and crime victims who have suffered at the hands of those who were illegally in this country.

"In terms of employment, the Americans hurt the worst are the ones least able to respond, namely our own poor and low-skilled folks who are competing directly against foreigners who willingly work for far less than a survivable wage for citizens living one family to a house.

"The bottom line is that illegal immigration is not a victimless crime."

Stories About the Real Victims

Among the many victims chronicled on Walker's Web site, ImmigrationsHumanCost.org, are Kris Eggle and David March. Eggle, a U.S. Park Service Ranger, was murdered in Arizona by a Mexican illegal alien smuggling drugs and weapons into the U.S. through Organ Pipe Cactus National Monument. March was a Los Angeles County Sheriff who was murdered when he pulled over a car for a routine traffic stop. The driver was a Mexican drug dealer, Armando Garcia, who had been deported twice and has a long history of violent crimes. As this book was going to press, Garcia was arrested in Mexico and U.S. authorities were preparing to extradite him for trial.

On the next several pages are short stories by Americans who have suffered and watched their communities deteriorate because of our government's out-of-control immigration policies. The stories were compiled by ProjectUSA for VictimsVoice.org, a Web site that is no longer active. ProjectUSA is a Washington group "dedicated to raising public debate about immigration."

"My 23-year-old son, James, died in the World Trade Center on 9-11-01. A major factor in allowing these terrorist attacks to occur was the failure to enforce existing laws on immigration and visas. This failure is due to members of Congress and Presidents Bush-Clinton-Bush. All cared more about getting votes and support from those who profit from open borders than they did about Americans' security. They are in major part responsible for the dead of 9-11."

Peter Gadiel
Kent, Connecticut
(Gadiel founded and heads 9/11 Families for a Secure America.)

"My thirteen-year-old son was murdered by an illegal immigrant from Mexico. It disgusts me to know more and more illegal immigrants cross the border and hurt U.S. citizens for no justifiable reason. To imagine more men like the man that took my little boy away from me forever are still coming—I can only hope that the laws on illegal immigrants get better so that innocent citizens aren't killed. If our laws were enforced, my son would be alive today. We as American Latinos should not be scared to say that we are proud to be American."

Angie Morfin
Salinas, California

"My husband was outside the gate at Padres Stadium in San Diego selling his four season tickets to a football game. Three men in a car, requesting the tickets, approached him. As he held them out, the passenger grabbed his arm and they entered the freeway, dragging him. While one passenger covered the license plate with a towel, the other two beat him, took his money and tickets, and then threw him onto the freeway at 55 mph, seriously injuring him. The three were later arrested sitting in the season ticket seats. During the trial, the three made death threats (mouthed and simulated 'bang bang'). They belonged to a Los Angeles gang and began drive-bys at our house, while my two-year-old, my husband, and a pregnant me were home. Ultimately the three were jailed for six months; it was their third felony arrest in California in a year. They were identified as illegal aliens from Mexico, but when they were released from jail, they never paid the restitution that was ordered, nor were they deported for being illegal aliens in this country."

Marty Lich
Gypsum, Colorado

"I feel everyone should know what's going on in North Carolina. Since NAFTA (North American Free Trade Agreement), we have lost over 48,000 textile and furniture jobs, yet illegals are pouring in. Also, as a health care worker, we are exposed to tuberculosis and other diseases we did not previously see here. A message to federal and state-level politicians: You took an oath of office to uphold the Constitution of the United States. Allowing illegal immigrants into our country without fear of punishment is treason."

A. V.
North Carolina

"One day in October 1995, a woman from Mexico ran a stop sign and collided with my little pick-up truck. After the police arrived, I was told she didn't have insurance, or a driver's license. She was here illegally. This accident caused damage to my right ankle, right knee, left rib cage, neck, and back. These injuries put me out of business forever, since my work required a lot of ladder climbing. My lawyer said it would be a waste of money to go after her, because she didn't have anything, and all she would do would be to split back to Mexico.... Because of that illegal alien, I will probably die alone, and in pain. I know illegal aliens want a better life, but what in hell about mine? I earned this as a veteran of Viet Nam?"

Ray W.
Phoenix, Arizona

"When one travels to a foreign country it's wise to buy a book to help translate their language into ours. Here in California I also need a wide assortment of foreign language books if I want to understand the Spanish, Vietnamese, Chinese, Iranian, etc. 'Babel' of my fellow citizens. The ever-growing invasion of third world people here legally and illegally, who choose not to speak English (or only speak it when they want to sell you something or need something from you or from the system) makes me feel like I'm in a foreign country. My President and the political hacks here in California turn a blind eye to the invasion and pander for the 'diversity' vote. They are destroying my state and my country."

Bob T.
Spring Valley, California

"My experience has to do with loss of job, family, savings and future as a result of cheap foreign labor, i.e., work visas and now the new threat of outsourcing skilled jobs in my profession to India, China, Russia and the Philippines. I was replaced along with the rest of an American IT staff only to have our jobs and futures taken over by cheap foreign visas and outsourced jobs to India. What ever happened to America?"

Mike S.
Melrose Park, Illinois

"An illegal alien has messed up my life, as I knew it. He took my son's life and put my wife in a wheelchair coming up on three years as of June 16, 2003. We were going to the mountains that day. We were stopped at a red light and he ran into us at an estimated 64 mph. I just want to try to get something done about this problem."

Billy Inman
Woodstock, Georgia

"Having lived in Laredo for many years I see the effects of this human wave of illegals from Mexico. It has caused a general breakdown at our local schools as well as in our medical units. There are diseases here that were wiped out in the U.S. years ago. And the crime in this border city has skyrocketed—from sex crimes against children and women to murder. Local stats show that the majority of these crimes are committed by illegals."

Bradley S.
Laredo, Texas

"I live in Miami, Florida, a city dominated by legal and illegal immigrants. I moved here from Arizona hoping I could land a better paying job. The newspaper want ads all say, 'must be able to speak Spanish.' I can't believe that the native people of this city can't get the best jobs. This city's politicians are bending over to accommodate the non-English speakers, while in the process pushing out the English speakers. Classes in schools are taught in Spanish. I can't believe that they are teaching high school English in Spanish. Kids who graduate that don't speak Spanish are at a disadvantage. There is a saying in Miami—'I like to visit Miami because it's so close to the United States.' That is exactly how I am beginning to feel—like I have moved to a foreign country and I need to learn to speak their language."

Crystal S.
North Miami, Florida

"I spent 15 backbreaking years building a business only to have it ruined by folks here illegally, and our government not protecting me. Like many employers across this county, we were forced into making a big decision, violate our laws by hiring illegal aliens or do what is in the best interest of our country, and not hire them. I used to pay my people a living wage back when I could have employees—it was $15 per hour. Since this flood of illegals who will work for poverty level wages, I cannot compete anymore paying those wages, so citizens have lost jobs and I have lost business. Those that employ these folks beat my bids by not having to pay workers comp, taxes, Social Security, etc. I will not violate our laws, so I am down to me as the only employee. I have lost major income and struggle to pay my bills and take care of my son, as I am a single father."

Alan C.
Carson City, Nevada

"In my occupation, warehouse supervisor, wages have dwindled in the past 10 yrs. The reason is that all the companies' shipping departments have been flooded with cheap Mexican labor. Illegal aliens have driven down the wages of numerous occupations—all the way from the fast food industry or restaurant industry to construction. I'm just seeing a lot of corruption around me and it sickens me to see the town I grew up in starting to look like a Third World village in Mexico. My niece is in a school where there are so many non-English speaking Mexican kids that it is deterring the American kids from learning. This is not a funny or passing fad—this is a major problem and all the politicians ignore it."

Jerry W.
Redwood City, California

"I have always been able to stay off unemployment because I am a skilled dry-wall finisher, a trade learned in my youth, and one that has often proven very handy. Unfortunately, there are no openings anymore for English-speaking dry-wallers. Two years ago I worked for a company in Dallas and I was the only employee who was American born and spoke English. Now needing work again I can't find it. When calling companies they question my qualifications, even though I have years more experience than my young Mexican co-workers, many under 17."

John C.
Dallas, Texas

"I lived in Dade County and saw in just 20 years after the Mariel Boatlift how the boatloads and the sheer numbers of Spanish-speaking third world immigrants impacted the county and brought about a banana republic. The immigrants then, due primarily to their large numbers, began to win political office and control most political positions. That's when the third world banana republic mentality set in. The criminal element is also heightened. My neighborhood in Dade was a fine neighborhood until the element began stealing cars and burglarizing homes in that neighborhood. I awakened one morning to find my son's car up on blocks after his expensive rims and tires were removed from his car. What happened in Dade is an outrage, but cannot be understood unless you have lived it. I have lived it, and do not want to see the banana republic mentality push me completely out of this state."

Linda D.
Charlotte County, Florida

"I live in a large mobile home park, and it is at least 75 percent illegal immigrants. The trailer behind me has eight adults living in a three bedroom. There is a prostitute at their trailer every day. I would love to move but houses are so expensive. I have three boys and it isn't safe to let them go outside without me. One Mexican told me that they would take over America and that we could go live in Cuba. Then he laughed about it. They are getting food stamps, Medicaid and WIC, and they don't report all their income. They get fake IDs made in Atlanta, and I even know one woman here in the park that makes them on her computer. One Mexican is using his son's Social Security number and had an ID made with his son's name on it. He uses it for everything. It makes me so angry that all this is going on. It seems like no one cares about the American people anymore."

Sharon D.
Carrollton, Georgia

"I have been programming for over 20 years. All those years I worked in Silicon Valley. I almost never had trouble finding good paying programming jobs. I have been a programmer, Project Manager, and Technical Lead. Now, it is nearly impossible for American IT workers to find work in Silicon Valley. All of my friends are out of work. Correction: all but one. He was out of work for 2.5 years and got a job only by moving out of state. I defy anyone to say that mass immigration is good for America. No other country in the world would tolerate this. It is destroying the living wage in this country and it is destroying our quality of life."

Michael A.
San Jose, California

"My family has recently had the pleasure (tongue in cheek) of moving around the country, due primarily to lack of work. My husband is a computer techie, native Californian, whose industry has been taken over by immigrants from India on H-1B Visas. After spending several months each in Chicago, Maryland, Ohio, various cities in Michigan, I can tell you the problem plagues the nation. I'm tired of all the immigrants.

Yes, I'm against all immigration at this point. Our country is being taken over from within and I'm not happy about it."

Annette H.
Leslie, Michigan

"Up until 1988 I worked overseas with our U.S. Dept. of State as a member of the Diplomatic Corps. When I returned to the states, I was shocked at the influx of illegal aliens all across the country. However, the enormity of this devastating problem didn't hit me until I moved to Arlington, Virginia. After eleven years of living in this intolerable situation, I've come to the conclusion that it's not just a 'problem' any longer; it's now a terrifying crisis—one that is growing by the day and one that is destroying America inch by inch. This great land is fast turning into a Third World ghetto and its inhabitants are ignorant, aggressive, maniacal human beings whose only desire is to rape this land, grab the goods and then trash the place."

Andrea R.
Arlington, Virginia

Those are just some of the stories the mainstream media ignore. Those are the real victims of our country's mass immigration nightmare: American citizens.

Part Two

The Patriots

Introduction and Photos

The following chapters tell the stories of eight courageous citizens and others who answered their country's call to battle the powerful forces behind open borders and who have made a difference in preserving a recognizable America. If not for these citizens and many others like them, America's immigration and overpopulation problems would be far worse today, and so would our quality of life.

Woven throughout these personal histories are the related topics of mass immigration: the economy and jobs, national security, crime, education, health care, welfare costs, public health, language, assimilation, culture, national unity, resources, sprawl, and congestion.

The people featured are among the leaders in the political and grassroots movement to end illegal immigration and re-establish national borders. These individuals have courageously defended our country's immigration laws and sovereignty while uncovering the truth about the powerful forces sponsoring mass immigration. Along the way, these patriots have made many personal sacrifices, repeatedly overcome adversity, and inspired other Americans with their tireless will to win. They are Republicans, Democrats, and Independents. They are of different races and ethnicities. Their career paths range from auto mechanic to Wall Street banker.

Their courage and honesty have brought them admiration and support from many Americans. Their words and activities have also brought them condemnation, slander, ostracism, property destruction, death threats, and in the case of one, the end of a career.

These real-life heroes may sometimes disagree with each other on tactics and on the rationale for immigration reductions. But, like most Americans, they agree that immigration must be legal, controlled, and reduced. These individuals love America and are deeply worried about what is becoming of our country. They fear that the U.S. as we know it will be ruined unless immigration policies are changed and laws are enforced.

Four of the eight featured patriots live in California: Terry Anderson, Barbara Coe, Jim Gilchrist, and Joe Guzzardi. Glenn Spencer and Chris Simcox reside in Arizona. Roy Beck makes his home in Virginia. Congressman Tom Tancredo lives in Colorado and Washington, D.C. Californians are emphasized because their state has suffered the longest and the most from uncontrolled immigration.

The immigration fight began in earnest in California in the early 1990s with Proposition 187. This would have denied most social services to illegal aliens in the state. Voters passed this measure overwhelmingly. Several years later, pro-illegal-immigration politicians and organizations killed it. The proposition was never implemented. California and the rest of the nation are paying the price.

Since then, the illegal-alien invasion has spread across the country. Angry citizens in other states are fighting to keep their states from ending up like California. They are learning from Proposition 187 and writing their own initiatives, as well as taking many other actions. Citizens in Arizona passed one such ballot measure in November 2004.

The information about the eight featured patriots was gathered from interviews with them and with people who know them, and from news media reports, letters, books, video and audio tapes, speeches, press releases, congressional testimony, radio shows, rallies, and other sources. Their stories follow.

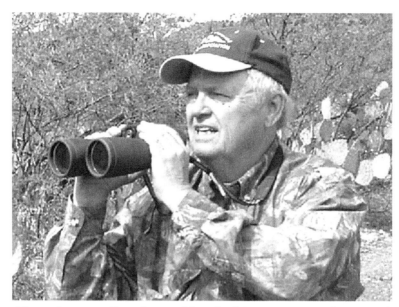

Glenn Spencer, founder and head of American Border Patrol, looks for people illegally entering the U.S. near the southeastern Arizona-Mexico border.

Terry Anderson, shown in 2004, launched his radio talk show on illegal immigration from KRLA in Los Angeles on November 26, 2000. (Photo by Cherilyn Blenkhorn.)

Roy Beck, founder and executive director of NumbersUSA, warns that unless Congress dramatically reduces immigration our population will surge to half a billion by 2050 and America as we know it will cease to exist. (Photo by Shirley Beck.)

Colorado Congressman Tom Tancredo accepts a plaque inscribed with the words, "#1 Immigration Reform Patriot," at a rally honoring him in the Los Angeles suburb of La Canada Flintridge on November 1, 2003. Barbara Coe (right), founder and chair of the California Coalition for Immigration Reform, presented the plaque. Lupe Moreno (left), president of Latino Americans for Immigration Reform, gave the congressman a certificate of appreciation from the Coalition of Latin American Republican Organizations. (Photo by David Moore.)

Supporters of Joe Guzzardi for Governor in the 2003 California recall campaign gather in Walnut Creek at the September 3 candidates' debate. Left to right are Tim Aaronson, Brenda Walker, Joe Guzzardi, and Carol Joyal. They are holding a giant check made out to "Illegal Immigrants" for billions of dollars, signed by John Q. Citizen, to emphasize that the enormous financial burden open-borders levies on taxpayers should be debated in the election. (Photo by Arnold Joyal.)

Minuteman Project founder Jim Gilchrist speaks to volunteers and the news media in Schiefflin Hall in Tombstone, Arizona, on April 1, 2005, the first day of the Minuteman campaign. Colorado Congressman Tom Tancredo, right, was the keynote speaker. Minuteman co-founder Chris Simcox, left, also spoke. (Photo by Fred Elbel.)

4 | Glenn Spencer

"If our government doesn't stop illegal immigration and secure the border, America will become a Third-World nation and Mexico will have achieved the conquest of Aztlan."

—Glenn Spencer, founder of American Border Patrol

On the night of July 19, 2004, two members of Glenn Spencer's citizen border watch group, American Border Patrol, showed how easy it would be for terrorists to bring a weapon of mass destruction (WMD) into the United States undetected.

That night, Technical Director Mike King and Director of Operations Mike Christie carried a simulated WMD from southeastern Arizona into Mexico then returned across the fence. While "in" Mexico, they remained within three feet of the fence, which is still part of the U.S., to avoid any border violation. The fake weapon consisted of foam rubber inside a hard-sided case marked "WMD," with international graphic symbols indicating nuclear and chemical danger. It was carried in a backpack.[1]

King and Christie were able to elude U.S. Border Patrol units on the ground, an agency helicopter, and an unmanned aerial vehicle (UAV) overhead to rendezvous with a waiting truck. They hid with the mock WMD in the bed of the truck, which took them to American Border Patrol's headquarters in Sierra Vista, a city of about 40,000 residents in Cochise County just a few miles from the border. They completed the mission without being apprehended by any law enforcement agency. Spencer videotaped every step of the operation.

King, a high-tech wiz and former army sniper who was assigned to Sierra Vista's Fort Huachuca as a national guardsman after the September 11 terrorist attacks, hoped the demonstration would help convince U.S. government leaders that America's southern border is a national security risk.

In the federal fiscal year—October 1, 2003, through September 30, 2004—U.S. Border Patrol agents in the Tucson sector apprehended nearly 490,000 illegal aliens. This region includes all of Arizona, except for the western area near Yuma. Of that number, more than 235,000 were taken into custody in Cochise County, with eighty-three miles of border with Mexico. (There are nearly three hundred miles of border in the entire Tucson sector.)[2]

But for every illegal alien taken into custody, the U.S. Border Patrol estimates that three to five others make it into the U.S. Assuming the more conservative estimate means that approximately 1.5 million foreigners successfully invaded the Tucson sector in just that twelve-month period. That region is by far the heaviest corridor for illegal-alien traffic, with more illegal border crossers than all other states combined.

King and Christie planned to repeat their experiment and guaranteed they wouldn't be caught.

They were right. A week later, the two American patriots smuggled their second fake WMD across the border about a quarter-mile from the spot where they conducted their first dramatic operation. Even though the first mission had been reported in the press, King and Christie noticed no increased enforcement in the area. Christie videotaped this mission. Again, the pair took the "weapon" to American Border Patrol's headquarters. But this time they didn't stop there. They drove the mock WMD seventy miles to the front entrance of the Federal Building in Tucson. As they approached the building, a federal officer appeared and asked them not to videotape the area. The officer asked for their IDs, but did not inquire as to what was in the backpack.[3]

On his popular Web site, American Patrol Report (www.AmericanPatrol.com), Spencer said right after the mission that his organization did not seek to embarrass the U.S. Border Patrol by smuggling fake weapons into the country. Instead, his goal was to point out the need for more resources to protect our borders. Spencer also said that he, King, and Christie were careful when making the videos of their operations "to avoid giving terrorists any aid in performing a real mission."

That same month, July 2004, terrorism expert Steve Emerson told Joe Scarborough on MSNBC's *Scarborough Country* about some shocking revelations in the 9/11 Commission's report, completed that summer, describing how al-Qaeda exploited the U.S. immigration system, set up a virtual document factory to make and manipulate passports, and how Arizona was ground zero for Muslim extremism and al-Qaeda training.[4]

During my four-day visit to southeast Arizona in November 2004, Spencer mentioned the smuggling of the simulated WMD to be among his most significant accomplishments in a long line of activities fighting illegal immigration and porous borders. "I think that's had more of an impact than people realize," he said proudly, referring to some media reports about the mission. But, he added, the big broadcast and print outlets did not cover the story. "They don't want to give us credit because that would help our cause."

Spencer also pointed to American Border Patrol's unmanned aerial vehicles, first launched in 2003, as one of his organization's most important achievements. Discussed later in this chapter, his group uses the UAVs to spot people illegally entering the U.S.

Threatening the Bonds of Our Union

Spencer said his most significant accomplishment was a forty-eight-minute video documentary he wrote and produced in 2001 when he was living in Los Angeles County's San Fernando Valley and heading an organization named Voice of Citizens Together. Titled "Conquest of Aztlan," the documentary is the third in a series under the heading

Immigration: Threatening the Bonds of Our Union. The others, also written and produced by Spencer, are "Courage and Capitulation in California" and "Treachery and Treason in America."

The "Conquest of Aztlan" is about the Mexican colonization of the American Southwest, which many Mexicans call "Aztlan." Aztlan includes California, Arizona, Nevada, Utah, Colorado, New Mexico, and Texas. Aztlan activists in the U.S. and in Mexico say this territory was stolen by the U.S. and must be re-conquered for Mexico. Actually, the region changed hands at the end of the Mexican-American War when Mexico signed the 1848 Treaty of Guadalupe-Hidalgo, and the U.S. paid $15 million for the land.[5]

Spencer, who narrates the "Conquest of Aztlan," opens the documentary by asking viewers to "demand that our laws be enforced. Do not attack anyone because of their race, language, or national origin. Americans of Mexican descent are some of our finest citizens."

Spencer then dramatically illustrates how the dream of radical Hispanics to retake the Southwest is becoming a reality with the aid of Mexican and U.S. policies and a number of powerful individuals and organizations. He says some of the organizations behind this movement include the Ford Foundation, which created and funds the Mexican American Legal Defense and Educational Fund (MALDEF) and the National Council of La Raza (The Race); the Southwest Voter Education Project; and big media outlets such as the *Los Angeles Times*.

According to Spencer, "A combination of legal and illegal immigration, coupled with citizen children or 'anchor babies,' born to illegal aliens, is allowing Mexico to colonize the American Southwest. And this colonization is being done with the tacit approval of the American government."

Here are some quotes from the documentary that help connect the dots the establishment media ignore:

- 1995 – Art Torres, former California state senator and current chairman of the California Democratic Party: "Remember, [Proposition] 187 is the last gasp of white America in California." The proposition, passed by

California voters in 1994, would have denied non-emergency public benefits to illegal aliens. Pro-illegal-immigration politicians and organizations prevented the proposition from being implemented.

- 1997 – Mexican President Ernesto Zedillo, speaking in Chicago: "I have proudly affirmed that the Mexican nation extends beyond the territory enclosed by its borders and that Mexican migrants are an important, a very important, part of it."

- 1998 – Mario Obledo, chairman of the California Coalition of Hispanic Organizations: "We're going to take back all the political institutions in California in five years. We're going to be the majority population of this state."

- 1999 – Democratic California Governor Gray Davis: "In the near future, people will look upon California and Mexico as one magnificent region."

In one scene showing illegal aliens walking in a long line through the desert into the U.S., Spencer asks:

Why aren't the American people outraged at this invasion of the United States? Why do they stand by and allow dual citizenship and blatant colonization of America? Why do they allow illegal aliens to take over entire unions and threaten our economic stability? Why do they allow corrupt, subversive organizations to tamper with our democratic process, often at the expense of taxpayers they intend to displace? Why? Because for the most part, they are unaware of it. They are unaware of it because the media want it that way.

More Americans are aware of the invasion today and what it is doing to the nation than in 2001 when Spencer made this documentary, thanks to the Internet, talk radio, cable TV, and books. The Minuteman Project in April 2005, discussed in chapter ten, was incredibly successful in drawing public attention to the invasion, but the mainstream media put their usual multicultural spin on the coverage and still refuse to tell Americans the truth because they are devoted to open borders, globalization, and socialism.

Spencer closes his narration of the documentary with these comments:

> It took hundreds of years to make America herself. From the pilgrims, to the founding fathers, to the pioneers, to today, through struggle, and—yes—conflict, America has been on the ascent. Lives, fortunes, and sacred honors have been laid down for that ascent. Laid down for the dream of a great nation. America is now at a crossroads. Will the children of the greatest generation preserve this nation, or will they willingly sacrifice it on the altar of globalism?
>
> America must now gain control over its borders and remove illegal aliens from its midst. This will not be easy. As we attempt to defend the homeland, we will face resistance as we go forth.

Phyllis Schlafly, a national leader of the conservative movement for decades, saw "Conquest of Aztlan" and called it "a stunning video." She invited Spencer to present it to her national Eagle Forum meeting in St. Louis on September 22, 2001. Schlafly is president of Eagle Forum, described as "a national organization of citizens who participate as volunteers in the public policymaking process." After the documentary was shown to Schlafly's group, Spencer received a standing ovation.

Schlafly then invited Spencer to show the documentary at a meeting of the Council for National Policy, another conservative organization, in early 2002. Among those attending the meeting were commentator Michael Reagan, the son of former president Reagan, former U.S. attorney general Edwin Meese, and Spencer Abraham, secretary of energy under President George W. Bush. "I felt that that video had quite an impact on some very high-level people," Spencer said. He was told that the video would be shown to Bush, but he doesn't know whether this actually happened.

Even though Spencer is concerned that another terrorist attack will occur in the U.S. because of our government's open-borders policy, he believes the massive Mexican invasion is a greater threat to America.

"Mexico has to unload one million of its people a year to avoid a revolution," Spencer told me. "I figure they've been doing just about that since 1984. In 1986, there were three million illegal aliens living in the U.S. Now [2004] there are up to 20 million illegal aliens in our country." Spencer's estimate includes the children born in the U.S. to illegal aliens.

A person born in the U.S. is automatically a citizen, regardless of the mother's citizenship status. Spencer and others in the pro-borders movement say that is a misinterpretation and abuse of the U.S. Constitution's Fourteenth Amendment, added shortly after the Civil War. In part, the amendment states, "All persons born or naturalized in the United States and subject to the jurisdiction thereof are citizens of the United States and of the state wherein they reside." It was drafted to guarantee that newly emancipated black slaves would never be denied citizenship by the states. However, when the amendment was crafted, the U.S. had no immigration policy. The authors had no idea that the amendment would be used to make a mockery of our immigration laws years later. It was never intended that an illegal alien could cross the borders into our country, have a baby a few minutes later or some time after that, and then the baby would automatically be declared a U.S. citizen.[6]

Automatic citizenship means that the illegal family is entitled to federal, state, and local welfare benefits paid by American taxpayers. Illegal-alien parents who have children born in the U.S. are seldom, if ever, deported. These children are called "anchor babies" because they anchor their families securely in the U.S. When the anchor babies turn twenty-one years of age, they become eligible to sponsor the immigration of other members of the family.

In the U.S. each year, hundreds of thousands of anchor babies are born to illegal-alien mothers. In Los Angeles, for example, more than two-thirds of the births are to illegal aliens, mostly from Mexico. In 2003 in Stockton, California, 70 percent of the 2,300 babies born in San Joaquin General Hospital's maternity ward were anchor babies.[7]

"I call children born here in America to illegal aliens 'illegal aliens,'" says the sixty-six-year-old Spencer. "It's illegal immigration by the birth canal. I've never been big on the abortion issue, but the fact is we are killing our babies, then replacing them in the schools with Third-World people. It's national suicide. And we are watching it before our very eyes, and it is inconceivable."

States Spencer: "Here we are going halfway around the world to attack a country [Iraq] that is no threat to us, while at the same time, every night, thousands of people invade our country from a nation that thinks this is their land.... The real war is not in Iraq, but on the Mexican border."

Educating Americans Since 1990

Since 1990, Spencer has been educating Americans about the invasion across our southern border, the forces behind it, and how the invasion is destroying America fiscally and culturally. He has founded several grassroots organizations, organized large rallies, produced many full-page newspaper ads, created video documentaries, produced newsletters, published Web sites, appeared on numerous radio and TV programs, hosted a radio program, and launched the first unmanned aerial vehicles on the U.S.-Mexico border. He even initiated an effort to recall California Governor Gray Davis for killing Proposition 187.

During his long campaign, Spencer has endured death threats and government investigations and been labeled a "vigilante," "racist," and "white supremacist" many times. But he keeps on working, hoping that enough Americans will wake up in time. At one point, he strongly considered retiring and ending his fight, but he found that he couldn't give up.

"The one thing that really gets me going is when I feel we [Americans] are being screwed over by people who are dishonest and underhanded," he told me, referring to government officials and the big media. "If there was a public debate over the issue of illegal immigration, and it was honest and open, and the American people decided we should keep the borders open, okay, that's the way life is. But when they [politicians and media] use unlawful, immoral, dirty, evil tactics to keep the truth from the people, that is something I cannot let stand. I cannot walk away from this. There has to be justice. These people have to be held accountable for what they have done. To the extent I can do something to help that out, I'll do it. I'm clearly not doing it for money."

Spencer began to publicly express his concerns about illegal immigration with letters to newspaper editors in 1987, the year after Congress, for the first time ever, amnestied about three million illegal aliens through the Immigration Reform and Control Act (IRCA). That year he also learned about the Federation for American Immigration Reform, or FAIR, (www.fairus.org) and became interested in the work they were doing.

In 1990, Spencer used his analytical skills to research the number of illegal-alien arrests on America's southern border. He had received a degree in economics, with a minor in mathematics, from the California State University, Northridge, in the San Fernando Valley. He worked his way through college programming computers and became an expert in statistical analysis. After college he worked in management and as a consultant for various companies and for the federal government. He specialized in computer simulations, energy development, and oil exploration. Through his 1990 research on illegal-alien arrests, Spencer realized that the large numbers of people illegally crossing the border amounted to an "invasion" by Mexico.

Spencer was deeply troubled by his findings and felt he needed to do more than write letters to newspapers, so he published a newsletter about illegal immigration that included data from his research. He then walked through his San Fernando Valley neighborhood distributing copies of the newsletter in mailboxes. Spencer said he thought this was all he had to do to alert people to the problem and get them to take action. He was wrong. Few people seemed interested in doing anything, but that would soon change as the problem of unrestrained immigration continued to worsen in Southern California.

Two years later, in 1992, Spencer attended his first FAIR meeting in the San Fernando Valley. He was inspired by the meeting and wanted to start a chapter there, but FAIR told him he couldn't. So he founded his own organization, initially calling it Valley Citizens

Together. He later changed it to Voice of Citizens Together and coined the motto "Citizenship/Sovereignty/Law" for his group. It was the same year Barbara Coe, in neighboring Orange County, launched the California Coalition for Immigration Reform. Outrage was growing among the citizenry.

In January 1994, citizen groups such as Coe's and Spencer's began collecting signatures from concerned voters for the statewide initiative that became Proposition 187. At about the same time, Spencer's group attracted national attention when one of its meetings was part of a CBS News *48 Hours* story on how immigration was impacting California. Charts created by Spencer showing that America was "importing poverty" were displayed in the broadcast.

The Cover-Up by the Power Brokers

Throughout his crusade, Spencer has not been afraid to take on the rich and powerful in public debates, written correspondence, or through any other means when he feels they are aiding and abetting illegal aliens. Here's what he wrote in a May 16, 1994, letter to Los Angeles Mayor Richard Riordan:

> Voice of Citizens Together [VCT] supported your candidacy when you told us that if elected Mayor you would seek to rescind Special Order 40, which restricts cooperation between the LAPD [Los Angeles Police Department] and the INS [Immigration and Naturalization Service].... You now refuse to do so.
>
> VCT worked to get over 2,000 people at a demonstration at Valley College when the President [Clinton] arrived to endorse Michael Woo [for mayor]. We helped defeat Michael Woo because he was behind the sanctuary movement in L.A. Our members went door-to-door to support you.
>
> Despite many attempts to get you to complete our "Feet to the Fire" questionnaire on illegal immigration, you refused to do so. We figured that you really supported us, but felt that it was politically dangerous to say so. Boy, were we wrong.
>
> You support those who are invading the United States. You are selling our seed corn in order to cover up the devastating

impact which illegal immigration is having on the budget of the City of Los Angeles.

You can fool some of us some of the time and all of us some of the time, but not all of us all of the time.

When it comes to the defense of the United States, I don't mince words. Mr. Riordan, you are a traitor.[8]

One year later, on May 14, 1995, Spencer's Voice of Citizens Together ran a full-page ad in the *Daily News* of Los Angeles about the invasion and the elite power brokers behind it. The ad was titled "Proposition 187 was the last gasp of white America in California," a statement made by former state senator Art Torres at a conference at a California university in January 1995 before hundreds of Hispanic activists, university professors, and elected officials. That conference is discussed in detail in chapter seven. Torres later became head of the California Democratic Party and holds that position as of 2005. The ad went on to say, in part:

> Can you imagine a prominent American saying that Proposition 187 was the end of the brown invasion of America? There would have been media outrage, that's what.
>
> But what happened when former state senator Art Torres said that Proposition 187 was the "last gasp of white America in California?" Nothing. In fact, the words were kept from you. What is going on here?
>
> An invasion of America covered up by the power elite, that's what....
>
> On October 16, 1994, 100,000 people marched through downtown Los Angeles carrying Mexican flags. One huge American flag was displayed on the main stage, but it had only thirteen stars—a statement as to the "true ownership" of California....
>
> Americans working on construction jobs throughout southern California are now being physically attacked by Mexican nationals under the guise of a union movement.
>
> Hundreds of these illegal-alien attackers have been arrested and then released by law enforcement even though they were in the country illegally.

Despite its tough provisions, five million California voters approved Proposition 187—after one of the most extensive public debates in our history and millions spent in opposition. They knew what they were doing. Now it has been stopped by one federal judge, Mariana Pfaelzer. The people speak but our government refuses to listen. In light of the clear and present danger of Mexican irredentism, this is an outrage!

So what can we do? Organize and spread the truth. Those who are determined to "reconquer" California are well financed and organized. They even have the government of Mexico behind them—and the American media. It is time to talk real about the invasion of the United States.[9]

In 1995, Spencer was using more than full-page ads in Los Angeles newspapers to talk about the invasion. Among other activities that year, he took advantage of the Internet—still in its infancy then—to spread the truth with his new Web site called American Patrol Report (www.AmericanPatrol.com). By this point he was seeking to awaken all of America about the growing crisis, not just immigration-ravaged California. Initially, the site attracted only a couple hundred hits a day. But as more people went online and illegal immigration spread across the country, the site's popularity grew. Eventually the site, which carries Spencer's Voice of Citizens Together motto "Citizenship/ Sovereignty/Law," became the place to go for news and commentary about illegal immigration. In 2005 the home page recorded its 13-millionth hit and was getting up to 25,000 visits a day.

In a January 2004 letter to Spencer about the site, Robert Bettes from El Paso, Texas, wrote: "You will never comprehend the effect you are beginning to have in transforming this nation from an oblivious, ignorant bunch of voters to an informed, passionate legion of activists, all united in the fight to halt and reverse the devastating effects of illegal immigration. The tide is turning.... You and your team will have as big an impact on America as Alexander Hamilton!"

'Good Fences Make Good Neighbors' Rally

But Spencer doesn't just report the news. He also makes news. On March 22, 1997, his Voice of Citizens Together organized what Spencer says was the biggest rally ever held on the U.S.-Mexico border up to that point. That Saturday, more than six hundred brave Americans, facing threats from supporters of illegal immigration, walked up to the border at San Diego, raised American flags, reaffirmed the sovereignty of the United States, and voiced their support for the completion of a new border fence. The demonstration, called "Good Fences Make Good Neighbors," is featured in Spencer's video documentary, "Courage and Capitulation in California."

Among those who spoke at the rally were Bill King, former chief agent of the Border Patrol's El Centro, California, sector; Richard Mountjoy, California state senator; Diane Jacob, San Diego County supervisor; and John Coleman, talk show host on KOGO radio in San Diego.

"There's a crime that has been committed," Jacob told the crowd. "It's a crime that's been committed by two governments: the United States government and the Mexican government against their citizens. Our government has failed to enforce our borders, failed to protect the lives and property of the United States citizens, and has ripped off U.S. taxpayers."

Coleman asked, "Those of us who are here today, those few of us who are here, are we the last patriots, or are we just the beginning? I pray we are just the beginning."

The demonstrators were urging the U.S. government to complete construction of a fourteen-mile fence at the Otay Mesa, the flat grassland east of the port of entry at San Ysidro, California. Construction on the fence had begun three years earlier, thanks to the efforts of citizen activist Muriel Watson.

By late 1989, Watson, the widow of a U.S. Border Patrol agent, was fed up with illegal aliens and drug smugglers crashing the border at Otay Mesa. She wanted the federal government to put up lights and a fence on the border, so she started a grassroots protest to bring attention to the problem. Watson and her fellow organizers called their protest movement "Light Up the Border."

On November 4, 1989, protesters in twenty-three cars beamed their headlights southward from Otay Mesa. This was the first of many "Light-Up" protests over a nearly one-year period. With each demonstration came more protesters and more cars. At one time, the headlights of about 1,800 cars were shining across the border, Watson said. The demonstrations attracted the attention of the local U.S. congressman, Republican Duncan Hunter. "He heard what we were doing and sent his aides down to watch," said Watson in another Spencer video documentary. "He realized we probably had a good idea."

In 1994, work finally began on the lights and fence. Construction was completed after Spencer's "Good Fences Make Good Neighbors" protest in 1997.

Watson's "Light Up the Border" demonstrations would eventually inspire Spencer to leave California for Arizona to show how technology could be used to help control the border and spot illegal aliens and drug smugglers. But in 1997, Spencer wasn't ready to leave behind his work in California. Staying in the Los Angeles area, he continued to hold protests, produce newspaper ads, host a radio program, disseminate press releases, and write commentaries, among other activities.

Bilingual Education and the Spanish-Language Media

In a 1997 commentary for the UCLA *Daily Bruin* student newspaper, Spencer wrote that the motive behind bilingual education is to accelerate the Mexican conquest of the American Southwest. Part of the plan of reconquista, he wrote, is to ensure that Mexicans in the U.S. retain Spanish as their primary language so they are dependent on the Spanish-language media for their "information and guidance." He said the print and electronic Spanish-language media are used as propaganda tools to criticize anyone opposed to illegal immigration, run stories about hardworking "immigrants," and teach "immigrants" how to take advantage of the social services provided by and for U.S. citizens.[10]

Spencer and others in the immigration reform movement say that organizations such as MALDEF (Mexican American Legal Defense and Educational Fund) and MEChA (Movimiento Estudiantil Chicano de Aztlan, a radical student group) block the assimilation process in America by advancing bilingual education, emphasizing racial identity, and manufacturing bogus grievances against the larger society.

Elected representatives also use their power to advance bilingual education and prevent children from learning English and assimilating. For example, in January 2005, Hispanics in the California state legislature refused to reappoint to the state Board of Education Reed Hastings, a businessman opposing bilingual education. Despite the fact that Hastings is a liberal and a major financial contributor to the Democratic Party, Hastings lost the Hispanic legislators' backing because of his "support of English-language reading instruction for immigrant children while he was the board's chairman," the *Los Angeles Times* reported. The Hispanic lawmakers said Hastings "did not show enough empathy for the concerns of Latino parents," the paper wrote.[11]

Spencer also explained in his 1997 *Daily Bruin* commentary that the English-language media rarely discuss illegal immigration, but when they do take up the subject, they don't do so honestly. For example, his Voice of Citizens Together had run a full-page ad in the *Los Angeles Times* in 1997 exposing Mexico's plan to retake the Southwest. Spanish-language television Channel 34 (Univision) covered the ad as a major news event, but there wasn't a word about the ad on the local English-language TV stations.

I have witnessed this phenomenon on several occasions. For example, in January 2005, in a live broadcast of the *John and Ken* talk-radio show at a hotel in Manhattan Beach, California, members of the California Coalition for Immigration Reform were collecting signatures for the "Save Our License" state initiative to prevent illegals from getting drivers' licenses. Thousands of people from all backgrounds fought late afternoon traffic to stand in line to sign the petitions and attend the show, hosted by John Kobylt and Ken Chiampou of KFI-AM. The duo's in-person guests were Colorado Congressman Tom Tancredo and California Assemblyman Mark

Wyland, co-chairman of the initiative campaign. The event was well publicized by the radio team and an important news story. However, the only Los Angeles media at the hotel were from Spanish-language outlets.

"Los Angeles is a city of two worlds," Spencer wrote in that 1997 *Bruin* article, "the English-language world and the Spanish-language world. ["The two worlds"] get different views of the unfolding immigration crisis."

That observation now applies across America with the proliferation of Spanish media outlets.

The First Effort to Recall Governor Davis

In September 1999, Spencer's Voice of Citizens Together initiated one of their biggest actions. They launched a ballot measure to unseat California Governor Gray Davis for killing Proposition 187, which the state's voters passed overwhelmingly in 1994.

Illegal-alien advocacy groups such as MALDEF, the League of United Latin American Citizens, and the American Civil Liberties Union immediately challenged the proposition as unconstitutional. Legal delays barred 187 from being enacted. Federal District Judge Mariana Pfaelzer ruled the proposition unconstitutional in 1998. The next step in the legal process should have been an appeal to a higher court. But Spencer and others featured in this book said Davis entered into an artificial "mediation" with Mexico's President Ernesto Zedillo and others to prevent 187 from going to the U.S. Supreme Court. No one from the side supporting the measure was allowed to participate in the closed-door negotiations.

"Here we have a ballot measure passed by 59 percent of the people, and Davis pulled this mediation trick and outright kills it," Spencer told the *Long Beach Press-Telegram* in October 1999. "We cannot let this stand. Then the governor makes a deal with Mexico. Davis thinks he can say and do anything he wants. When are we outraged? When?"[12]

In that same story, Barbara Coe, who joined with Spencer in the Davis recall effort, said, "This is tyranny we're talking about. [During his campaign for the governorship,] Gov. Davis repeatedly stated that he would uphold the will of the people. He betrayed that commitment."

Spencer, Coe, and others realized that recalling Davis was a monumental task. Organizers needed to collect one million signatures from California voters by early 2000 to place the recall issue on the ballot. Rallies were held and money was raised for paid signature gatherers. In the end volunteers collected only a few hundred thousand signatures. Spencer concedes the effort failed because of a near total "news blackout" by the English-language media.

In a second recall effort launched three years later, Davis was thrown out of office. This campaign is discussed in chapter eight.

'Her Work Was an Inspiration'

In 2000, after his effort to recall Davis failed, Spencer was weary from battling the powerful forces sponsoring illegal immigration. "I fought it for so many years," he told me. "I tried to expose the politicians, media, and judges. I tried to recall Gray Davis. I was going to retire in Lincoln, Nebraska, but I couldn't give up. I couldn't walk away. I was going to make one last stand so I decided to devote all my time and energy to the border."

For years, Spencer had wanted to do something on the border—not just the "Good Fences Make Good Neighbors" rally his organization held near San Diego in 1997, but something that would continually show citizens across America what was happening on the border. The more he thought about Muriel Watson's "Light Up the Border" campaign, the more he realized that's what he wanted to do, but in a different way. "Her work was an inspiration," Spencer said.

On May 12, 2000, Spencer returned to Otay Mesa near San Diego to videotape an interview with Watson just a few yards from the border fence and lights that were built because of her grassroots demonstrations. In the interview, Spencer discussed his idea of using the Internet to "light up the border." Here's part of the exchange:

Spencer: "We could have a snapshot at the border."

Watson: "That's a good idea. Have folks take pictures."

Spencer: "And we could put them on the Internet so everybody could see."

Watson: "Absolutely, and the rest of the country. You know the folks in Iowa and North Dakota and all of those areas have absolutely no idea of the problems we have down here."

The next day, Spencer held a public meeting at a hotel conference room in Sierra Vista, Arizona, located in Cochise County and just a few miles from the border, to introduce his plan for a new organization called American Border Patrol. The meeting was called "Illegal Immigration: What Can Citizens Do?" Spencer showed his interview with Watson from the day before and distributed flyers explaining how the Internet could be used to stream video pictures of people entering the U.S. illegally. Speaking before a packed room of concerned and angry citizens were several illegal immigration fighters:[13]

- Rick Oltman, western field director for FAIR: "The U.S. Border Patrol is apprehending 2,000 illegals per day in Cochise County. On their best day they only catch one in three. I've heard in this area [Sierra Vista] they may only be catching one in eight or one in ten. That means that every day and night there are 10,000 to 20,000 illegal aliens on the move in Cochise County spread out over the desert. They move north towards Tucson and Phoenix, bound for California, Washington State, Salt Lake City, Des Moines, Chicago, New York, and a thousand other destinations in our country."

- Ron Sanders, retired chief U.S. Border Patrol agent for the Tucson, Arizona sector: "Arizona has become the doormat for all illegal immigration throughout the United States. But more frustrating, the illegal aliens know that. They know that the Border Patrol is going to patrol two miles east of Douglas, Arizona, and two miles west of Douglas. The other three hundred miles are wide open, and the illegals are taking advantage of this to go through your property and to destroy your property rights. The government of Mexico has stated that they intend to sue the property owners that are trying to protect their property from the invasion of illegal aliens.

I say that it is time that we sue the INS for failing to provide us with the protection that we are entitled."

- Larry Vance, Cochise County resident: "We need to educate ourselves and other Americans as to the size, depth, and seriousness of this most dangerous problem. Contact your local representatives and demand action. They work for us. We don't work for them. This is an issue of American sovereignty and American citizenship. And, by God, it's time we stand up and fight back."

- Roger Barnett, Cochise County rancher: "The U.S. government won't protect my property, and I am prevented from doing so. Since the U.S. Border Patrol admits it doesn't have any resources to control the border, I call upon [Arizona] Governor Hull to deploy the National Guard to the border immediately. I will make my ranch available as a bivouac area. I have water, roads, and other facilities at their disposal."

- Larry Dever, Cochise County sheriff: "Be a good friend. Be a good neighbor. Report these things that you see. Don't give up. One of the biggest heartbreaks of this whole thing is I see hard-driving, hardworking fighters give up. Don't do that, please."

The meeting was a success for Spencer. Spirits were lifted and there was tremendous interest in his plan to use the Internet to show the American people what is really happening along the border. But it would be two more years before Spencer would be ready to move to Arizona and begin making his dream a reality.

Newspapers Cancel Spencer's Ad Warning Voters

Spencer returned to the San Fernando Valley to continue his work. Among other activities, he wrote and produced his three-part video documentary, *Immigration: Threatening the Bonds of Our Union*, discussed earlier in this chapter.

Also in his campaign to educate Americans were his full-page ads in newspapers. Spencer purchased the ads with donations from supporters of Voice of Citizens Together and AmericanPatrol.com. The first full-page ad appeared in the *Daily News* of Los Angeles in October 1994 and dealt with Proposition 187. Since that year, Spencer had run nineteen full-page ads in the *Los Angeles Times* and *Daily News*.

On May 3, 2001, Voice of Citizens Together announced in a press release that they would be carrying another full-page ad in the *Daily News* in three days. In the release, Spencer said the ad would represent the launch of a campaign to inform voters of Los Angeles mayoral candidate Antonio Villaraigosa's close ties to the Mexican government and bias toward the Latino community, including illegal aliens. The ad was to carry the headline, "Does Los Angeles Need a Mayor Who Reports to Mexico City?"

The ad would include a reproduction of the front page of the *Los Angeles Times* of August 4, 1999, showing Villaraigosa alongside Mexican President Zedillo applauding the demise of Proposition 187. Spencer said the ad would raise "serious questions about the loyalty of Villaraigosa to all Americans."

Villaraigosa, a Democrat, was Speaker of the California State Assembly at the time. He is a former chairman of the reconquista Chicano organization MEChA, an acronym for Moviemiento Estudiantil Chicano de Aztlan.

"Do we need a mayor whose public record strongly suggests that his primary loyalty is to an ethnic group, including illegal aliens, rather than all Americans?" Spencer asked in the press release. "For ten years our issue has been illegal immigration, and right now, Mr. Villaraigosa is the number-one advocate for illegal aliens in America." The ad would show a photo of Villaraigosa at a rally for illegal-alien amnesty held at the Los Angeles Sport Arena on June 10, 2000, attended by more than 20,000 people.

"Villaraigosa, Gov. Gray Davis, and the president of Mexico joined to keep Proposition 187 away from the U.S. Supreme Court because they were afraid it would be found constitutional," Spencer said. "Does Los Angeles really need a mayor who thwarts the will of the people?"

However, the *Daily News* canceled the ad just before it was scheduled to run. Voice of Citizens Together quickly filed a lawsuit in Los Angeles Superior Court against the *Daily News* and the *Los Angeles Times*. According to the lawsuit, the *Daily News* pulled the ad because of claims by the *Los Angeles Times* that it violated their copyright, a claim denied by Spencer's organization. The complaint said that the *Daily News* had accepted the ad and payment in full before canceling it at the last moment, thus breaching its contract. The complaint also pointed to "anti-competitive behavior" by the *Times* and *Daily News*, which together controlled newspaper advertisement in the San Fernando Valley, the target of the ad campaign.

"This action by the *Los Angeles Times* and *Daily News* sends a chilling message to American citizens," declared Spencer. "If we are not allowed to have a public debate over the issue of illegal immigration and the role politicians play in it, we are a doomed society."

Later, Spencer said, Los Angeles Superior Court Judge Emilie Elias tossed out the lawsuit on the claim that Voice of Citizens Together was trying to suppress the *Times*' freedom of speech.

"This outrageous ruling is a clear demonstration of just how lawless our nation has become," Spencer stated. "The *Los Angeles Times* sought to stifle our free speech, not the other way around. Each and every time anyone seriously threatens the established power structure over immigration issues, they are slapped down. Proposition 187 was killed by an illegal act by Governor Davis, following an outrageous ruling by a federal judge.

"The *Los Angeles Times* is an open-borders advocate and resists all serious attempts of dissension. It owns the Los Angeles Superior Court system. It was so desperate to keep this suit out of court, it persuaded a judge to violate the Constitution. We are all in danger."

Spencer was asked why the *L.A. Times* is such a strong advocate of illegal immigration and open borders. "You have no idea of the forces at work behind the scenes to make sure this process [illegal immigration] continues," he explained. "There are billionaires behind this.... The *Times* is a socialist newspaper. They subscribe to this global village concept. They are behind it because the banks, homebuilders, retailers, and all of the big people are behind it. More illegal immigration means more cheap foreign labor and more people to buy things. And since these big corporations and billionaires are the ones who advertise in the newspaper, they can influence the paper's editorial position. The people at the *Times* are whores. They have sold out to the power system."

As for Villaraigosa, he lost the mayoral race in 2001 to Democrat and city attorney James Hahn by a 54–46 percent margin. Four years later, on May 17, 2005, Villaraigosa ousted Hahn by 17 percentage points after capturing 58.7 percent of the vote.[14] The former head of MEChA became the first Los Angeles mayor of Mexican descent in more than 130 years.

Spencer Takes Battle to Arizona

In April 2002, Spencer had given up his twelve-year fight in California, but he still had hope that the rest of the nation could be saved from the flood of illegal aliens across the border. In September he moved to Arizona, the gateway to America for illegals, to work full-time on his new nonprofit American Border Patrol organization in Sierra Vista.

As president of the organization, Spencer recruited two former chief U.S. Border Patrol agents to join his board of directors: Bill King of the El Centro, California sector and Ron Sanders of the Tucson, Arizona sector. Later, three more patriots joined the board: Richard Humphries, a former agent and pilot for the Arizona Drug Agency; Henry Harvey, former city manager of Big Bear, California; and Iris Lynch, a recent California transplant who would serve as Arizona community organizer. Spencer also hired Mike King as technical director of American Border Patrol and Mike Christie as director of operations.

In September 2002, Spencer, Sanders, and Bill King held a public meeting at a Sierra Vista hotel to tell citizens about the new organization and the deteriorating situation on the border. They asked for financial support and volunteers to assist in the effort.

King characterized the situation as the worst he's seen in forty-five years. He said the U.S. Border Patrol is a great organization made up of dedicated field agents led by weak people.

"The Republican Party is stupid," King told the gathering, as reported in the *Sierra Vista Herald*. King said he believes President

George W. Bush is an open-borders supporter and is allowing Mexican President Vicente Fox to manipulate U.S. policies for Mexico's advantage. King said that in 1986 the U.S. Border Patrol did more with 3,000 agents and 1,000 criminal investigators to apprehend illegal aliens than in 2002 with 10,000 agents and 2,000 investigators.[15]

Spencer told the crowd that the goal of his new organization was to get live video of people entering the U.S. illegally, report them to the U.S. Border Patrol, and show the invasion to the American people on AmericanPatrol.com.

His organization, with the help of citizen volunteers working in teams, would conduct surveillance missions near the border. The volunteers would be positioned near ground sensors, planted by Spencer's group to detect the presence of border intruders. Once the sensors were triggered, the teams would move into position with cameras to record the intrusion. Spencer said no attempt would be made to apprehend the intruders. The video would be shown on AmericanPatrol.com.

Spencer also said his organization would patrol the border with small-scale unmanned airplanes that weigh about eighteen pounds and have a ten-foot wingspan and are equipped with electronic guidance systems and cameras. The sensors already planted along the border would detect the presence of people and guide the unmanned aerial vehicles, or UAVs, to those locations. The planes, ranging in cost from $12,000 to $21,000 each, would then transmit live video feeds to a van where members of Spencer's organization would monitor computer screens. The video would be uplinked to the Web site. Initially, the group would monitor the border between southeastern Arizona and Mexico. But the eventual goal was to monitor the entire U.S.-Mexico border and have border surveillance twenty-four hours a day, seven days a week. Spencer would use $180,000 of his own money to help fund his American Border Patrol organization, but he would also need regular contributions from citizens.

About his decision to leave California and move to Arizona, Spencer told the Sierra Vista gathering: "I fought in California for twelve years.... There is nothing I can do for California." But he hoped to do something for the rest of America.

In July 2003, one year after he left California, Spencer talked about the immigration disaster in the once-golden state in a lengthy letter posted on AmericanPatrol.com. Here is part of that letter:

California has been destroyed by illegal immigration. Most of the budget deficit can be traced to illegal immigration, past and present. Its schools have been destroyed, its health care has been destroyed, and now its entire social and physical infrastructure face collapse....

I have seen the power that runs California at work; it is awesome. They will allow the people to vote to recall Gray Davis, just as they allowed the people to vote on Proposition 187, but they will not permit serious consequences. They see the ballot box as a public pacifier. If the 'children' misbehave, they will be bludgeoned in the courts, the media, and, if necessary, through outright lawlessness as in the case of Proposition 187.

The establishment will destroy anyone who threatens their control, including the unpredictable Arnold Schwarzenegger.

California has one last chance to save itself. It must replace Gray Davis with a governor who will send Proposition 187 back to the courts and send the National Guard to the border. The new governor must also enforce those parts of Proposition 187 that are already on the books. [Spencer said this includes the manufacture, distribution, sale, and use of false documents to conceal true citizenship or alien status, mandating cooperation between local law enforcement and the federal government, and the reporting of suspected illegal aliens.]

If the appeal is allowed to go forth, the U.S. Supreme Court will find Proposition 187 constitutional and, faced with a total cut off of services and stringent law enforcement, millions of illegal aliens will leave California. Soon thereafter, Americans would end their exile in the deserts and return to the shores of the Golden State.

Short of this, California will sink into an abyss. It will become a Mexican state, just as Mario Obledo predicted.

Three months after Spencer's commentary, movie star Schwarzenegger replaced Davis as governor in the October 2003 recall election. However, as of early 2005, Schwarzenegger had done nothing about California's immigration crisis, even though voters tossed out Davis in large part because he consistently supported illegal-alien measures, including signing a bill allowing illegals to obtain drivers' licenses.

In November 2004, a report by FAIR showed that California's illegal immigration population was costing the state's taxpayers more than $10.5 billion per year for education, medical care, and incarceration, the three largest cost areas.

Even if the estimated tax contributions of illegal-alien workers are counted, FAIR pointed out, net expenditures still amount to nearly $9 billion per year.

The largest cost is for education. Californians spend approximately $7.7 billion annually on K-12 education for illegal-alien children and for their U.S.-born siblings—anchor babies.

FAIR said the total burden of illegal immigration to California's taxpayers would be much higher if other costs such as special English instruction, school feeding programs, or welfare benefits for Americans displaced from their jobs by illegal-alien workers were added into the equation.

In his annual State of the State address to Californians on January 5, 2005, Schwarzenegger talked about the state's staggering debt and said it would worsen. He proposed remedies, but none dealt with California's biggest problem, illegal immigration. He never mentioned the crisis.

As for education, Schwarzenegger blamed the high rate of high-school dropouts—30 percent, according to the governor—on teachers. There was no reference to the fact that many of the students—in some cases, most of the students—don't speak English and have no desire to learn the language.

Just two months later, a Harvard University report said the dropout rate is significantly higher and the California government uses "misleading and inaccurate" reporting methods. In the Los Angeles Unified School District, the report said, more than 60 percent of Hispanics drop out of high school, by far the highest rate for any group. More than 70 percent of the students in the district are Hispanic. The shockingly high dropout rate promises higher unemployment, increased crime, a bigger prison population, more pregnant teenagers, and other huge social and economic costs.[16]

Patrolling the Border

On September 20, 2003, one and a half years after moving to Arizona to work full-time on his American Border Patrol organization, Spencer and his team held a public meeting at a hotel in Sierra Vista to show their unmanned aerial vehicle, called "Border Hawk," and announce that missions on the border would begin in two days. They had been conducting test flights since April. Spencer's group worked with some small, independent companies, including Border Technology Inc. and UAV Flight Systems Inc., to design and build Border Hawk from scratch. More than five hundred people attended the meeting, including some from nearby Fort Huachuca, where the U.S. Army's UAV operator training takes place.

However, the September 22 launch was grounded by the remnants of a hurricane. That day, Spencer received a call from the army. "They wanted to see our Border Hawk in action," Spencer said. "Two days later, just as the weather was clearing, two army civilian employees showed up to see a demonstration. They were very impressed and said they needed our help in the Middle East protecting our troops. We explained that our primary role was to patrol the border, but we would do what we could to help our troops."

"The army asked us to reprogram the Border Hawk so it would stay ahead of a convoy by one kilometer, flying S-turns as it went," Spencer explained. "This was not easy, but we did it. The army sent brass out, and we ran a test of the system, flying the Border Hawk ahead of our Ground Control Van for twenty-two miles. It worked. Despite the fact that the army promised to buy fourteen of the aircraft, we never heard from them again.

"Six months later, we learned that the army had let a contract to another company to do the same thing, but that they were in financial trouble and hadn't produced anything. The army incident cost our organization a six-month delay in deploying the Border Hawk."

Spencer said some people suggested that the Department of Defense was showing interest in the Border Hawk to keep his group from deploying it along the border. "I am as cynical as the next guy, maybe even more so," Spencer said, "but this just isn't the case."

In the spring of 2004, the Border Hawk performed its first full border mission, sending high-quality video images over the Internet via AmericanPatrol.com. The Border Hawk showed that it could easily spot people entering the U.S. illegally.

Later, Spencer's organization expanded the duration and capability of the Border Hawk missions. The plane spotted hundreds of border intruders near the border in Cochise County.

Then Border Hawk II was launched. The newer version included a pan and tilt camera system designed and built by Border Technology, an upgrade from the fixed camera. The company also developed other improvements, including an infrared camera that permits use at night, the time when most illegal border crossers are on the move.

In addition to the Border Hawks, volunteers working with Spencer's group have conducted numerous day and night surveillance missions on the ground, getting video pictures of people entering the U.S. illegally and reporting them to the U.S. Border Patrol. The missions are shown on AmericanPatrol.com.

Thanks to the pioneering efforts of Spencer and his group, along with the financial and volunteer support of many citizens, the federal government began patrolling the border with UAVs. On June 24, 2004, the U.S. Border Patrol launched an Israeli Hermes 450 aircraft to help surveil the nearly three hundred miles of border in the Tucson sector. "I'm delighted they're doing it," Spencer told the *Arizona Daily Star*. "They may be able to save some lives."[17]

Four months later, during the third and final presidential debate on October 13, 2004, President Bush commented on the government UAVs patrolling the border, in response to the only question about illegal immigration during the debates. "We're using new equipment; we're using unmanned vehicles to spot people coming across," Bush said. "And we'll continue to do so over the next four years."

Spencer told me Bush's answer wasn't entirely true. "When the president was asked about border control," Spencer explained, "he bragged about their unmanned aerial vehicles flying the border. Well, at that time, they were not flying. They had been grounded. But we will take full credit for forcing the government into using that technology, and I don't think you'll find a journalist in southern Arizona who would disagree with that statement."

Spencer's Border Hawks, as well as his group's surveillance missions on the ground, have attracted print and broadcast media attention from all over the world. However, most of the time, the U.S. press has wrongfully portrayed his group as a vigilante organization made up of racists. Here's one example that appeared in the September 7, 2003, edition of the *Atlanta-Journal Constitution*:

> Spencer's group and others like it have alarmed immigration advocates, who say the citizen patrols are vigilante mobs motivated by xenophobia and racism.
>
> The Border Action Network, an advocacy group for immigrants, has launched a campaign to find Mexicans and other immigrants, who have been mistreated by citizen border patrol groups while trying to enter the United States illegally. The idea behind the effort—which includes billboards, posters, and radio spots—is to help the immigrants file civil cases against the groups.
>
> "Enough is enough," Gustavo Lozano, a member of the network, said at the campaign's launch earlier this year. "These groups have hunted Mexicans and other immigrants with dogs, guns and high-tech surveillance equipment. We've heard reports of beatings, deaths and other abuses."
>
> Spencer denied the American Border Patrol is a vigilante organization or engaged in any such actions.
>
> "We've never stopped anybody. We do not apprehend anyone," he said. The group simply spots illegal immigrants and calls the authorities, he said.

And while the *Atlanta-Journal Constitution* presented Spencer's point of view in three sentences, the paper had already used several paragraphs to plant the idea in the reader's mind that Spencer and his group are racists who kill people coming across the border illegally.

During my time with Spencer on the border in November 2004, he told me he's pleased with what his American Border Patrol organization had accomplished, but his goal is to monitor the entire U.S.-Mexico border around the clock so citizens can see the magnitude of the invasion. He likened his vision to a daily traffic report, with his team having the resources to report that 10,000 people crossed the border yesterday, the Border Patrol caught 2,000, and 8,000 are en route to Americans' jobs, schools, and hospitals.

"I am very pleased with what we've done down here at the border," he said, "although some of the technology has taken a little longer to develop than what I would have hoped. But I know we are on the right track.

"If I had $5 million, we wouldn't have a border problem. We could have border surveillance twenty-four hours a day. Americans could log on to the computer and see people crossing the border any time of the day or night. That would be incredible. Then people would pick up their phones and call their congressman and say, 'Did you see what's going on? You can see them right there. What are you going to do about that? And if you aren't going to do something, I want to find out who's running against you. And if there's nobody running against you, then I'll do it.' That's my goal. [Billionaire financier] George Soros could write a check and solve the border problem and wouldn't even miss the money. There are very wealthy people who could do this, but they choose not to. They don't care."

Citizens Say 'Militarize the Border'

In 2003, Spencer circulated petitions across the country asking citizens to sign on the line if they wanted the Bush administration to put the military on the southern border to keep illegal aliens, terrorists, drug smugglers, and dangerous criminals out of the U.S. Spencer's goal was to collect 100,000 signatures by January 2004 and send the petitions to Secretary of Defense Donald Rumsfeld. Spencer surpassed his goal, collecting 115,000 signatures.

On March 6, 2004, Spencer's American Border Patrol held a rally near the Federal Building in Tucson to publicize the collection of signatures and demand that the government put the military on the border. The rally was held on the same day that Mexican

President Vicente Fox was visiting President Bush at the Bush ranch in Crawford, Texas.

About two hundred people attended the demonstration. Two TV stations and two newspapers were on hand. Speakers included several well-known names in the immigration reform movement: Arizona State Assemblyman Randy Graf; Bill King, former chief U.S. Border Patrol agent and a director of Spencer's American Border Patrol; Los Angeles radio talk-show host Terry Anderson; D.A. King, founder of The American Resistance Foundation in Georgia; and Yeh Ling-Ling, executive director of the Diversity Alliance for a Sustainable America.

The speakers wondered how our elected officials in Washington could use hundreds of thousands of American soldiers to guard borders and protect citizens in other countries, but not use them to protect our own citizens from an invasion across the U.S.-Mexico border.

Also speaking at the gathering was Rick Oltman, FAIR's western regional representative. He presented a $50,000 check from FAIR to help put the Protect Arizona Now (PAN) initiative, which would combat voter and benefits fraud by illegal aliens, on the November 2004 ballot.

Following the rally, there was a short march to the Federal Building to deliver boxes containing the 115,000 petitions.

While the American patriots were holding their rally to save the nation, Bush was hosting Mexico's Fox at Bush's 1,600-acre property in Texas and pledging to exempt certain frequent Mexican visitors from new security checks at the border.[18]

Under the US-VISIT program, travelers from certain countries must be fingerprinted and photographed before entering the U.S. VISIT is an acronym for Visitor and Immigrant Status Indicator Technology. Bush said he wanted to ease those checks for Mexicans.

"Mexico and the United States are more than neighbors," Bush told the press at his ranch, sprinkling Spanish throughout his remarks. "We are partners in building a safer, more democratic, and more prosperous hemisphere."

Fox applauded the work by the two presidents to advance Bush's so-called guest-worker proposal, announced by Bush just two months before, in January 2004. Discussed extensively in chapter nine, the plan would give amnesty to the millions of illegal aliens, mostly from Mexico, already working in the U.S. The proposal also calls for the admission of countless family members of those amnestied and would allow U.S. employers to seek unlimited numbers of workers from other countries who are "willing" to work at whatever wages the employers determine.

Proposition 200: 'A Turning Point'

In 2003, a citizens group in Arizona called Protect Arizona Now (PAN) took matters into their own hands to help save their state from the illegal-alien invasion. The grassroots group launched a state initiative that would require proof of citizenship to register to vote, photo ID when voting, and proof of eligibility to receive non-federally mandated public benefits. It also required local and state government employees to report illegal aliens to federal authorities or face criminal penalties. A total of 122,612 valid signatures were required to certify the initiative for the November 2004 ballot.

The initiative was a scaled-back version of California's Proposition 187, passed overwhelmingly by voters in 1994 but killed by Governor Davis several years later.

"Local, state, and federal officials steadfastly refuse to protect our borders and enforce our immigration laws," said the members of PAN on their Web site, www.pan2004.com. "But why should the citizens of this state allow the hundreds of thousands of illegal aliens in Arizona to vote or collect welfare? With an estimated 5,000 to 10,000 illegal aliens crossing our border each day, including who knows how many Muslim terrorists, clearly the numbers and time are not on our side."

"Our Medicaid costs have exploded from $200 million in 2001 to $1.2 billion in 2003," the members of PAN said. "Hospitals are in trouble financially. Maricopa County Hospital is losing $2 million weekly. The education system is overburdened. There is a huge crime impact, neighborhoods are in trouble, and we suffer from drug trafficking, home invasions, and see our election process violated. We have a $1 billion deficit going into 2005. We believe enough has been too much and we intend to set things right rather than sit idly by."

The sponsors of PAN included grassroots civic leaders, Arizona elected officials, patriotic businessmen, and environmental activists.

Those opposing the citizens' initiative included Hispanic separatist organizations, major newspapers, and virtually all of the political, business, and religious establishments of the state. Among the politicians against it were the state's leading Democratic and Republican elected officials, Governor Janet Napolitano and Senator John McCain. Republican Congressmen Jim Kolbe and Jeff Flake also opposed it. The politicians said PAN was misguided and unnecessary.

In 2004, the initiative grew from a volunteer effort with citizens collecting signatures door to door to a statewide campaign funded mostly by Washington, D.C.-based FAIR. Because of PAN's national significance, FAIR and other immigration reform organizations independently supported signature-gathering efforts to ensure that the initiative appeared on the November 2004 ballot.

On June 3, 2004, some lawmakers and leaders in the pro-borders movement held a rally in Phoenix to encourage volunteers to succeed in getting the initiative qualified for the ballot. Among those at the rally were Colorado Congressman Tom Tancredo, Team America Chairman Bay Buchanan, FAIR Executive Director Dan Stein, FAIR Western Regional Representative Rick Oltman, Arizona State Representative Russell Pearce, and Los Angeles radio talk-show host Terry Anderson.[19]

"This is not just a local issue," Tancredo told PAN volunteers. "You are the front line and will send a message" across the country.

FAIR's Stein announced that his organization had just released a report showing that Arizona's illegal-alien population was costing the state's taxpayers about $1.3 billion per year for education, medical care, and incarceration.[20]

"Each year," Stein said, "special interests are involved in this Ponzi scheme. There is no cheap labor, just cheap employers. We are supposed to sit idly by while they ask us to subsidize college for illegal aliens. We are in this mess because special interests for thirty years opposed efforts to strengthen border control. Leaders of the two parties say, 'Shut up; we are moving to a free-trade zone.' And they are letting the middle class dissolve. Both political parties conspired to stifle debate and thwart this effort."

Arizona Representative Pearce, a senior co-advisor for PAN, told the crowd: "Shame on us for wanting to have standards as high as Blockbuster, which requires two forms of ID to check out a video, to vote. This is a very simple, modest initiative. It requires us to enforce the laws. People who don't uphold the oath of office they took ought to be removed from office. That Constitution does mean something."

Terry Anderson told the volunteers: "You are going to be in the history books forever…. You guys have to prove you can do it here. You must get it done…. I want to come back again to celebrate when PAN is put on the ballot and again when it passes."

Two months later, on August 16, Arizona's secretary of state certified that PAN, now known as Proposition 200—the Arizona Taxpayers and Citizens Protection Act—qualified for the November ballot. At least 152,187 valid signatures were collected for the initiative, far more than the 122,612 it needed to qualify. [21]

Public support for Proposition 200 was strong, despite a well-financed effort by cheap-labor interests and pro-illegal-immigration groups to discredit it, as well as prominent opposition from Governor Napolitano and Senator McCain. Initial polling showed that between two-thirds and three-fourths of those polled favored the measure. [22]

On the day of the general election, November 2, 2004, Arizonans passed Proposition 200 by a substantial 56-44 margin. In the months prior to the election, opponents spent hundreds of thousands of dollars in advertising to defeat the measure. In addition, the state's major newspapers—the *Arizona Republic, Arizona Star,* and *Tucson Citizen*—carried many articles opposing Proposition 200. If not for this opposition, supporters of Proposition 200 said, the measure would have won by an even wider margin.

Despite attempts by Hispanic organizations and others to portray Proposition 200 as racist, 47 percent of Hispanics voted for it. Also on board were 70 percent of Republicans, 42 percent of Democrats, and 51 percent of Independents. [23]

The passage of Proposition 200 drew immediate reactions from opponents and proponents. Supporters of open borders said legal challenges would be coming. Many leaders in the immigration reform movement considered the victory to be the biggest grassroots triumph in the fight against illegal immigration since the approval of California's Proposition 187 in 1994. They predicted it would inspire similar citizen efforts in other states and put more pressure on Congress to get tougher on illegal immigration.

"I think Proposition 200 was a tremendous success," Glenn Spencer told me just two weeks after the election. "It allowed the people to express themselves at the ballot box, and that's the last thing the power structure wants. It was a great victory from that standpoint, and I think it will encourage others to repeat Proposition 200s in their states."

Yet barely a week after the November 2, 2004 election, President Bush sent Secretary of State Colin Powell to Mexico, where he met with Mexican officials and indicated the administration's strong desire to revive the amnesty plan that Bush first proposed in January 2003.

On November 30, just like they had done ten years earlier with California's Proposition 187, MALDEF filed suit in federal court against Proposition 200. U.S. District Court Judge David Bury granted a temporary restraining order against the state to prevent it from implementing any of Proposition 200's measures into law until December 22. Ford Foundation-funded MALDEF said the newly passed legislation would "violate the U.S. Constitution's Supremacy and Due Process clauses, as well as the federal Voting Rights Act of 1965, a law to protect minority voters."[24]

But Proposition 200 doesn't say minorities can't vote, only people who aren't U.S. citizens.

On December 22, Judge Bury lifted the order, putting the law into effect. MALDEF officials vowed to continue their fight to defeat Proposition 200 in the federal courts. "We know that Proposition 200 is illegal, and we will fight it all the way to the U.S. Supreme Court, if necessary," said MALDEF President and General Counsel Ann Marie Tallman.[25]

One American patriot who worked mostly behind the scenes to ensure Proposition 200's triumph was FAIR's Rick Oltman. A long-time immigration reform activist, Oltman has spent years trying to prevent the California legislature from "handing over the state to illegal aliens," as he puts it. He's also been fighting illegal immigration in other states such as Arizona. Spencer said Oltman was the "key to success" for Proposition 200 and named him American Patrol's 2004 Person of the Year.

"Arizona's Proposition 200 will go down in history as a turning point in the battle against illegal immigration," Spencer predicted in his December 26 commentary on AmericanPatrolReport.com. "While many played a part in the success of this ballot initiative, the one person who made the difference between victory and defeat was Rick Oltman. Rick went out on a limb to raise the funds to gather the signatures needed to get the initiative on the ballot. He used his excellent diplomatic skills to keep the Protect Arizona Now team together despite severe internal stress. The success of Proposition 200 is but one of the many major contributions he has made in the fight against illegal immigration."

'Pre-War America'

During my time with Spencer in mid-November 2004, he was a constant whirlwind of activity. He shuttled from American Border Patrol's computer-filled office in Sierra Vista to the site of the organization's new headquarters just a stone's throw from the border, then back to town again to manage his high-tech operation and monitor the news media. His employee team of Mike King and Mike Christie was making preparations for the new command center, and Billie Palmer was helping supervise the busy office. Employee Jerry Deebach built the fuselages for the UAV Border Hawks, and citizen volunteers offered their time for missions.

Spencer's schedule is usually hectic, but this was a particularly crazy time because of the upcoming move to the new headquarters, an eighteen-acre site in Palominas in southeastern Arizona just 1,200 feet north of the border. Spencer's operation had been based in nearby Sierra Vista for two years, but the property association evicted him in 2004 for running a business—American Border Patrol—out of his home. Spencer called it a "blessing in disguise."

The new site, leased to American Border Patrol, looks out over miles and miles of open desert. It is surrounded by majestic mountain ranges and located near the San Pedro River. This vast expanse is one of the major pathways into America for illegal aliens and drug smugglers, and probably terrorists.

Spencer said the new site, where two runways had been built for the UAVs, would allow his organization to monitor a large section of the border, from Naco, Arizona, to the Coronado National Memorial, on a 24/7 basis. The headquarters would be named the Alan C. Nelson Center, after the former INS commissioner "who was instrumental in the passage of California Proposition 187."

Spencer's goal is to improve performance by the U.S. Border Patrol and show over the Internet even more of the invasion to the American people. "We want to statistically measure a section of the border and see how many illegal aliens are getting past the Border Patrol. We want to continue to show ways of detecting, identifying, and catching suspected border intruders." Spencer estimates that his organization has helped agents apprehend thousands of illegal aliens.

However, elected officials in Washington have already allowed millions of illegal aliens from totally different national and cultural identities to successfully make it across and illegally take American jobs and overwhelm schools, hospitals, and prisons. Most are poor, illiterate, and Mexican. Many believe they are reclaiming Mexican territory in the American Southwest. Increasingly, Americans, not just in border states, but also far removed from the Mexican border, are frightened and angry. Spencer believes serious trouble is coming.

"I call this time period pre-war America." He cautioned, "There is going to be a civil war of a kind we've never seen before, because our government hasn't allowed the problem to work itself out in the public arena. They've allowed the cancer to grow, with no treatment, by covering up the symptoms. They've allowed the cancer to grow to where now it is going to take a massive, possibly fatal process."

He warned that those in government, big business, and the media "who continue to thwart the will of the people when their nation, their culture, and their standard of living are being attacked are skating on very thin ice."

Spencer said Americans "should do what people do in a free society, a democratic republic. You demand action by your elected officials. You start grassroots organizations like I did with friends and neighbors. I'm not that special. There are other people like me. We need more people to take charge of this thing. We need more good people running for office to go up against congressmen like Jim Kolbe, Chris Cannon, and Henry Waxman [who support open borders]. We need more people donating to organizations like mine."

He said immediate steps must be taken to save the nation. The border must be shut down. There must be a humane but effective repatriation of all illegal aliens now in the U.S. The practice of granting automatic citizenship to children of illegal aliens must end. The U.S. must end all bilingual education programs and the broadcast of other-than-English programs.

"If our government doesn't stop illegal immigration and secure the border," Spencer warned, "America will become a Third-World nation and Mexico will have achieved the conquest of Aztlan."

5 | Terry Anderson

"Stupid people of America, if you ain't mad, you ain't payin' attention!"

—Terry Anderson, auto mechanic and talk-radio host

Auto–mechanic-turned-radio-talk-show-host Terry Anderson begins his broadcasts from the KRLA studios in Los Angeles every Sunday night with the attention-grabbing line quoted above. For several years his broadcast, *The Terry Anderson Show* (www.theterryandersonshow.com), has been the only one in the nation devoted entirely to the subject of illegal immigration.

He didn't always open his broadcast by calling Americans "stupid." When Anderson launched the show in November 2000, he opened by saying, "Good people of Los Angeles, good evening." After the show grew in popularity and went nationwide, he changed the opening to, "Good people of America, good evening."

But the pleasant greeting ended in late 2002. "I began getting angry because people weren't responding to this issue of illegal immigration," Anderson told me during one of several interviews. "Not enough people were getting involved. They weren't circulating petitions and calling their representatives in Congress. They weren't standing up and doing what's right for America. So on one of my broadcasts I said, 'You people out there are stupid!' That's when I decided to change my opening to, 'Stupid people of America, if you ain't mad, you ain't payin' attention!'"

While some listeners tell Anderson they're offended that he calls them stupid and sometimes uses rough language, most don't mind his blunt street-talk at all. His five-year-old show is more popular than ever. What began as a show broadcast only in Los Angeles is now heard on many stations across the nation.

"People are calling the station here in Los Angeles and saying, 'We want this show in our city,'" Anderson said. "That's because illegal immigration has become a problem across our country and more and more people are being affected by it. People are getting angrier about it."

If you think Anderson is an angry, middle-aged white guy from the Republican Party, you're only half right. He is middle-aged (fifty-five) and he is angry, but he's not white or a Republican. He's black, poor, and isn't tied to any political party.

"I can't stand the Republican or Democratic parties," he said. "Most politicians stink. There are a few good ones out there, but not many."

Anderson lives in South Central Los Angeles. It is an area that has undergone a dramatic shift during the past two decades from mostly black to mostly Hispanic because of illegal immigration from Mexico. He said South Central no longer looks like America—it looks like Mexico. The illegals have brought with them their own culture and language and are thumbing their noses at America's laws and customs. And they are taking jobs away from American citizens. This is why Anderson calls himself "The Prisoner of South Central."

"I feel like a prisoner in my own community," he said with anger and sadness. "I don't feel like an American citizen anymore. I feel like I'm in jail because I don't have the freedom that I once had. I'm living in a foreign country, and I've been to foreign countries and I know what they look like. This is what it looks like. I don't want to live in a foreign country. I'm an American, and I'm proud of my nation and my race."

Anderson has lived in South Central nearly his entire life. When he moved there from Oakland, California, in 1954, the area was largely white. Most of the white people treated his family with "dignity and respect." He and his brother went to the same schools as the white kids, and "no special arrangements" were made for them. White people gave them jobs, and everyone spoke the same language, English.

"We were all Americans," he said. "We had a common culture, the American culture."

From the 1950s through the civil rights movement of the 1960s and to the 1970s, the community gradually changed from mostly white to mostly black but still remained American.

In the 1970s and early 1980s, Anderson remembers, the quality of life for blacks in Los Angeles was becoming better each year.

"We were making strides in every avenue of society," he explained. "I'm not trying to paint all blacks as nice, caring, non-violent people, but we were really coming into our own. My neighborhood was a respectable, blue-collar area of hardworking black folks living in their bungalows and going to their jobs."

Corn, Rabbits, Roosters, Chickens

In the late 1980s, Anderson's neighborhood began to change. "That's when this illegal-alien invasion from south of the border started," he recalls. "The first thing that really grabbed me was when I saw the billboards start to change into Spanish. Then it really got bad in the '90s. The water and power company, gas company, telephone company, Seagrams, Kellogg's, Colgate, you name it, all of a sudden they were all in Spanish.

"Since the invasion began, jobs, schools, and crime are much worse. The average black guy in the community has lost most of his employment possibilities because the area has been invaded by illegals willing to work for less than a living wage. Now everything's gone to hell."

The massive invasion began shortly after 1986 when Congress and President Reagan granted legal status to about three million illegal aliens living in the U.S. The amnesty was called the Immigration Reform and Control Act (IRCA). It was supposed to solve the illegal immigration crisis, but it only legalized the lawbreakers and worsened the problem.

"In 1986, the American people were promised a well-run, one-time-only amnesty program for illegal aliens living here at the time," the Federation for American Immigration Reform said after President George W. Bush announced his guest-worker amnesty proposal in January 2004. "The 1986 amnesty was neither well run nor apparently a one-time offer. It was riddled with fraud and did nothing to solve the illegal immigration crisis. In fact, judging by the fact that we have an estimated nine to eleven million illegal aliens living in the U.S. today, it exacerbated the problem.[1]

"The second part of the 1986 immigration act was the promise of employer sanctions that would punish employers who continued to hire illegal aliens. Employer sanctions have never been enforced, and there is no reason to believe that the government will be any more serious this time."

After the 1986 amnesty, millions of poor and uneducated people from south of the border illegally flooded into the U.S. to seek jobs and take advantage of welfare, "free" health care, and "free" education. These invaders hurt poor and middle-class Americans, but especially Americans on the lowest rungs of the economic ladder such as those in Anderson's neighborhood.

Today, Anderson said, 60 percent of his neighborhood is Hispanic, almost all are from Mexico, and "99 percent" are illegal aliens. The population is constantly growing from new illegal arrivals and from their high number of births.

One day, Anderson gave me a tour of his neighborhood and pointed to houses where his black American neighbors once lived.

"Thirty illegal Hispanics live in that three-bedroom house. That's fairly typical—lots of families living in one house." Pointing to another house, Anderson said the Hispanic woman living there was growing corn in her front yard. Still another house "had lots of rabbits in the yard. They're raised for food. The house next to it had roosters."

During another visit to Anderson's home, I nearly drove over chickens crossing his street. Remember, this is happening in the middle of the second largest city in America, not out on a farm.

Anderson's home is near the University of Southern California and the Coliseum.

Anderson said officials with the City of Los Angeles don't care about the zoning violations resulting from so many people crowded into one house or the farm animals in a residential neighborhood. He said enforcing the laws might get in the way of political correctness.

Then there's the music and parties. "Mexican music is played all day and all night," Anderson said. "We didn't have a problem with loud music on my street before. The Mexicans play it louder at night and from many households. There's lots of partying."

The invasion has driven many black Americans out of Los Angeles. Some have moved east of L.A. County, toward the desert, Anderson said. But most have moved to the Southeastern U.S., to states such as Mississippi, Alabama, and Louisiana, "usually where the family was from."

How are they displaced from their homes? Anderson explained it this way: "A Mexican family moves into the middle of the block. They have their parties and play their music loud. There's not one black family on my street that has parties. The black family next door can't take it so they move. Well, who's going to buy the house next to these loud people? It's another Mexican family. Now he's next to another black family, and that family moves out too. It's a cycle, and before you know it, you've got an eight- to ten-house wedge in the middle of the block where they've come in and nobody wants to live next to them, and it's not for racial reasons; it's for cultural reasons. And that's how they take over a neighborhood—house by house, block by block."

Over the years, hundreds of thousands of Americans of all backgrounds have abandoned Los Angeles and other California cities and communities because of the invasion. However, many people who fled are finding that the problems they thought they left behind soon show up in their new hometowns.

One was Marty Lich. She and her family left San Diego County in 1994 for several reasons—all related to illegal immigration.

"We wanted to raise our two children away from schools ridden with non-English speakers," Lich told me. "We wanted them to have a good education like we had gotten. My husband also was nearly killed by illegal aliens who dragged him on the freeway at 55 miles per hour. They belonged to a Los Angeles gang and were identified by law enforcement as illegals from Mexico." (That crime is one of many short stories featured in chapter three.)

The final straw for the Lich family was the financial impact the invasion was having on her husband's business. "He no longer had a competitive contractors business," she explained. "He hired the legal day workers and paid workmen's compensation, but he couldn't compete with employers who were hiring cheap illegal labor and paying them in cash. So we moved to escape all of it." Or so they thought.

The Lich family moved to Gypsum, Colorado, which is about forty miles from Vail and Aspen. Illegal immigration was not a problem when they first moved to the small town, but soon thereafter the invasion began to make its way there. "They began infiltrating about ten years ago," she said. "Eight years ago we had less than one hundred ESL [English as a second language] Spanish-speaking students. Today there are more than 2,200. They are enrolling here daily. I moved my son and daughter out of the public schools, where the illegal aliens steal school supplies and tag the facilities with graffiti. We now spend a lot of money on private schools, which is very costly to us, and I drive 80 miles a day to take them to school. All of these problems are caused by our politicians in Washington who refuse to secure our border with Mexico and deport illegal aliens, who are destroying our country."

Others who left California in recent years are Randy Lewis and Phyllis Sears. Lewis left in 1998 after living in the state for thirty-five years. "I saw it go from the best state to the worst," he said. Lewis moved to North Carolina, hoping to get away from the troubles, but encountered the same problems there. He became so fed up he started a group called Stop the Invasion![2]

Sears left California and moved to the Phoenix area, where she served on a city council. She then moved to St. George, Utah, because she thought it would be relatively crime-free. Within a year, problems that plagued California and Arizona began to surface in the St. George area.[3] "When we moved here seven years ago," Sears wrote in a 2004 commentary, "there had not been a murder in the county in ten years. Now there are the murders of at least two citizens at the hands of illegal aliens and possibly two other murders as well."[4] Because of those crimes and other problems, Sears and other residents founded the Citizens Council on Illegal Immigration. There's more about the efforts of Lewis and Sears in chapter eleven.

In a May 2002 article, Patrick Buchanan, author of the bestselling book *The Death of the West*, wrote about Americans escaping California and warned that the crisis plaguing the state is a harbinger of what's coming to the rest of the nation:

> What kind of country will our grandkids live in? If immigration is not brought under control, tomorrow's America will resemble Los Angeles today—a multicultural, polyglot nation, most of whose people trace their ancestry to the Third World, and a country where the extremes of wealth and poverty mirror the Third World.
>
> In the 1990s, poverty in Los Angeles County did not decline, it rose 28 percent.... In Orange County, south of Los Angeles, once the bastion of Goldwater Republicanism, the poverty rate soared 44 percent. East of Los Angeles, in the Inland Empire counties of San Bernardino and Riverside, on the road to Palm Desert and Nevada, poverty soared by 51 percent and 63 percent.
>
> White folks are fleeing California at a rate of 100,000 a year. Black folks are following. La Reconquista is at hand. Well over half of Los Angeles County residents—54 percent—now speak a language other than English in their home.[5]

Mr. Anderson Goes to Washington

Twice, Anderson has traveled to Washington to tell members of Congress how illegal immigration is hurting citizens in his neighborhood and across America. He first testified on June 10, 1999, before the House Judiciary Subcommittee on Immigration. This was before he became a radio talk-show host. Here is most of his written testimony:

> When you here in Washington hear about illegal immigration you will only hear about 'the poor immigrant

who comes here for a better life' or the poor, poor immigrant child who 'must' have an education. You hear about how 'hard working' they are and about their great work ethic. You hear the lie about how they don't use public services and how they only take the jobs that nobody else wants.

You hear from all of the liberal organizations who advocate for the illegal aliens. You also hear from the racist organizations like the Mexican-American Legal Defense and Educational Fund (MALDEF), the League of United Latin American Citizens (LULAC), Movimiento Estudiantil Chicano de AZTLAN (MEChA), and the National Council of La Raza, The Race. They will tell you why the illegal alien is good for America.

What they don't tell you about is the 17-year-old kid on my street that can't get a McDonald's job because he can't speak Spanish. They don't tell you about the 8-year-old boy on my street who like thousands of other black kids is thrown into a bilingual classroom and listens to translations all day long. His six-hour school day is turned into three hours. When his mother asks for an English-only classroom she is told 'there are none.'

They don't tell you about the $100,000 house in my neighborhood that sold for $137,000 because the real estate company put five families of 'newly arrived Hispanics,' who spoke no English, on the deed. Now when a black family wants to buy a house, they too have to find four other families to share the ridiculous cost.

They won't tell you how skilled black workers in Los Angeles can no longer apply their trade—body and fender, roofers, framers, drywallers, gardeners, and now even truck drivers.

They won't dare tell you about all of the race riots in our schools where the blacks are told to take their black asses back to Africa. Even the news media has refused to tell of this while we know that they are aware of it.

There is never a mention of all of the billboards in Spanish and how Chevron is now advertising in Spanish on English-language TV.

The illegals won't hire us and won't buy from us. But still our elected black officials won't help us.

We black Americans are being displaced in Los Angeles. We are being systematically and economically replaced.

And the next time somebody tells you that the illegals only take jobs that blacks won't do, just remember that we were doing those jobs before the illegals got here. And in places of the country where there is not yet a problem with illegals, you can still get your grass cut, your dinner served, your dishes bussed and your hotel room cleaned. Funny how in those places Americans are doing those jobs. We would still be doing them in Los Angeles if it was not for the fact that the illegal will work for $3 an hour.

I could go on for a week. I would just ask you to help us. Enforce the laws we have. Guard our border like we guard the borders of the world. Find these people and deport them. Remember those of us at the bottom who have no power.[6]

In fact, a number of Hispanic politicians and labor leaders in California and other states boast about how both black and white Americans are being displaced by illegal aliens. California State Senator Gil Cedillo is one. He is a former member of MEChA, the radical Hispanic student movement that demands annexation of all Southwestern states. Cedillo, a Democrat, is best known for writing a number of illegal-alien driver's license bills. Some Los Angeles talk-radio hosts call him "One-Bill Gil." Before Cedillo was elected to the State Assembly and later the Senate, he was manager of the Service Employees International Union. Here's what he said as a union boss in June 1997 before a Southwest Voter Registration Project (SVRP) Conference meeting in Los Angeles:

We move the union movement deep into the Latino community. Latinos are central to union revitalization. Our problem in America is our inability to get power in our own interests. Latinos are now the employment foundation. We have displaced other work communities. Clothing, hotel, and restaurant industries used to be done by blacks and Anglos. Now we need to organize to be in a position to lead this country. SVRP can activate the base, and then more partisan elements can move in. Unions can be partisan for full empowerment. Because of immigration and the birth rate, our population is growing; so we help people become citizens, work with Spanish language media. Latinos are all over this nation.[7]

A little more than four years after his appearance on Capitol Hill, Anderson was back in Washington for a second time testifying before the same House Subcommittee. It was October 30, 2003. What were some of the significant developments that occurred between his first testimony, when he asked the lawmakers to enforce our immigration laws and guard our borders, and this latest turn on the Hill? Foreigners who broke U.S. immigration laws murdered thousands of Americans on September 11, 2001. Our government leaders created the Department of Homeland Security and sent 130,000 American soldiers to spread "democracy" in the Middle East while telling us they won't secure our borders. Several million illegal aliens invaded our nation and began colonizing more American communities. And our government allowed employers to illegally hire hundreds of thousands of illegal aliens, putting more American workers in the unemployment line.

However, this time when Anderson testified, he had his own national radio talk show and thousands of concerned and angry listeners from all backgrounds hanging on his every word.

At the hearing, Anderson was one of four witnesses testifying about immigration's impact on American workers. The others were Steven Camarota, director of research at the Center for Immigration Studies; Vernon Briggs, Jr., professor of labor economics at Cornell University; and Daniel Griswold, associate director of the Cato Institute's Center for Trade Policy Studies.

Representatives attending the hearing were Democrats Sheila Jackson-Lee, Zoe Lofgren, Howard Berman, and John Conyers, and Republicans Steve King, Lamar Smith, Chris Cannon, Jeff Flake, and Chairman John Hostettler. Except for Hostettler, King, and Smith, these are among the most ardent congressional supporters of massive illegal and legal immigration.

Camarota and Briggs spoke in support of American workers. Camarota said that massive immigration has resulted in significantly reduced wages for native workers in low-skilled occupations. He called for legal, controlled, and reduced immigration.

Briggs mentioned organized labor has shifted its support from citizen workers to illegal aliens and legal immigrants over the past decade.

Said Briggs: "It's not going to be long before most American workers begin to realize, if they haven't realized it already, that the labor movement, the champions of all kinds of American workers, have now turned against them and advocate for lax immigration policies, amnesties, and all the rest of these things."[8]

Griswold spoke in favor of cheap labor, open borders, increased immigration, and legalizing illegal aliens, echoing the Cato Institute's libertarian philosophy.

Rather than reading from his written testimony, Anderson spoke extemporaneously. As he explained to his radio audience a few days later: "Most people read from their written testimony. Me, I shoot from the hip. I wrote a nice one, but I went in there sayin' all the things they wouldn't let me say in the written testimony. It was my opportunity to let them know how I felt."

Anderson told the representatives that massive illegal and legal immigration is "killing" the American worker. He mostly focused on the impact of illegal aliens. He also told the elected officials that Americans are growing so angry over this issue that "this country is going to boil over" if the crisis is not fixed. Here is much of his spoken testimony:

> I don't have the credentials of these gentlemen [who are testifying], but I have an advantage that they don't have. I have lived my entire life in the streets of Los Angeles. I am a person from the streets, not homeless, but from the streets, and I have my finger on the pulse of Los Angeles and the rest of this country now.
>
> I have a radio show. I never thought I would be there, but I am, and I am telling you folks something. There is a

huge disconnect between the people in this room and the people in this country. The people in this country are angry over this situation of these guest-worker programs, and these amnesties, and all these other things that are being proposed.

We just threw a governor out of office in California. A Democratic state threw a Democratic governor out of office. Why? Because the many policies he's had, one of them was to get rid of one of our propositions, Proposition 187. The other was signing a driver's license bill for illegal aliens so that they could go to work.

Illegal aliens in California are killing the economy there. Yes, they're making money for their bosses, but they're killing the worker.

We had a strike with janitors in Century City and Beverly Hills back in the 1980s. The janitors there, predominantly black, were making $13 an hour. The union was broken by the ruthless employers. They hired all illegal aliens from Central America and Mexico, and as a result, those black janitors were out on their ear. The wages then went to minimum wage and then those people went on strike and that wage then went up to $6, $7 an hour. That is not progress to me. And nobody stood up for those black janitors.

But let me say this. That is not an isolated incident. I've got an article right here that I just found. This is printed in *Newsday*, July 29 of this year. It talks about Pictsweet Frozen Foods, who would not hire blacks and whites. They only hired Hispanic immigrants, and there was a [federal proceeding] that they lost because they would not hire black Americans, white Americans.

The people that call my radio show—blacks, whites, American Hispanics, American Asians—are angry over this issue, and you folks should understand, this is going to boil over. They are angry over this issue because nobody is listening to them.

I've got kids in my community who cannot work at McDonald's because they don't speak Spanish. You know what they're told? "Well, we can't hire you because our entire kitchen is Spanish speaking." Now, is that fair for a kid who's been in this country his whole life, that he cannot get a job flipping a hamburger because he can't speak a foreign language? That is not fair, and the reason why the numbers are so high is because of illegal immigration in California.

But it's happening everywhere. The people that call my show—and I'm on in eight states and get calls from all fifty because I'm on the Internet—these people are angry, and I don't think you understand it. They are being displaced from their homes, their neighborhoods. They are being displaced in the workforce. And if something's not done, this country is going to boil over. That is not a threat; it's a prediction, and it's the voice of the people.

I get many, many calls from very liberal Democrats, and they are against this issue also. They want the immigration issue fixed because they are worried about their jobs.

Illegal immigration is killing the workforce. Legal immigration is killing the workforce. And the American worker is the guy that's coming up short, and I don't understand why this body of people in this city does not understand that.[9]

Two days after his testimony, Anderson was back in Los Angeles speaking to hundreds of Americans from all backgrounds at a large outdoor event honoring Representative Tom Tancredo. Anderson told the crowd that according to most of the congressional representatives who heard his testimony the solution to fixing illegal immigration is to make it legal:

I talked to the usual suspects. I was eye to eye with quite a few people I do not align myself with, but the worst of the bunch that day was Howard Berman. He said to me, "We have a lot of immigrants coming to this country, and some of them are even illegal, if that's what you want to call them." And I said to him, "That's what they are. Why can't you say what these people are? They are in this country illegally. They are illegal aliens. Call them illegal immigrants if you want, but just use the 'I' word." He could not bring himself to say it. And the attitude at that meeting was, "We've got to fix this problem, and the way to fix it is to make them legal; then they won't be illegal." I said, "Let's leave the banks open so the bank robbers aren't criminals anymore. Let's make sure the child molesters have plenty of kids to molest so they won't be illegal anymore." I talked to both sides. I talked to the Republicans and to the Democrats and, let's be honest, the Republicans aren't much better.[10]

No Support from Black Politicians

While Anderson is angry with any politician sponsoring illegal immigration, the members of the Congressional Black Caucus irritate him the most because they refuse to fight for the thousands of black Americans displaced by illegal workers across the nation. Neighbors and listeners to his show regularly express their frustration.

"In the black community you hear people talking about the illegal-alien problem and the loss of jobs all the time," Anderson told me. "I also get tons of e-mails from black people who listen to my show. Oh, man, they're fed up. They're sick of it. They wonder why their black representatives don't help them."

Not only are blacks losing jobs to illegal workers, they also are losing work to legal foreign labor imported by Congress each year.

An astonishing 40 percent of high-school-educated black American men are jobless,[11] but do not expect the mainstream media to tell you this is largely because illegal aliens and legal immigrants have undercut blacks from the jobs they once held. The establishment media will not address the issue because they support open borders and, for them, political correctness takes precedence over the truth. Yet, media elites continue to tell readers and viewers how much they care about black Americans.

Anderson told me that the thirty-eight-member Congressional Black Caucus will not help their black constituents for two reasons. First, they hate white people. Second, they hopelessly believe in increased power by pandering to Hispanics, or "hispandering," a term Anderson uses on his show.

"A lot of these black Congress people hate whitey," he explained. "They see this as a way to get whitey, pay him back for whatever he needs payin' back for. Another thing is they see this as a way to get power with another minority, Hispanics."

In June 2003, the U.S. Census Bureau announced that Hispanics had surpassed blacks as the largest minority in America. The Hispanic population stood at 38.8 million in July 2002, an increase of nearly 10 percent from the 2000 census. The black population was estimated at 38.3 million in July 2002.[12]

The *Los Angeles Times* relished the news. In the lead paragraph of a front-page news story titled "Latinos now top minority," reporter Ricardo Alonso-Zaldivar called the development "a much-anticipated milestone that demographers said is a sign of more rapid growth in the years ahead."[13]

Two paragraphs later, Census Bureau Director Louis Kincannon was quoted saying to a convention of the League of United Latin American Citizens (LULAC) meeting in Florida: "This is an important event in this country—an event that we know is the result of the growth of a vibrant and diverse population that is vital to America's future."

There was nothing in the story about the millions of Mexicans and Central Americans who have illegally invaded the U.S. in recent years.

Instead of "hating whitey," wouldn't the members of the Congressional Black Caucus do more good for their constituents by addressing this crisis and pushing for enforcement of America's immigration laws?

Anderson, whose great grandfather was a slave, said black politicians can hate "whitey" and "hispander" all they want, but in most cases it will not prevent them from being replaced by Hispanic politicians. "Black politicians talk about minorities and people of color," Anderson explained. "Hispanic politicians talk about Hispanics. They don't include blacks. They don't want us. They only want us until they get enough power that they don't need us anymore. Hispanics will vote for black politicians as long as they pander to Hispanics and don't have one of their own running for office. If they have one of their own running, they aren't going to elect some black politician."

Influenced by a Legendary Broadcaster

So how did a poor black man from South Central Los Angeles become host of a national radio show on illegal immigration? Years ago, blacks were making economic progress in South Central and elsewhere. With his own thriving auto repair business, Anderson was prospering and moving up the ladder of financial success.

"The '70s and early '80s looked very promising for blacks," Anderson explained. "My neighborhood was a pleasant district of lower-middle-class black families. I remember that in 1982 and 1983 I had a great business. I was doing fiberglass-repair work at the time and had a fabulous business where I was makin' good money. I loved my work. Then illegal foreign competition began moving in and taking our jobs. They took wages far below the going rate. They undercut my rates, and they undercut everyone's rates—in auto repair, hotels, restaurants, construction, you name it. For my business, it was a slow, gradual decline through the late '80s and into the '90s.

"And it wasn't just the jobs. It was also the schools and crime. The Hispanics crowded our schools and didn't speak English, making it hard on our kids. And the Hispanics started race riots in our high schools. We didn't have that before the invasion. There are race riots every single day now. They attack anyone who isn't Hispanic. And the crime went up all over South Central. The police have been shot at for years, but today these illegals aggressively get out of their cars and start shooting. There's no words exchanged. They just start shooting. That's unbelievable now. There's no fear of the police anymore. La Times and TV news are only giving us the tip of the iceberg as to what's really going on."

Anderson calls the *Los Angeles Times* "La Times" because "they hispander to the Latino community and to illegal aliens more than any other race. It's like Hispanics are 'the chosen people' and nobody else matters."

In 1993, as Anderson's auto repair business continued to go down hill, something happened that set him on a new course. It was a voice from his distant past. One day, Anderson's son Adam was at work and was tired of listening to talk on the radio about the Los Angeles Rams football team. He searched on the dial and came across something that grabbed his attention. The man speaking was talking about the same issues his father often talked about, including illegal immigration, so he called his father to tell him.

"Pop, there's a guy on the radio that sounds just like you. He's saying the very same things you say. He's on 870 AM."

Anderson turned on the radio and immediately recognized the voice. It was that of legendary newsman-broadcaster George Putnam. Anderson was more than surprised. He thought Putnam was dead because he had not seen him on TV or heard his voice in years.

"George was talkin' about the same things that concern me and my community," Anderson recalls. "I was lovin' it. So I listened to him for several weeks and got up the nerve to call his talk show and got on the air with him. I called his show several more times. About a month later, George called me at home and invited me out for lunch. As a result of that, we became friends."

It is important to digress here to talk about George Putnam for several reasons. First, for seventy years he has worked as a newsman, reporter, and commentator for most of the major broadcasting organizations in the U.S. He has talked and written about important chapters in American and world history. His historical memory is vital for people to hear, especially younger people. Second, Putnam has had the courage to talk honestly about the problem of illegal immigration since the late 1960s, when few people recognized the immense problems it would bring to the U.S. Third, Putnam's knowledge of history and his broadcast experience have been major influences on Anderson as a radio talk-show host.

Putnam started out in radio news in Minneapolis in 1934. Since then, he has worked for NBC, ABC, Mutual, Dumont, and Metromedia. He has covered every president since Herbert Hoover and Hollywood legends going back to the days of Mae West.

During World War II, Putnam served in the army and later as a first lieutenant in the Marine Corps.

The award-winning broadcaster has been a part of the Los Angeles news scene since 1951. Over the years, Putnam has not been afraid of tackling the tough issues or going up against powerful forces.

Putnam told *Insight* magazine that the most important fundamentals in a newsman's character should be "an insatiable curiosity, objectivity, perseverance but, most of all, integrity." About his own approach to journalism, Putnam said, "I'm not an expert on anything. But I'm an observer, and what I do have, I think, is common sense."[14]

Putnam has observed illegal immigration over the years. "I began talking about an invasion by illegal aliens thirty-five to forty years ago," he told me. "People pooh-poohed me and said, 'What the hell are you talking about?' I said it's an invasion. They're destroying our sovereignty, our culture."

As we now know, Putnam was prophetic.

Illegal immigration was one of the issues he discussed on his daily radio show, *Talk Back*, from 1974 to 2000 on KIEV (now KRLA) in Los Angeles.

In late 2001, Putnam took his program to another radio station, KPLS in Orange County, one of just three 50,000-watt powerhouse stations in Southern California. His program was broadcast throughout much of the region and heard across America via the Internet. Putnam and his guests frequently talked about the illegal immigration crisis. Here are some sample comments from Putnam:

- "The Mexican government plans a takeover of America. President Fox is determined to bring about dual citizenship and to wipe out all borders on his drive toward globalization."

- "Hundreds of thousands of pregnant, illegal-alien women wait near our borders then rush across to deliver an instantaneous American citizen. Suddenly they're on some form of welfare. Next, the extended family arrives and additional births are counted. At L.A. County Hospital alone, 66 percent of babies are born to illegals at our expense."

- "Our border patrol agents are no longer allowed to make arrests on city streets or question suspected illegal aliens except along the border and at highway checkpoints."

- "We are conducting a growing battle against terrorism worldwide while Governor Gray Davis signs a bill allowing illegal aliens to obtain drivers' licenses."

- "More than 75 percent of all illegal drugs come across our borders. More than 25 percent of the prisoners in our federal prisons are illegal aliens. And how about diseases? In three years 7,000 new cases of leprosy have crossed over from Mexico, India, and Brazil. We now have 16,000 new cases of drug-resistant tuberculosis that is incurable. Venereal disease is rampant among illegals."

- "Congressman Tom Tancredo went to the White House and talked for a moment about our illegal-alien crisis. What did it get him? It got him a phone call from President Bush's advisor, Karl Rove, who actually said to this hero, 'Don't ever darken the doorway of the White House again.'"

Putnam's phone lines lit up when he talked about illegal immigration. Some callers shared personal stories about how they had been victims of the invasion. Others suggested ways to battle the problem. A few expressed total despair and said there was nothing to stop the U.S. from becoming a Third-World country.

Ironically, in August 2003, Putnam and his producer Chuck Wilder learned that *they* had become victims of the invasion. Their station was being sold to a new Hispanic radio network and would broadcast entirely in Spanish. In the closing months prior to the transfer of ownership, Putnam mostly refrained from discussing the sale on the air, but his callers expressed sadness, frustration, and anger.

One day in November 2003 he did tell his audience, "I never thought that after seventy years in broadcasting I would be thrown off the radio for speaking out about defending our nation's laws and sovereignty."

On December 11, Putnam broke disturbing news to his audience. In Miami, Department of Homeland Security Secretary Tom Ridge said the U.S. should "legalize" the millions of illegal aliens currently living in the U.S. (A few weeks later, President Bush announced a massive guest-worker amnesty proposal for illegal aliens.)

"Is this the age of insanity?" Putnam asked his audience. "Does our sovereignty no longer mean anything? I can't believe I'm witnessing this. What is this about? I think this is a conspiracy. This is the new world order. They are doing this out of sheer greed. Big business. Money, money, money. If this continues, we're going to end up with three classes: elitists, a large peasant class, and a small middle class."

Putnam's last live broadcast on KPLS was on December 24, 2003. Putnam graciously invited me on as one of several guests that day. This book was discussed. At the end of the broadcast, Putnam and Wilder were displaced from their jobs, just like the invasion displaced Terry Anderson, his black neighbors, and millions of others from their jobs.

Only a few days after Putnam's departure, KPLS joined scores of other stations across America broadcasting in Spanish.

Although Putnam lost his job at KPLS, he continued writing about illegal immigration in his weekly commentaries for NewsMax. com. On January 2, 2004, he wrote:

> It is this reporter's opinion that America's national security is not the only thing being compromised by the invasion of illegal aliens. The lack of enforcement of our nation's immigration laws has threatened our national media, our language … indeed, our ability to communicate with each other as America is under attack.
>
> There are actually measures before Congress that would force privately owned television and radio stations to broadcast in foreign languages.
>
> Let's face it: The real purpose of [these bills] is to set in stone policies of the multilingual crusade—to make government

the enforcer of a multilingual marketplace—and to pander to those who come to this country and refuse to learn English.

This reporter ... has recently felt the results of our media invasion.

But this is only one such transfer of ownership to foreign interests. In the greater Los Angeles area, there are more than 22 foreign language broadcasters, all broadcasting exclusively in a foreign tongue. This has, amazingly, been approved by the FCC.

It is difficult, as one scans the radio dial, not to conclude that you're listening to radio in a foreign land. We know the problems we face with the illegal-alien invasion. Our sources of water are being threatened, areas devoted to food growth, housing, the repeated power threats, strangling transportation, education, law and order, crime, pollution, health care, the importation of diseases that were all but nonexistent in this country ... and the list goes on.

How can one emphasize the power of the media to those of us who lived through the '30s when Adolf Hitler took over Germany through just such power. He used the newspapers and radio stations to spread the venom of the Nazis. How can one question the power of media—in this case, foreign media, within our own country.

The late Professor and U.S. Senator S.I. Hayakawa repeatedly stated, "A common language is the glue that holds a people and a nation together." Years ago, it was a source of great pride for an immigrant to immediately learn the English language. Now it's to be avoided.

Three months after Putnam and Wilder lost their radio jobs, they returned to the air in Southern California on KSPA-AM in Ontario. In March 2005, they left that station and took their program to the Cable Radio Network (www.crni.net).

Joining the Movement and Becoming a Broadcaster

In 1993, Anderson became a devoted listener to Putnam's broadcasts and also began tuning in to other radio talk shows. "I noticed that other people were talking about illegal immigration too, although not like George. No one's like him."

At the same time, Anderson had become so fed up with the mass of illegals descending on South Central that he decided it was time to do more than just complain about the problem—he had to take action.

"I saw what was goin' on in my neighborhood and decided somethin's gotta be done," he told me. "And I'm lookin' for somebody to do it, and I'm lookin' and lookin' and there's nobody. And I said maybe it's time for me to step up, so I joined the immigration reform movement."

A new ballot initiative called Save Our State, which would have denied most social services to illegal aliens in California, was heating up in 1993. (Save Our State later became Proposition 187.) Battle lines were being drawn between American citizens and the illegal aliens and their sponsors including Hispanic separatist organizations, labor unions, politicians, immigration lawyers, the Catholic Church, and others.

Anderson began attending rallies in Los Angeles and Orange counties that were organized by the newly formed California Coalition for Immigration Reform, founded by Barbara Coe, and Voice of Citizens Together, founded by Glenn Spencer.

"I started going to their meetings and that's how my name got around," Anderson explained. "I went to a lot of rallies at the Federal Building in Westwood and met a lot of people. And I was always asked to speak at the rallies."

Anderson is a natural public speaker with a strong, resonant voice. He also has a powerful physical presence, towering over six feet with "two hundred and a bunch of pounds."

As Anderson's public speaking appearances increased over the years, the audience suggested he talk about illegal immigration on the radio.

"They told me, 'You've got a lot to say.' George Putnam also told me I'd be good on the radio."

Anderson's fans heard their wish come true on November 26, 2000, with the debut of *The Terry Anderson Show* on KRLA in Los Angeles.

Anderson did not have formal training for his new role as a broadcaster and commentator, but he had the benefit of informal training at the hands of his friend Putnam.

"George taught me a lot of things, but mostly I think the thing I learned from George was there's nothing wrong with being patriotic. I used to think that was dumb. It was okay to think it but you shouldn't tell anybody.

"The other thing I learned from George was you have to let it out if you want people to listen to you, so I let it flow. You may not like what I say on the radio, but you can believe what I say. There's no PCBS [politically correct bullshit] on my show. I serve it up raw. I don't serve it up like a bowl of yogurt, but that's to get your attention. I won't wake anybody up if I'm just another guy on the radio. I gotta be myself."

Even with advice from Putnam, Anderson still felt like a child who is thrown in a pool and told to sink or swim.

"When they put me in the studio to do my first show, they said, 'There's the mike.' I didn't know what I was doing. At first, I didn't have a monologue. I'd just get on, and we'd start taking a few calls from listeners, then we'd have a guest, and sometimes the guest was in the second half-hour. It was kind of a loose-knit thing. I knew we had to come up with a format, and eventually we did."

Most Horrible-ist Clown of the Week

Today the one-hour Sunday night show is divided into four segments: Anderson's monologue, "the most horrible-ist clown of the week," a guest, and listener phone calls.

Anderson develops the monologue on the day of the show, after reading dozens of articles and hundreds of e-mails throughout the week. He gets most of his news and information from the Internet, where there is no shortage of material about illegal immigration.

"The most horrible-ist clown of the week" is the name Anderson gives to the person—usually an elected official—who said or did something "really stupid" during the previous week. Anderson said choosing whom to talk about is one of the hardest parts of preparing for the show.

"The problem is not coming up with a horrible-ist clown, the problem is, 'which one do I use?' There were three last night and eight last week, and I had to decide which one."

As for the word "horrible-ist," Anderson said he's "pretty good at speaking Ebonics" and thought this would be a catchier name than "ridiculous idiot." Anderson's never afraid to poke fun at himself.

Among his guests are grassroots activists, elected officials, and candidates for office.

The listener phone calls take up the second half of the program, and the lines are full from the show's start to its finish.

If you want to know how angry people are over illegal immigration, tune in, and you will hear plenty of callers "articulating the popular rage," the show's slogan. Here are a few caller comments from various nights in 2003 and 2004:

- "Bush has gotten a pass on this issue. I voted for him last time but wouldn't this time."

- "Terry, the situation here in North Carolina is awful."

- "I was at the so-called Freedom Ride at Liberty State Park in New York, and I can tell you that the police were there to protect the illegal aliens. It was frightening."

- "Terry, our hospitals in Arizona are bankrupt because of this invasion."

- "I predict that in the not-too-distant future, when Hispanics are the majority in California, they will vote to secede from the Union."

- "Don't our laws mean anything to these politicians? What's next?"

Anderson also gets an occasional call from someone who disagrees with him. Sometimes it's more than a disagreement.

"We're going to take over America," a Los Angeles caller with a Spanish accent said one night.

Every few weeks someone will call the show and call Anderson a racist. He has a commonsense response: "What if a hundred thousand Vietnamese were suddenly dropped into Guadalajara? And what if those newcomers didn't speak Spanish and further insisted that their children be taught in Vietnamese? What would you think if they were happy to work for half the normal wages for any job they could get, thereby putting thousands of your local Guadalajarans out of work? Would it be racist to say there was a problem?"

Over the years Anderson has faced far worse situations than merely being called a racist.

"I've been threatened many times—phone calls, mail, e-mail. In 1995, my brother and I were shot at fifteen times. They just drove by and filled his truck with holes. There was nothing we could do. Luckily, neither one of us was hit. People have thrown bricks at my house. Once somebody shit on my front porch."

While Anderson has enemies, he is a hero to many people across the country. He is considered a leader in the immigration reform movement, although he doesn't look at himself that way. He enjoys the camaraderie in the movement and appreciates the fact that no one has looked down on him because of his background.

"No one has ever turned their nose up at me and said, 'Terry's from the ghetto, and he's black.' I never got that from anybody. I've always been treated with the utmost respect and dignity. And I appreciate that. We've got people in the movement from different walks of life, different races, different cultures, but we're all the same. We're all on the team. There are some leaders. I consider myself a soldier. I'd rather be a soldier.

"It's an amazing thing to me that so many people are giving so much of their time—free—to try to save our country. I never made a dime on this. I'd rather be spendin' all day doin' my thing—go to work, come home, and maybe go to the club or the gym. But there's no time for that anymore when millions of people are invading our country and our government isn't doing anything about it."

Now that you've read Anderson's story, you can understand why he tells his radio listeners each Sunday night: "Stupid people of America, if you ain't mad, you ain't payin' attention!"

6 | Roy Beck

"The members of this national community should themselves determine their quality of life, not the elites."

—Roy Beck, founder of NumbersUSA

In the summer of 2003, Roy Beck and his wife, Shirley, drove more than 6,000 miles across America. Much of the trip was to be for non-business purposes. But since Roy's job as head of NumbersUSA is fighting the effects of over-immigration and over-population, it was difficult to experience a true holiday.

For a few days, the Becks enjoyed the rolling hills and lakes of northwest Wisconsin. They lodged over the Independence Day weekend near the city of Barron with the army officer under whom Roy served in the early 1970s. They visited farms where the officer and his wife grew up, with no subdivisions or massive development in sight.

But their pleasant journey abruptly ended while heading back south on a Sunday afternoon. The interstate highway became a stop-and-go nightmare when they were still 250 miles northwest of Chicago. After an hour of inching along, the Becks stopped at a truck stop to eat. "When I pulled out a map," Roy recalls, "a truck driver called across the room, 'Getting the map out to find an escape?' The truck driver then said that typically, at the end of a holiday, the last 200 miles or so outside Chicago turn into a rush-hour-like urban traffic jam.

"My wife and I spent several hours zigzagging on county roads westward and then southward before turning east below Chicago," Roy remembers, "but from every direction, traffic was stopped or crawling toward Chicago. Near midnight, halfway across Indiana, the traffic headed toward Chicago was still stop and go.

"What kind of society do we have in which regular citizens of the cities of the Great Lakes Midwest cannot escape on holiday to open country without enduring endless hours of traffic jams? Yet, the *Chicago Tribune* and all of the senators from Wisconsin, Illinois, Indiana, and Michigan consistently speak for and act for immigration increases to speed up the massive population boom. Wouldn't it make more sense to stop nearly all federally forced population growth until the infrastructure could meet the needs of the current population size?"

Of course, urban sprawl and traffic congestion don't affect only the vast Chicago metropolitan area, as Beck was reminded that summer when he and his wife journeyed from their home in Arlington, Virginia, for weekend trips.

"Every time we left the Washington, D.C. area on a Friday, at any time of the day, it took nearly two hours to get out of town," he remembers. "We missed a theater performance of our son in New York City because we foolishly thought we could average 40 miles per hour on the trip. The next week, we were late for the performance because we figured on averaging 30 miles per hour on a trip in which all but about ten miles is interstate highway. Yet, every year the congressional delegations of every state along the way overwhelmingly vote to add several hundred thousand more residents and road-users to this already terribly congested real estate."

When it comes to unrestrained immigration and overpopulation, Beck knows all about the voting records of those congressional delegations between Virginia and New York and between Wisconsin and Michigan. In fact, this former award-winning newspaper reporter knows how all the members of the U.S. Senate and House of Representatives vote on immigration bills. As executive director of NumbersUSA, it is his job to know—and to let American voters know.

Founded by Beck in 1997, with the help of a second mortgage on the family house, NumbersUSA is a grassroots Internet organization that tracks the role of each member of Congress in forcing or reducing U.S. population growth and educates Americans about the effects of federal immigration policies.

Beck's nonprofit, nonpartisan organization includes a team of fifteen highly educated and skilled people working on the shore of the Potomac River in Arlington, Virginia, on Capitol Hill in Washington, D.C., and in Maine, Florida, upstate New York, and Wisconsin. Beck manages a range of programs that educate and mobilize Americans using a variety of tools, including three Web sites in addition to NumbersUSA.com. They are: www.BetterImmigration.com, which grades the immigration voting records of each senator and representative; www.SprawlCity.com, a site showing how growth in both population and per capita consumption forces urban sprawl to increase; and www.SmartBusinessPractices.com, which assists owners of businesses in obeying hiring laws and in reporting other businesses that gain unfair competitive advantages by hiring illegal aliens. Other tools are videos, posters, studies, books, and articles.

Amassing a Small Army of Citizens

The NumbersUSA.com site has become a powerful tool for citizens to contact Congress with their concerns about moderating immigration. People registering at the site receive regular e-mailed "action alerts" on legislation before Congress based on intelligence gathered by NumbersUSA's legislative team on Capitol Hill. Registrants can send free faxes from the Web site to members of Congress. Phone numbers for congressional members are also provided.

In an interview in his Arlington office in July 2004, Beck told me the number of citizen volunteers in the NumbersUSA network has jumped in recent years, primarily because of two events: the terrorist attacks on September 11, 2001, and President Bush's guest-worker amnesty proposal in January 2004. Those two events were wakeup calls.

"On 9/11," Beck noted, "fewer than 3,000 Americans were working with us to change immigration policy. Nonetheless, this still was the nation's largest group of activists directly pressuring Congress. But after the attacks, active participation rose steadily for months. By the end of 2003 we had 12,000 participants. Then after Bush's amnesty proposal thousands of people were joining every couple of weeks. People were outraged over the president's plan."

In July 2004, the organization had 43,000 participants faxing and phoning Congress. By January 2006, the number had jumped to 135,000.

Said Beck: "We are amassing a small army of citizens to battle Congress."

Beck, who has a view of the U.S. Capitol across the Potomac from his office, concedes that many Americans believe it is a waste of time to contact their representatives in Washington. But through the NumbersUSA fax system, participants have helped block all amnesty efforts between 2000 and 2005 and helped pass at least two bills to reduce illegal immigration significantly.

"Too often," he says, "Americans lose heart because they don't believe there is anything they can do to make a difference. We fill that void. In fact, the amnesty lobby in its internal communications to members and in quotes to journalists has blamed its failure to pass an amnesty [in 2004 and 2005] on our ability to mobilize citizens."

Beck says if Americans do not stop Congress from pushing massive U.S. population growth through amnesties for illegal aliens and increased importation of foreign workers, our country as we know it will cease to exist.

"We are indeed trying to stop terribly misguided and often greedy forces," he explains. "If left unchecked, these forces will eventually destroy our quality of life, our culture of individual liberties, our high mobility and ability to treasure natural open spaces, and our American ideals of economic justice and environmental sustainability."

Growing Up in the Ozarks

It was while growing up in a small town in the Ozarks of Missouri in the 1950s and 1960s that Beck discovered the freedom of mobility and access to natural open spaces America offered. He loved floating along the rivers and exploring the caves and forests in the Show-Me State.

His family's house was sandwiched between old Route 66, also known as the "Main Street of America" (because it stretched across the center of the country from Chicago to Los Angeles), and the Frisco Railroad, which also crisscrossed the nation. As people traveled back and forth, Beck got a taste of America.

"The highway ran right through my front yard, and the railroad ran through my back yard," he told me. "Since Missouri is located in the center of the country, I had a parade of America going past my house. Several times during the day, the Frisco would go past my house, and all day long, people were going from coast to coast. And there were two gas stations across the street where cars were always broken down. I would get to talk to the people, and they were from everywhere. I felt like, 'This is America!'

"In many ways, the 1950s was the time that Americans discovered America. For all of its negative effects, the internal combustion engine and the privately owned automobile have been this gigantic source of liberty. I am for improvements in mass transit and for autos to run as cleanly and energy-efficient as possible, but, in my view, part of what it is to be an American is to explore America. And in a country like this, there's only so much exploring you can do without getting in an automobile.

"But if you live on the East Coast today like I do, or in other parts of the country where there are big metropolitan areas, you're trapped because of all the sprawl and congestion. That is not America. Most of the time when I try to leave the city to get to nature, the experience is so awful that any psychological benefit that comes from being in nature is lost on the trip there and back."

In the 1960s when he was a high-school student in Missouri, Beck knew he wanted to be a newspaper reporter. He did not have to search far for a top-notch journalism school since one was in his home state: the University of Missouri School of Journalism.

While attending school there, the environmental movement was beginning to spread across the nation. With Beck's love of nature, that movement was a perfect fit for him.

One of the First Environmental Reporters

Beck's career in newspapers began with special training in environmental journalism at the university and the general-circulation morning newspaper, the *Columbia Missourian*, where he became one of the nation's first environmental-beat reporters. It was the start of a twenty-year career for Beck as a journalist for Midwest newspapers.

"I was part of the vanguard of environmental reporters," Beck recalls. "As a result, I met most of the seminal characters in the environmental movement such as Gaylord Nelson, who was such a huge character in the beginning of the movement in the '60s."

In 1969, as a U.S. senator from Wisconsin, Nelson came up with the idea of Earth Day. First held on April 22, 1970, Earth Day has become an annual national event for people to learn about ecology and what can be done to reduce environmental harm.

"But I was not part of the original movement," Beck explained. "I covered it. I learned what it was, and privately, it matched my own personal principles."

To the dismay of Beck and many others, the environmental movement in the 1990s retreated from one of its main goals: protecting and preserving the environment by stabilizing U.S. population. Instead, environmental groups such as the Sierra Club, the nation's largest with 700,000 members, were taken over by people who pushed other issues such as human rights, social justice, and ethnic preferences to the top.

In 1996, the Sierra Club declared that it would discontinue its opposition to mass immigration, which is responsible for most U.S. population growth. Today, the Sierra Club's ruling clique leaders tar anyone who advocates lower immigration, legal or illegal, as "racist."[1]

The Sierra Club's integrity on the matter of domestic overpopulation has been severely compromised by accepting "donations" of $100 million from Wall Street investor David Gelbaum. "I did tell [Sierra Club Executive Director] Carl Pope in 1994 or 1995 that if they ever came out anti-immigration, they would never get a dollar from me," said the investor.[2]

In 1970, the U.S. Army drafted Beck. He served in Italy from 1970 to 1972 and was a recipient of the Army Commendation Medal for non-combat service.

After his service, Beck returned to journalism and won national awards for his coverage of urban expansion issues, including honors from the U.S. Environmental Protection Agency and the Izaak Walton League of America, one of the nation's oldest conservation organizations.

In the late 1970s, Beck focused on business news at the *Cincinnati Enquirer*. It was at this time he realized that six years after the American fertility rate had gone below replacement level in 1972, the nation was on a course to grow forever at baby boom proportions because of the government's mass immigration policies. "I realized right then that immigration was absolutely at the heart of everything I had ever done."

His final stint as a newspaper reporter was as chief Washington correspondent for the Booth chain of daily newspapers. While covering Capitol Hill, it dawned on him that most of the national problems Congress was trying to solve or minimize were made worse by Congress allowing immigration numbers to rise dramatically ever since the Immigration and Nationality Act of 1965, which opened up extended-family chain migration to every corner of the world.

"I discovered that nearly every measure Congress was taking to improve the American quality of life was being undermined by congressional immigration policy," Beck explained. "This was no more evident than the week in 1990 when Congress passed major new regulations to decrease Americans' per capita air pollution. During that same week, Congress drastically undercut the benefits of the Clean Air Act by passing the 1990 Immigration Act. This would increase the number of immigrants each year by about 35 percent, which would result in tens of millions more people in the country contributing to air pollution. Yet not a single member of Congress commented on the inconsistency. There was no debate. They just passed the bill. And I was one of the very few reporters covering it."

That's when Beck concluded that governmental and journalistic work on most issues is pointless until the country's immigration policy is brought back under control.

"I had a total crisis of confidence and sort of a mid-life career crisis," he told me. "I loved being a newspaper reporter, but at that point I was forty-two and had lost all interest because I thought I am not in a position as a journalist to break through the avoidance and denial that was going on through all the news media, politicians, and academia. It was clear to me that all the elites were ignoring one of the two or three largest dynamics in the country—immigration. Nobody was looking to see if this was a change we wanted and where it was taking us."

Beck quit his job as a newspaper reporter. His wife, a physical therapist then running a small pediatric clinic, "was kind enough" to support Beck for ten months while he studied immigration. Later, he began making "a little bit of a living" writing about the subject as a freelance writer and editor for various publications.

"My freelance writing allowed me to express my personal opinions more strongly," Beck said. "It was absolutely clear to me what had been clear to the original environmental leaders, and that is you cannot meet the environmental goals of this country and constantly have rapid population growth."

Beck's big breakthrough came in April 1994 when the *Atlantic Monthly* magazine published his article "The Ordeal of Immigration in Wausau." The article looked at how the quality of life rapidly deteriorated for Americans in Wausau after a few churches and individuals decided to resettle poor Southeast Asians—refugees from the Vietnam War and most from the nomadic Hmong mountain tribes of Laos—to the small Wisconsin city. Schools became overcrowded and experienced gang violence and guns for the first time. Hmong girls in junior high and even elementary school were having babies. Most of the immigrants and their descendants ended up receiving public assistance because there were not enough jobs for them. So costs rose dramatically for native-born taxpayers. The story of Wausau's experience with the Hmong was featured on *60 Minutes* in October of that year.

The article led to two publishers asking Beck to write books. One book was *Re-Charting America's Future: Responses to Arguments Against Stabilizing U.S. Population and Limiting Immigration*. The other was *The Case Against Immigration: The Moral, Economic,*

Social, and Environmental Reasons for Reducing U.S. Immigration Back to Traditional Levels, which received favorable reviews in several dozen newspapers and magazines.

The Case Against Immigration examines how our government has waged war on Americans for decades through forced mass immigration that benefits the rich at the expense of virtually everyone else in America, including previous immigrants. The book shows how high immigration drives down wages and salaries, especially harming the middle-class and poor. It also describes how immigration-driven population growth has crippled environmental progress.

The books led to national book tours and speaking engagements for Beck, as well as more articles by him in publications such as the *New York Times, National Review, Washington Post*, and *Christian Science Monitor*. Beck was becoming one of the most visible chroniclers and spokesmen on mass immigration and its affects on American business and local communities.

NumbersUSA Enters the Fight

In 1996, as Beck crisscrossed the country talking about his book *The Case Against Immigration*, people encouraged him to create a Web site to help citizens use the information in the book to pressure Congress for change. "I'd never even visited a Web site," Beck recalled. "My friends called me Low-Tech Beck. But after some persuading, I decided to do it."

In 1997, Beck, high-tech expert Jim Robb, and former Senate staffer Jon Eifert introduced a Web site featuring a "Fax-Congress-Free" system for citizens. They named the site NumbersUSA, in reference to the growing number of people in the country.

"At that time," Beck remembers, "NumbersUSA was only Jim, Jon, and myself. And I was attempting to get back in my wife's good graces by raising enough money to pay back the second mortgage I'd taken out on our house to put up the site. Today, Jon is the person still taking care of every Web site need of our users. Jim is director of technology for the organization."

When NumbersUSA was launched, the immigration reform movement consisted of a number of national, regional, statewide, and local organizations. But the movement was weak in a critical area: the halls of Congress. Many congressmen and staffers today have told Beck that if NumbersUSA had existed in the mid-1990s, the movement might have been able to enact deep cuts in immigration then.

"We missed our chance in '95 and '96 when [former congresswoman] Barbara Jordan's bipartisan U.S. Commission on Immigration Reform and [President] Clinton's Council on Sustainable Development came out with recommendations that were absolutely on target," Beck explained. "They said we couldn't reach population stabilization and reach our environmental goals unless we greatly reduced immigration. We had bills in both Houses of Congress. We had people chairing key committees that were introducing the bills. But the movement was absolutely not ready for the moment. It did not have a major Capitol Hill operation. If the NumbersUSA activist mobilization system had existed in '96, we very well could have won. But we had no mass grassroots pressure whatsoever."

To fight "economic injustice," Representative Jordan's commission urged reducing immigration numbers so that the most vulnerable American workers and their families would not be hurt. The commission wanted to eliminate both chain migration and the visa lottery. Clinton's council, in an effort to achieve an "environmentally sustainable society," urged reducing immigration numbers to a level that would allow the U.S. population to stabilize. Since its inception, NumbersUSA has aimed to make all of those recommendations a reality.

Another goal was to get citizens involved in the process. "Our dream," Beck explained, "was to create a team of top-notch professionals operating daily in the halls of Congress and the administration so that the will of the vast majority of Americans would start to be a player on immigration decisions here in Washington."

However, running a grassroots organization, managing a large staff, and raising money to keep NumbersUSA going are activities Beck never envisioned for himself.

"Career-wise, I ended up doing something totally different, and raising money is something a journalist would hope to never have to do," Beck told me. "But I've always been smack in the middle of public policy that affects how people pursue their happiness in this country. I've always thought of myself as being a journalist. I think most journalists think of themselves as being representatives of the common man. Unfortunately, especially with the bigger newspapers, journalists are more representative of the elites, and the elites want mass immigration. But our organization is a crusade of the common man and woman in this country who want substantially less immigration."

Decades of Massive Population Growth

The Great Wave of Immigration in America began in 1880, when there were about 70 million people in the country. But immigration exploded during the first decade of the twentieth century with 16.3 million new entrants. This population boom began to significantly change the character of America from one primarily of towns and farms into one of densely packed urban centers. "The rapid population growth was destroying huge sections of the country's once bountiful natural resources, leading to the establishment of federal systems of parks and other preservation programs," says a NumbersUSA review of U.S. population growth.[3]

World War I slowed immigration considerably during the middle of the 1910 decade. However, high immigration at the beginning and end of the decade, coupled with high immigrant and native fertility, kept total population growth high, adding another 14.1 million people.

In the 1920s, according to the review, Americans "rose up in revulsion" at the amazing pace of change and congestion caused by the previous two decades of immigration-driven population growth. In 1924, Congress passed an act that reduced immigration numbers toward more traditional levels, starting the next year. But very high immigration during the first half of the decade, and the momentum caused by the high fertility of the greatly enlarged population, still resulted in a record 16.6 million people.

The 1924 immigration law and the Great Depression kept immigration below traditional levels during the 1930s. Americans significantly reduced fertility to respond to the terrible economic times, lowering total population growth for the decade to nine million.

After the end of World War II in 1945, Americans began to have large families. "The giant spike in fertility came to be known as the baby boom, a demographic phenomenon that changed every aspect of American society and that continues to drive a lot of the social and political agenda to this day," explains NumbersUSA. The population in the 1940s grew by a record 20.1 million.

The 1950s was the peak of the baby boom. Combined with other factors, this led to a huge conversion of farmland and natural habitats into sprawling suburbs. This new record—28.4 million people—was "thought to be a special phenomenon reflecting pent-up pressures from the Depression and the war and one that would never be repeated or exceeded," according to the review.

In the 1960s, Americans began reducing their fertility, thanks to a social and political movement to stabilize the population. However, Congress opened the door to massive immigration with the Immigration Act of 1965, which ended quotas based on national origin and started chain migration. This decade saw the addition of 24.2 million people.

In 1972, according to NumbersUSA, the American fertility rate fell to replacement level, making it possible for the nation to eventually reach a stable population. Experts predicted that subsequent decades would see lower and lower population growth until early in the twenty-first century when there would be no growth at all. However, America's population rose by 22.2 million people in the 1970s.

Despite Americans choosing to have smaller families, population growth continued in the 1980s at the level of the previous decade, 22.2 million. This growth resulted from a congressional system of chain migration that multiplied annual legal immigration over traditional levels. Also adding to the population was the Immigration Reform and Control Act of 1986, when Congress for the first time ever rewarded about three million illegal aliens with amnesty and a path to citizenship.

The 1990s saw the heaviest population boom in U.S. history—32.7 million people—wiping out the goal of a stabilizing population. Three factors were to blame. First, with the 1990 Immigration Act, Congress further increased immigration to a level almost four times America's full (1776–1965) traditional level of about 250,000 immigrants a year. Second, the federal government stopped enforcing most laws against illegal immigration in the interior of the country. Third, although American natives maintained a below-replacement-level fertility rate, immigrant fertility was at a rate similar to the U.S. baby boom fertility of the 1950s.

Says Beck: "No wonder Americans in the 1990s became increasingly alarmed at their deteriorating quality of life due to sprawl, congestion, overcrowded schools, lost open spaces, and increasing restrictions on their individual liberty in order to handle the new population explosion."

In 2005, America's population stood at almost 300 million, rising by approximately 100 million people just since 1970. Most of the increase comes from immigrants, illegal aliens, and the children born in the U.S. to both groups, according to Beck. Decades ago, native fertility caused most of the growth. The post-1970 increase is a direct result of our government's relaxed immigration policies and refusal to enforce laws against illegal immigration. If immigration into the U.S. is not dramatically reduced, we will be a half-billion-person nation by 2050.

Return to Exploitation

For many years, Beck has helped lead teenagers in a week of building houses for the working poor in various states. In 2003, Beck and a group of teenagers worked on houses in Scranton, Pennsylvania. One day, they took a break to go down deep in an abandoned coal mine to learn about the brutal working conditions of one hundred years ago. The kids were startled to see what it was like. He refrained from reminding their tour guide that the corporations could treat the miners as "more expendable than mules" because immigration at that time brought fresh new workers by the thousands every month. Later he told the kids that safety and pay for miners only rose toward humane levels after immigration was substantially reduced in the 1920s. But Beck sees those same terrible conditions returning to the U.S. today because of high immigration.

"All across America," he explained in a letter to supporters of less immigration, "jobs are slowly drifting back toward earlier conditions due to a glut of labor. Above ground in Scranton, the economy has been depressed for decades for a number of reasons. But if Congress didn't pour nearly a couple of million new foreign workers primarily into the coastal cities each year, corporations might have a need to try to take advantage of the excess labor forces of under-performing interior communities like Scranton."

Among the many places employers are taking advantage of American workers are hospitals, Beck says. In the summer of 2003, his nephew was just out of college and beginning to work in hospital administration in Oklahoma. The new college grad was struck by the inefficient way that nurses are scheduled and organized so that they feel frustrated, demeaned, and under-appreciated. He said nurses are leaving the profession—not because of pay, which Beck thought was "quite good, especially at Oklahoma cost of living"—but because of job dissatisfaction. His nephew said Oklahoma hospitals are starting to import nurses, especially from India, in large numbers. Beck's response: "If the hospitals didn't have that option, somebody might have to figure out how to treat American nurses like professionals and human beings."

Decades ago, Samuel Gompers, founder and president of the American Federation of Labor, condemned the push by unsympathetic employers for more and more immigrants at the expense of American workers. An immigrant himself, Gompers said racial groups also are responsible for advocating increased immigration of more people like themselves. In a letter to Congress in 1924, Gompers warned:

America must not be overwhelmed. Every effort to enact immigration legislation must expect to meet a number of hostile forces and, in particular, two hostile forces of considerable strength. One of these is composed of corporation employers who desire to employ physical strength (broad backs) at the lowest possible wage and who prefer a rapidly revolving labor supply at low wages to a regular supply of American wage earners at fair wages. The other is composed of racial groups in the United States who oppose all restrictive legislation because they want the doors left open for an influx of their countrymen regardless of the menace to the people of their adopted country.[4]

Between 1924 and 1970, America became a mostly middle-class society because immigration was significantly reduced by Congress and other factors, Beck says. As a result, people at the bottom of the economic ladder saw their wages rise rapidly. And because the immigration stream was reduced, immigrants assimilated into the American society. Then along came the Immigration Act of 1965, which opened extended-family chain migration into every country in the world. Senator Ted Kennedy, a liberal Democrat from Massachusetts who pushed the bill through the Senate, assured Americans: "The bill will not flood our cities with immigrants. It will not upset the ethnic mix of our society. It will not relax the standards of admission. It will not cause American workers to lose their jobs."[5]

But Kennedy's guarantee proved false. Immigration rose significantly primarily because of chain migration, based on family "reunification."

Today, legal and illegal immigration are out of control, with millions of new foreigners and their U.S.-born offspring added to the country every year. Employers are replacing poor and middle-class American workers with these foreigners, who are willing to work for far less money and, in many cases, without benefits. And illegal aliens, in particular, are afraid to complain about their work conditions because of their immigration status and because they are so easily replaceable with new illegals arriving every day. At the same time, hundreds of thousands of professional jobs are being outsourced to cheap-labor Third-World countries and millions more are predicted to leave America in the coming years. As a result of all these factors, wages have fallen in the U.S., the middle-class is shrinking, and the number of poor people is rapidly rising. More and more Americans are becoming waitresses and social workers. Economist and columnist Paul Craig Roberts says America "is a country on a path to the Third World."[6]

During the past few years, most politicians and newspapers have been criticizing the loss of American jobs and the fact that millions of Americans cannot find full-time work. The *Washington Post*, for example, published a major piece in 2003 about the plight of high-school-educated black American men nationwide, saying that 40 percent of them are jobless—a shocking statistic.[7]

At the same time, however, these same politicians and newspapers have been talking about looming labor shortages in the U.S. and pushing the need for guest-worker programs and amnesties for illegal aliens. In early 2005, there were nine amnesty bills in Congress, and the press regularly applauds all of them with sympathetic stories and op-ed pieces.[8]

Beck is outraged at this deception from our elected officials and the collaboration by the media, supposedly a watchdog on government. "This isn't just obfuscation, it is sophistry of a particularly amoral, and perhaps immoral, type," Beck wrote in a letter to thousands of NumbersUSA participants in August 2003.

He is especially angry about the troubles of black American men. "Nearly forty years after Congress passed laws to provide for the full assimilation of black Americans into our political, social, and economic life, the lack of job opportunities for these descendants of the American slavery system is scandalous," he raged. "But apparently, in the view of many elected officials, none of these men is looking for a job."

Some of the politicians selling out blacks and other Americans to cheap foreign labor are in Arizona, which has become the primary gateway to America for millions of illegal aliens pouring across the U.S.-Mexico border. In 2003, Senator John McCain, and Representatives Jeff Flake and Jim Kolbe, all Arizona Republicans, introduced legislation for massive amnesties for illegals.[9] Beck says that since these politicians knew that the truth about their legislation would not go over well with the American public, they disguised the facts.

"They claim their chief aim is to stop the deaths of illegal aliens trying to cross our borders in the desert," Beck told NumbersUSA participants. "They would allow the millions of illegal aliens in this country to apply for a work permit and a few years later to get a green card and become permanent residents. Their bill would also allow any worker in the world to apply to a U.S. business and ask for a job. Although the bill seems to provide a little bit of incentive for jobs to go first to American workers, any foreign worker who can get a job by mail would be allowed to enter the U.S. and once here to apply to remain permanently. The Arizona Obfuscators call this a guest-worker program, but these guests would never go home."

Beck is deeply concerned that America's elite is hooked on greed, no matter the cost to the country. "I fear that most politicians and journalists are addicted to the thirty-year trend of using foreign labor to slowly globalize the American labor market to drive down the wages of American workers," he told participants in his organization. "It is also a sign of the deep commitment of the opinion elite to force continuing mass population growth to further the economic interests of developers, land speculators, and retail concerns that do not believe it possible to prosper in a stabilized society. These same interests also are doing everything possible to make illegal immigration a natural and accepted part of our society."

Beck was even blunter on October 17, 2003, during an interview with broadcaster George Putnam on radio station KPLS in Orange County, California. The interview was conducted just two months before the station began broadcasting entirely in Spanish.

"The business lobbies in Washington are for these amnesties for illegal aliens," Beck told Putnam's audience. "It's a grand coalition of the far-left and the libertarian right. These aren't patriotic people. They are global, corporate types who have no patriotism. They think they can bring in the new world order [of erased borders, increased corporate power, and decreased individual rights]. It's an unscrupulous minority who want to do this. They will do anything to flood labor markets with foreign workers. They believe Americans are paid too much…. The grand plan is to merge the United States with Mexico."

However, most businesses are not in favor of mass immigration, according to Beck. Good employers are forced to hire illegals to compete with the businesses that are eagerly hiring them.

Report Cards for Congress

Unfortunately, many of our U.S. senators and representatives do not care about average American citizens, only about reelection, Colorado Congressman Tom Tancredo told me during an interview at his

Capitol Hill office in July 2004. They routinely sacrifice our quality of life and endanger our country by welcoming each year millions of legal immigrants and illegal aliens for their personal gain. Their pandering has been directed at pleasing those who provide most of their campaign money: giant Washington business lobbies, the huge leftist-illegal-alien lobby of Hispanic groups financed by the Ford Foundation, and the immigration lawyer industry. Businesses want cheap labor and open borders, Hispanic groups want open borders so a flood of their people will come to America, and immigration attorneys benefit by representing aliens, who have access to tax money through immigration laws.

"The game here in Washington is a very simple one," the Republican congressman explained. "It's called control. Maintaining control of this place, getting the power and keeping the power. Everything around here is designed to accomplish that goal. Both parties really and truly don't look at the long-range implications of their policies as much as they look at the immediate political impact.... Both parties and many politicians inside those parties are myopically focused on the next election. That acquisition and maintenance of power, that is the primary motivating factor for most everything that is done around here."

I asked Tancredo if those politicians would ever change their self-serving attitudes and stop forcing massive immigration on the American people and future generations of Americans.

"I don't know that they care," he responded. "And it's not just on the immigration issue. I've noticed this in other issues. In the past, you could make a case for any kind of issue if you could point out that what you are doing is really ruining things for your children and grandchildren. But I'll get people who will say to me, 'They're [children and grandchildren] going to take care of themselves. I'm taking care of myself.' And I say over and over, don't you realize that you're burdening your children and grandchildren? And, you know, down deep they don't care. We have become so focused on our immediate needs and gratification."

Tancredo said the American people must replace those power-hungry, nearsighted, and selfish politicians with "good people" and "patriots" who will battle the powerful forces profiting from open borders and careless immigration policies. That's where NumbersUSA comes in.

Since Congress is responsible for most of America's population growth, Beck and his NumbersUSA team work to hold those lawmakers forcing immigration accountable to the citizenry. They educate Americans about congressional actions using information gathered by the organization's staff on Capitol Hill, led by Rosemary Jenks, director of government relations.

Through NumbersUSA's BetterImmigration.com Web site, citizens can see the immigration voting records of each senator and representative. All 535 congressional members are graded on how they have used immigration to force population growth, sprawl, and congestion. An A+ means a member virtually always supports lower immigration and population stabilization. A grade of C means that half the time the member has acted for lower immigration and half the time has acted for higher numbers. An F- indicates the member has acted to force higher immigration and population growth. All congressional actions since 1989 are graded. The grades are based on principles that have been evaluated and reviewed by experts in immigration policy from government, think tanks with different viewpoints on immigration, and universities. Beck's organization examines how congressional members' votes and actions, such as signing a letter about immigration legislation, impact the following categories:

- Illegal Immigration – Illegal aliens are foreign nationals having entered the U.S. without legal status. The most common ways are by either crossing a land or sea border without being inspected by an immigration officer or simply by violating the terms of a legal entry document, such as a visa.

- Chain Migration – One of the reasons immigration is so high is chain migration, where one immigrant sponsors several family members for admission, who then sponsor several others themselves, and so on. Annual immigration has tripled since chain migration began after the Immigration Act of 1965 and has led to additional millions consigned to visa waiting lists.

- Anchor Baby Citizenship – An illegal alien can cross the border, have a baby five minutes later, and that baby is automatically declared a U.S. citizen. Illegal-alien parents are rewarded for disobeying U.S. law by having their children granted automatic citizenship. The family is entitled to welfare benefits, and illegal-alien parents of children born in the U.S. are seldom deported. That is why their children are called "anchor babies"—they anchor their families in the U.S. Hundreds of thousands of new "anchor baby" citizens are born each year.[10]

- Amnesty – A decision by a government to forgive people having committed illegal acts, in this case, living in the U.S. illegally.

- Worker Importation – This one is self-explanatory.

- Refugee – Any foreigner unable or unwilling to return to their country of origin because of persecution or fear of persecution.

- Visa Lottery – Each year, 50,000 immigrant visas are made available through a lottery to individuals without regard to their age, skills, education, our need for their labor, their ability to assimilate, family ties, or humanitarian need. Our government also welcomes cultures with practices contravening our criminal laws, specifically polygamy and female genital mutilation. The program promotes massive illegal migration by people believing they may some day win the lottery and be allowed to stay in the U.S. One having won the lottery and legally allowed to reside in the U.S. was the wife of Hesham Mohammed Hadayet, who on July 4, 2002, entered Los Angeles International Airport and murdered two innocent people and wounded several others before being shot by an El Al security agent.[11]

According to the report cards, most Republicans have acted for less immigration, while most Democrats have supported more immigration. At the top of the rankings, as of September 2004, seventy-two Republicans and six Democrats showed career grades of A+, A, and A-. In the middle of the pack with a grade of C were twenty-seven Republicans and eleven Democrats. At the bottom, 116 Democrats and seven Republicans showed career grades of D-, F, and F-. Of the thirty-six members receiving a career grade of F-, most are from states that border with Mexico.

Victories on Capitol Hill

After decades of losing the war to save the nation, citizens are fighting back and winning battles on Capitol Hill, thanks to Beck, his NumbersUSA group, and an army of loosely organized, modestly funded national and local organizations. Among the victories in 2004:

- The Save Our Summer Act 2004 that would have increased H-2B visas for temporary skilled and unskilled foreign workers from 66,000 to 106,000 never came up for a vote, despite intense pressure from the hotel and tourism industry. Businesses claimed that no American workers were available for summer jobs—the supposed "jobs Americans won't do." But the truth is American workers don't want to work for slave wages and be forced into overtime without appropriate compensation. Apparently, the additional foreign workers were not needed, because summer businesses operated normally.[12]

- The Agricultural Job Opportunity, Benefits, and Security Act of 2003, also known as the AgJobs bill, a massive illegal-alien amnesty, was not voted on, despite having a filibuster-proof majority of sixty-three cosponsors. Senate Majority Leader Bill Frist (R-Tenn.) maneuvered to kill the bill for that congressional session, probably because the White House was afraid of a backlash from angry voters. Senators Larry Craig (R-Idaho) and Ted Kennedy

(D-Mass.) introduced the bill. Of the 1.2 million illegal aliens currently working in agriculture, an estimated 860,000 plus their spouses and children could qualify for this amnesty, so the total could reach three million or more.[13]

- In September 2004, the House Judiciary Committee passed the Security and Fairness Enhancement for America Act of 2003. The bill, introduced by Representative Bob Goodlatte (R-Va.), would eliminate the visa lottery.[14]

Stopping various forms of amnesties for illegal aliens such as the AgJobs bill has been the most significant accomplishment for proponents of less immigration. After Congress passed six amnesties from 1994 through 2000, there have been no amnesties for five consecutive years, 2001–2005, despite many attempts by Republicans and Democrats.

"People in the most powerful corporate board rooms, money foundations, banks, and Washington lobbying offices are sobered because they have been foiled in what they believed was inevitable— that in fact was more or less a divine right, as they saw it," Beck told NumbersUSA participants in a letter. "Absolutely the only reason they failed to achieve any amnesty was the constant resistance from citizens.

"The only power that kept U.S. borders intact, that protected American workers from having to totally compete one on one with every worker in the world for wage and conditions, that protected our communities and open spaces from having millions upon millions of additional residents over the next few years at a minimum, was tens of thousands of citizens, each taking individual actions one by one and cumulatively forcing members of Congress and the president to tip-toe through the tulips that they otherwise would have stomped with nary a thought."

The Quality of Life

For the past forty years, the quality of life has rapidly deteriorated for the American people as tens of millions of people have come to the U.S. through reckless, greed-driven immigration policies.

It began in 1965 when Congress abolished quotas based on national origin and introduced chain migration. In 1986, Congress rewarded millions of illegal aliens with amnesty and a path to citizenship, which encouraged millions to come illegally in anticipation of future amnesties. Since 1986, Congress has increased immigration even further through scores of bills and by continuing to refuse to protect our borders. In the last forty years, 100 million people have been added to the nation's population, most of them a result of those policies. But most members of Congress act as if nothing has happened.

In a letter to tens of thousands of NumbersUSA participants on Independence Day, July 4, 2004, Beck talked about how elected officials have ignored the Declaration of Independence and the American voters' desire for a better quality of life in favor of small groups of elites who want high immigration and massive population growth.

> The Declaration of Independence can be very useful in our shared cause of restoring the rule of law to our immigration system and reducing the immigration numbers to a level that no longer deteriorates the quality of life of the American people. I believe one message of Independence Day is that, to keep faith with the aspirations our founders had for this nation, our immigration policy should first and foremost serve the interests of the "governed" who own and comprise this country....
>
> The central concept of the Declaration is that people have a God-given right to gather in communities and determine for themselves how they will be governed ... the right to determine how they will pursue happiness in all its rich texture of fulfillment, relationships, ambition, art, beauty, work, education, religion, and recreation.
>
> The Declaration suggests that the designated purpose of a proper government is to derive its power from the "consent of the governed" to provide the best way possible for the governed

to experience "inalienable rights." When Thomas Jefferson and his fellow founders listed specifics of those rights, they named "life, liberty and the pursuit of happiness."

I believe our political leaders need to be pressed to reacquaint themselves with this primal concept of our nation. How many members of Congress actually believe that their constituents have been "endowed by their Creator with certain unalienable rights" including the "pursuit of happiness"? Or that the reason they have been elected to Congress is to make sure that their constituents are able to maximize their pursuit of happiness?

How different might immigration policy be if politicians shaped it based on what contributed to the pursuit of happiness of those citizens who gave them the right to govern!

Perhaps it advances our thinking about the concept of "pursuit of happiness" if we use a similar term: "quality of life."

No single action of government has more impact on the quality of life of "the governed" in America than the addition of around 2.5 million people each year because of the federal government's immigration policies. Nearly every endeavor of the American people in their tens of millions of differing pursuits of happiness is changed because of this massive inflow of additional people....

You have probably noticed that the elites often wrap their desire for open borders in a supposed humanitarian compassion for all the people in the world. They tend to suggest that America should not be governed by the desires of the members of its community but by the desires of the billions of people who live outside the community.

Although very few of the elites are actually sincere in their claim of that ethical principle, it is helpful to note that that principle is profoundly undemocratic and the antithesis of the Declaration. If all humanity has the right to determine the policy of a country, then that country is no longer self-governed....

The elites of corporations, unions, religious bodies, universities, entertainment and the news media overwhelmingly want high immigration and massive U.S. population growth. The public overwhelmingly does not.

For the most part, the elites believe that their positions of privilege not only protect them from the deterioration in their quality of life but also allow them to profit by the unprecedented population growth. The only really valid explanation for why the tiny elite's ideas of pursuit of happiness in terms of immigration policy are burying the public's pursuit of happiness is that the public has not believed in the core principle of the Declaration of Independence....

The members of this national community should themselves determine their quality of life.

After Beck wrote that letter, I asked whether it is truly possible to stop the few but powerful elites from further destroying America. Is it possible to turn back the mass immigration threats and actions from Congress? Always the optimist, Beck believes that day could come relatively soon.

"None of the elites is involved in providing leadership on this issue," he responded. "On this one it's been the common people all by themselves. We are the leadership. When Tom Tancredo stepped up to the plate, it was a massive step forward because he was in a Congress where nobody would do that kind of thing—get in your face every day. Now there are a lot of people in Congress stepping up to the plate. Nonetheless, he's a marginalized member of Congress. We're not quite to the point where we've got a person truly in leadership taking it on.

"However, I'm still optimistic that we are going to substantially turn this problem around sooner than later. It would only take a few members of Congress to lose an election over their stance on immigration for the situation to dramatically change. It's a cliché, but the fact is it's darkest before the dawn."

7 | Barbara Coe

"Until the U.S. controls immigration, all else is a moot point, as it will no longer matter."

—Barbara Coe, founder of the California Coalition for
Immigration Reform

On the morning of December 8, 2001, about 250 American patriots held a "Defense of the Homeland" rally in front of Anaheim City Hall in Orange County, California. They were protesting the city council's recent decision ordering the Anaheim Police Department to accept Mexico's matricula consular cards as valid identification for Mexicans living illegally in the U.S.

The rally was organized by Barbara Coe's California Coalition for Immigration Reform (CCIR) and Glenn Spencer's American Patrol. Among other patriots participating were broadcaster Terry Anderson; Lupe Moreno, president of Latino Americans for Immigration Reform; Ezola Foster, Pat Buchanan's vice presidential running mate in 2000; and Reverend Jesse Lee Peterson, president of the Brotherhood Organization of a New Destiny.

The patriots carried signs that read, "No more phony IDs" and "What part of 'illegal' don't you understand?" They said the matricula consular cards were an attempt by Mexico's government to circumvent U.S. immigration laws and legitimize the presence of illegal aliens. The patriots were especially outraged that their elected officials would accept the matriculas for identification just three months after September 11, when terrorists, all of whom broke U.S. immigration laws, murdered several thousand Americans.[1]

Fifteen minutes after the protest began, over a dozen counter-protestors pushed their way into the middle of the rally. Some were carrying the communist flag and wearing black clothing, Marxist-themed shirts, hoods, masks, and combat boots. Those dressed in black called themselves anarchists.

A few minutes later, about twenty additional counter-protestors and self-proclaimed anarchists appeared across the street from the rally. They marched in a circle, chanting and screaming, "Fuck Nazis!" and "Fascists!" Then they began shoving, punching, and kicking the American patriots, and the patriots fought back.[2]

"I remember one agitator wearing a T-shirt with Zapata's face," recalled college history instructor Edward DiBella, as he recounted the incident to me in early 2004. (Emiliano Zapata was a famous leader of the Mexican Revolution.) "This agitator was assaulting some of the elderly men in our group. He began tearing signs away from people and swinging the stick from one of the signs at people trying to intervene. Eventually, about three or four men wrestled him down. He nearly got me in the eye with the nail from the stick. Luckily for him, he missed. A couple of men were injured, so I ran back to my truck and retrieved my first aid kit. I gave small bandages and antiseptic wipes to several men with cuts on their faces."

As the violence was occurring, an Anaheim police car drove by slowly but did not stop, even though several patriots were on the curb pleading for their help. Days before the rally, CCIR was given assurances that they would receive police protection.[3]

The fighting lasted a minute or two and broke up; then both sides went back to protesting.

About twenty minutes later, more violence erupted. Several patriots were shoved to the concrete. One patriot suffered a sprained hand and one broken finger and ended up in the hospital the next day. Others had teeth knocked out and bloodied faces.[4]

Despite the injuries, DiBella and others were proud that the patriots stood their ground. "It was an inspiring day, as patriotic Americans exercised their First Amendment rights and refused to be cowed," he noted. "One person who really inspired me was Barbara Coe. I vividly remember her down on the sidewalk, wearing some kind of red, white, and blue garment. She refused to be intimidated and was down there leading the patriots in chants demanding better homeland and border security."

Another patriot at the rally was real estate agent Sheri Crawford. "Barb Coe took immediate action in an attempt to resolve the problems created by the pro-illegal group when they attacked innocent citizens," Crawford wrote to me. "She was as courageous as she is in any situation, always prepared and willing to stand up for what's right. For how hard she tried to get the Anaheim cops to come and 'Protect and Serve' us, the entire force should have been there, sirens blasting all the way. Sadly, her cries for help fell on determinedly inattentive ears."

On May 8, 2002, Judicial Watch, a public interest group that investigates and prosecutes government corruption and abuse, filed a federal civil rights lawsuit on behalf of CCIR. The suit charged that police stood by and watched as citizens were "violently attacked during a peaceful rally" by "pro-Iranian anarchists, communists, advocates of rejoining the Southwestern states to Mexico, and other counter-demonstrators."[5]

Larry Klayman, Judicial Watch chairman and general counsel, said: "This case resembles violent encounters during the civil rights movement of the 1960s, when government officials in some parts of the country refused to uphold the law and protect marchers from violence."[6]

In December 2004, Judicial Watch reached a settlement with the Anaheim Police Department that prompted it to change its policy on public demonstrations to better protect peaceful protestors from violence. Judicial Watch President Tom Fitton said: "The California Coalition for Immigration Reform is to be applauded for not being cowed by acts of violence and for pursuing the cause of immigration enforcement. They have struck a blow for the First Amendment."

Five days after the attacks on the patriots at city hall, the anarchists struck again. It was early afternoon. Barbara Coe had left her Orange County home to run some errands. When she returned less than two hours later, she found her house spray-painted with graffiti. Sprayed on the sidewalk in front of her house were the words "FUCK WHITEY." The words "RACIST" and "ANARCHY" were sprayed on her garage. An "A" inside a circle was sprayed next to each set of words, the traditional symbol of anarchism and the same symbol used by the anarchists at the rally.[7]

The incident happened in broad daylight, but Huntington Beach Police said they could not find any neighbors on Coe's street who saw anything. Police classified it as a hate crime. Coe believes it was done in retaliation for the rally CCIR held at Anaheim City Hall.

The violent attack at city hall and the racist graffiti are just two of many episodes Coe and members of her CCIR organization have endured over the years for seeking enforcement of America's immigration laws and protection of citizens from the massive illegal-alien invasion.

Coe, a petite, seventy-year-old grandmother, was born and raised on the Pine Ridge Reservation in South Dakota and is part Sioux Indian. She has received numerous death threats and been smeared in the press and harassed by the federal government. She was even forced to resign from her management position with the Anaheim Police Department for reporting crimes committed by illegal aliens to her superiors. And Coe and her CCIR patriots have been violently attacked and bloodied on other occasions while police stood by.

Through it all, Coe and the members of CCIR have worked tirelessly on major campaigns, from California's Proposition 187 in 1994 to the measure's sequel in 2004. They have exposed pro-illegal-alien hate groups, corporations that support them, and corrupt elected officials who use immigrants and illegal aliens for profit at the expense of American citizens. They have initiated efforts to defeat pro-illegal-alien legislation that victimizes American citizens. And they have sponsored scores of meetings and produced stacks of materials to educate citizens on America's illegal immigration crisis.

Today, Coe and CCIR are recognized as immigration reform leaders in California and at the national level.

A Frustrated Cop

Long before Coe became a leader in the immigration reform movement, she worked in administrative positions at TRW's space and defense business in Redondo Beach, California, beginning in 1969. She started out in the Contracts Division and then moved to the Legal Department. Later, she transferred to TRW's Credit Division in Orange County. "That's where I found out I was a frustrated cop," she told me in one of several interviews in early 2004. Coe developed and administered the TRW Credit Fraud Control Unit and was "instrumental" in revising some credit fraud cases from misdemeanors to felonies.

In 1982, Coe began working for the Anaheim Police Department, where she developed and managed the department's Crime Analysis Unit. As a member of the Department of Justice Office of Criminal Justice Planning Technical Advisory Committee, Coe also trained police personnel throughout California on crime analysis techniques.

"The Crime Analysis Unit was a pilot program that was incredibly successful," Coe explained. "We tracked crime, incident, and arrest reports on a daily basis in a matrix to identify hot spots, month, time of day, place, and possible suspects. This information was extremely helpful to the patrol officers." Through this data Coe found that Mexican nationals committed much of the crime in Orange County. "I obviously knew that illegal immigration was a problem in California, but I didn't realize the seriousness of it until we analyzed the crime through our program."

However, as bad as illegal-alien crime was during Coe's early years with the police department, it became a far bigger problem after the federal government granted legal status in 1986 to about three million illegal aliens—mostly Mexican nationals—living in the U.S.

"Americans were told the amnesty would solve the illegal immigration problem, but it just got worse," Coe said. "As soon as these people got their amnesties, they were importing their families from Mexico, and crime started spiraling, primarily in the Latino areas. There was an almost immediate increase in narcotics, domestic violence, home robbery, and burglary. It was absolutely incredible."

Coe told her superiors about the jump in crime, but for political reasons, they did not want to hear about it. "The Hispanic community and the Hispanic power base were increasing appreciably," she explained. "The bureaucracy at the police department wanted their support. They didn't want any problems. Also, the powers within the community decided that we shouldn't take illegal aliens back to the border. When I first started working at the department, they would load up a bus almost every day with illegal aliens and take them back to the border. But after the amnesty, the Hispanic power base decided that was no longer acceptable, so the Anaheim police backed off and adopted L.A.'s Special Order 40 as their own."

Special Order 40, passed by the Los Angeles City Council in 1979, prohibits L.A. law enforcement from cooperating with federal immigration authorities on immigration matters. This pandering to Hispanics is what created the explosion of "sanctuary" cities across America where there are high numbers of illegal aliens.

Coe did not let the new policy stop her from trying to protect citizens from the growing illegal-alien crime problem. "I identified the rise in violent crime, and most of it was coming from the Latino areas. That was simply a fact. I remember that from 1987 to 1988 the number of violent crimes and drug-related crimes tripled over the norm in those areas. The chief did not want to see these reports. I said, 'Excuse me? I thought you and all the officers took an oath of office, when you were sworn in, to enforce our laws.' Well, I was speaking out to the officers in the department about what was going on. Of course, the vast majority of the rank-and-file agreed with me."

Today, because police commanders and other government officials in Southern California and across the nation ignored Coe and others echoing the same concerns for so many years, illegal-alien crime has wreaked havoc in communities. By definition, all illegal aliens are criminals because they have violated U.S. immigration laws. Although most aliens do not come to the U.S. with the intention of engaging in a life of street crime, many violent foreign criminals do come to America because it is an easy target.[8]

About 30 percent of federal and state prisoners are criminal aliens, non-citizens who commit crimes.[9] Most of those are Hispanic. There are 40,000 illegal-alien prisoners in California alone.[10] In Los Angeles, 95 percent of all outstanding warrants for homicide—totaling some 1,200 to 1,500—are for illegal aliens. Up to two-thirds of the fugitive felony warrants, about 17,000, are for illegals.[11]

Some Los Angeles police officers support Special Order 40 and apparently don't care that illegal-alien criminals are in our communities. Here's what two Los Angeles Police Department officers said in an April 2005 *Los Angeles Times* story[12] about the order: "Everyone here has their rights, whether they're legal or illegal," said Officer John Pedroza. His colleague, Officer Oscar Casini, agreed: "It doesn't upset me that you get arrested, you get deported and are back here."

However, other officers, who "refused to be named for fear of reprisal," are opposed to Special Order 40 and want permission from department brass to go after all illegal aliens. Said one: "Let us use all the laws," noting that entering the United States without papers is a crime.

Most of the illegals in L.A. and in the rest of America come from a country where crime apparently is part of the culture. In a March 2004 cover story in the *Los Angeles Times Magazine*, Dick J. Reavis wrote, "Crime has become the defining characteristic of Mexico City." He quoted Mexico City politician Aleida Alavez Ruiz saying, corruption is "not all up to the police—that would be too simple to say. It is part of our culture as Mexicans."[13]

In 1991, Coe learned about another side of the illegal immigration problem, one that would motivate her to take action as a private citizen to combat it.

"I was caring for a friend, a destitute and crippled World War II veteran," Coe explained. "He was like my brother. But this poor man who had risked his life in our military to protect our country was denied Medi-Cal and Social Security benefits. Since I personally could not attend to him or fund his needs, I was forced to put him in a low-cost nursing home in Orange County, where I found that the majority of the employees could not speak English and did not properly care for him. The result was an immediate deterioration in his health and his premature death.

"Through someone I met in social services, Erica Cook, I learned that the majority of these nursing facilities employ illegal aliens and most of the patients are illegal aliens. I also learned that illegal aliens were receiving Medi-Cal and Social Security benefits by the billions, but my friend was denied benefits.[14] This terrible injustice toward a loyal American citizen, combined with the Anaheim Police Department's refusal to deal with the illegal-alien crime explosion, was my incentive to do something about our immigration problems."

The California Coalition for Immigration Reform Is Born

Following the death of her military friend, Coe got together with Erica Cook, from social services, and Bill King, newly retired chief agent of the U.S. Border Patrol's El Centro, California sector, whom Coe knew. The trio agreed that something had to be done about illegal immigration. They placed a small ad in the *Penny Saver* publication, inviting anyone who was concerned about the problem of illegal aliens in their community to attend a meeting in Costa Mesa, a coastal city in Orange County. The trio called the organization, "Citizens for Action Now." In addition to the three organizers, eight people showed up for the first meeting. It was not much of a turnout, but at least it was a start, Coe thought. They discussed issues, strategies, and next steps.

In January 1992, Coe and the others listed all the citizen groups they knew in California, such as immigration reform organizations and taxpayer groups, and sent them a hand-printed invitation to meet and determine how they could strengthen their efforts on the illegal immigration issue. The invitation read:

With no threat to the autonomy of any group, we invite you to join us in a unified effort to effectively combat the "immigration invasion," which threatens our very sovereignty as well as our rights and freedoms for which our forefathers and loved ones fought and died and is now our responsibility to preserve.

This time they were far more successful, Coe remembers, as eight group leaders and "wall-to-wall" people showed up for the second meeting in a "ratty little room" they rented. They established a board of directors and agreed on a new name for the organization that was suggested by one of the group leaders from San Francisco. The California Coalition for Immigration Reform was born, and leaders of other immigration reform groups agreed to come under the CCIR umbrella to attract more members and strengthen their own organizations.

In the coming months, CCIR's board developed the organization's bylaws, philosophy, and goals. Their philosophy was two-fold:

First, "Until the U.S. controls immigration, all else is a moot point, as it will no longer matter." (Today, Coe says, "this fact was well illustrated by the terrorist attack on 9/11 by foreigners who are welcomed into our communities by corrupt elected officials for their own personal gain.")

Second, "Immigration is a legal issue, not a racial one." CCIR said this means U.S. citizens of every race and ethnicity are victims of our government's refusal to enforce our immigration laws. Existing law mandates immediate deportation and denial of employment to all who have entered the U.S. illegally, regardless of country of origin.

The board developed the following goals:

- Uphold Article IV, Section 4 of the U.S. Constitution, which guarantees each state protection from invasion

- Enforce U.S. immigration laws

- Protect the lives of U.S. citizens

In June 1992, CCIR was incorporated as a "nonprofit, nonpartisan public benefit educational organization representing law-abiding American citizens of every race, creed, color, religious and political preference."

Meanwhile, back at the Anaheim Police Department, Coe continued to speak out about the growing illegal-alien crime problem while her bosses tried to silence her. "I was getting warnings from my commanders who said, 'You've got to quiet down about this.'"

Political correctness and pandering to special interests continues today in police departments. Said one Los Angeles Police Department captain in a 2004 magazine article: "We can't even talk about [illegal-alien crime]. People are afraid of a backlash from Hispanics."[15]

In 1993, the Anaheim Police Department had had enough of Coe, her crime reports, and her repeated requests for commanders to enforce the law in Hispanic neighborhoods. The department filed a lawsuit that charged that Coe misused department property—a camera—and was destroying the image of the department. She had used the camera to take pictures of illegal aliens protesting against the Anaheim Police Department.

Coe was escorted out of her office by two armed officers and told not to return. She was put on administrative leave and demoted thirteen pay grades, from manager to records clerk. Coe filed a countersuit against the department and spent two years in arbitration, finally winning a settlement that included back pay and severance.

The First 'Save Our State' Initiative

By the summer of 1993, one year after CCIR was incorporated, Coe and her patriots had achieved notable gains. They were documenting the financial, social, and cultural cost of uncontrolled immigration to U.S. citizens, identifying pro-illegal-alien elected officials, and identifying race-activist hate groups seeking to abolish America's sovereignty. They shared this information with citizens at CCIR's monthly meetings in Orange County and with other groups in California and across the country that were affiliated with CCIR. The organization had thousands of members and was growing, as more people were becoming affected by illegal immigration.

At that time, Coe and her friend Bill King, the retired chief agent of the Border Patrol who helped create CCIR, wanted to launch a ballot initiative in California, but they didn't know how. "We weren't politically savvy enough," Coe said. But someone else was.

Ron Prince, an Orange County accountant active in politics, also was becoming an activist against illegal immigration. Prince wanted to use the California ballot initiative process, which allows citizens to shape public policy by collecting enough voter signatures.

He sought to put a measure before the voters to deny illegal aliens state benefits.

On October 5, 1993, Prince held a meeting in Costa Mesa to discuss the ballot initiative plan with several concerned citizens. Coe also attended the meeting. She had not previously met Prince. He showed the group portions of the initiative he had already written. The group agreed with Prince's plan, and Prince agreed to be chairman. California Republican Assemblyman Richard Mountjoy agreed to serve as the initiative's representative in Sacramento, the state capital. As a result of his leadership, Mountjoy later became known as the "Godfather of 187."

However, since the group was short on funds, volunteers were needed to take on the time-consuming job of distributing petitions and gathering voters' signatures at places such as grocery stores, swap meets, and gun shows. Prince asked Coe if she would spearhead the effort to collect signatures. "I'll do my best," Coe replied. They needed 384,974 signatures from registered voters by the qualifying date of April 22, 1994. Coe contacted group leaders throughout California and discussed the plan with them. They were fully behind the effort and ready to go.

During the next several weeks, Prince and other members of this new committee, including Coe, drafted the rest of the initiative. They called it "Save Our State" (SOS). The initiative would:

- Prohibit illegal-alien children from attending public schools. School districts would have to verify the immigration status of each student;

- Bar public health or social services to illegal aliens, except for emergency medical care. Hospitals would have to report suspected illegal aliens;

- Require police to verify the immigration status of suspects they arrest;

- Make the manufacture of false documents a felony with up to a five-year prison sentence.

On November 8, 2003, the Save Our State committee filed the initiative with the California Secretary of State's office.

On January 10, 2004, the secretary gave the committee permission to collect signatures from voters.

The next day, SOS members printed the petitions. CCIR members circulated the petitions around the state. With only one hundred days to gather 384,974 signatures from registered voters, the deadline loomed.

Prince and other committee members held news conferences in San Diego and Los Angeles to announce the initiative. Although the majority of California's citizens were opposed to illegal immigration, as they are today, the media gave the initiative "very little attention," Prince recalled. "When they did give us attention, they charged us with being racist."

Assisting Coe and her CCIR members with the gathering of signatures and distribution of petitions were volunteers from Ross Perot's organization, United We Stand America, although Perot himself was not involved. The California Republican Party and various clubs also helped out. Later, Prince raised tens of thousands of dollars, mostly from SOS committee members, to pay professional signature-gatherers.

At the end of the one-hundred-day period on April 22, the volunteers had collected about 400,000 signatures, and 200,000 were collected by the paid signature-gatherers, more than enough to cover any signatures that were invalid. The Save Our State initiative was renamed Proposition 187 by state officials, although the campaign was still called Save Our State.

Volunteers distributed 100,000 SOS campaign brochures written by Prince to educate voters around the state about the growing illegal immigration problems. On the inside back cover of the brochure, Prince described what would happen if the initiative failed or was struck down by the courts:

> The defeat of Proposition 187 would be a declaration of open borders. Millions of new illegals will flood into California, swelling the hundreds of thousands who already come here every year.

Public hospitals, strained by providing free care to illegals, won't be able to meet the increased demand. Diseases that are already beginning to spread will become epidemic.

Public schools, suffering from overcrowding now, can't add hundreds of thousands of new illegals. California's quality of education, already among the lowest in the United States, will be mined.

Welfare programs already cut back due to lack of funding will have to be cut back further. Benefits won't be enough for people to live on, and many of the poor will riot in the streets.

Wage rates will drop even further with so many unemployed illegals competing for scarce jobs.

Unemployed illegals will turn to criminal activity. They already commit crimes at a higher rate than the general population.

Crowding in many areas will get worse, and deteriorating neighborhoods will mean further declines in property values.

Over-crowding throughout the state will have a devastating effect on the environment.

No matter how bad it gets in California, it will still be better than many parts of the world. Illegal aliens will continue to come as long as we have anything that they want.

Virtually all of Prince's predictions have come true. Although the poor have not rioted in the streets of Los Angeles since 1992, they probably will, if California's financial situation continues to worsen (the state was about $40 billion in debt in April 2005[16]) and the federal government continues to allow millions of poor people to flood across America's border with Mexico. Regarding property values, prices have climbed dramatically due to mass immigration. If the quality of life continues to deteriorate in Los Angeles and other parts of California, property values may decline.

In the months leading up to the November 1994 election, the California Democratic Party and Hispanic leaders attacked Proposition 187, Prince, Coe, and anyone else associated with the initiative. They said it was racist to deny "immigrants" state benefits.[17]

Democrats and Hispanic leaders also went after California Governor Pete Wilson and his television advertisement accurately depicting illegal aliens streaming across the border. Wilson was running for reelection against Democrat Kathleen Brown. In a voiceover for the ad, Wilson said, "I'm suing to force the federal government to control the border. And I'm working to deny state services to illegal immigrants. Enough is enough.... Kathleen Brown thinks differently. She supports continuing state services to illegals and says illegal immigration is not a cause of problems in California. Where do you stand?"

Prince said he was opposed to the ad. He also said Wilson did not support Proposition 187 until after he saw it could help him get reelected. "Wilson was trailing Brown by a wide margin just weeks before the election," Prince said. "He joined our effort and his poll numbers shot up."[18]

Interestingly, calling people opposed to illegal immigration "racist" apparently was a tactic agreed to by Hispanic leaders at the "first-ever Hispanic Leadership Roundtable" in Washington, D.C., in 1990. Organizations such as the National Council of La Raza (The Race) and the Mexican American Legal Defense and Educational Fund (MALDEF) were planning a strategy to force the U.S. government to repeal the Employer Sanctions Law that prohibits the hiring of illegal aliens.[19]

Francisco Garcia, national director of the immigrant rights program for MALDEF, proclaimed that the conference was just "a first skirmish of a prolonged war" against American citizens. Andrew Hernandez, director of the Southwest Voter Registration Education Project, said the label of "racism" was the weapon to be used in that war, since it "would strike fear and dread into the heart of any politician."[20]

Since that conference in 1990, organizations such as La Raza, MALDEF, the Southern Poverty Law Center, and many others have launched scurrilous accusations of racism against courageous Americans such as Coe, Prince, and others discussed in this book for demanding U.S. immigration laws and borders be enforced.

For years, every poll shows that the vast majority of Americans want immigration to be legal, controlled, and reduced. But these organizations have made illegal immigration into a race controversy, when it is actually about sovereignty, law, fairness, and common sense.

On November 8, 1994, the word "racist" did not help Democrats and Hispanic leaders keep Pete Wilson out of the governor's office in 1994. Wilson easily defeated Kathleen Brown, 55 percent to 40 percent.

Charges of racism also failed to defeat Proposition 187, which won by an even wider margin, 60 to 40 percent. The voters overwhelmingly agreed to deny non-emergency public benefits to illegal aliens. Majorities of whites, blacks, and Asians voted for it, as did 30 percent of Hispanics, according to exit polling, wrote UCLA professor William A.V. Clark in his 1998 book *The California Cauldron*. But Prince believes that the number of Hispanics voting for the proposition was about 50 percent. "Prior to the election," he said, "the California Field Poll found that 50 percent of Hispanics were in favor of 187."

The day after the election, several lawsuits were filed against Proposition 187 in California state court by MALDEF, the League of Latin American Citizens (LULAC), the American Civil Liberties Union, and other organizations.

Years of legal delays prevented Proposition 187 from being enacted. In March 1998, U.S. District Court Judge Mariana Pfaelzer ruled the proposition unconstitutional. California Attorney General Dan Lungren promised to appeal the case to a higher court, but there was no appeal.

In 1999, Governor "Gray Davis settled the case 'out of court' in a mediated agreement, and Proposition 187 was killed in a back room deal," a Prince Web site reported several years later. "None of the supporters of Proposition 187 were allowed to speak in its defense. The judge sealed the only evidence presented to the state—a series of reports by public agencies showing how the measure could be implemented constitutionally. The public was not allowed to see it."[21] California voters were outraged.

Coe said there was a bright side: "Although Proposition 187 was 'mediated' into oblivion by Davis, it sent a loud and clear message to Congress, which in 1996 passed the first immigration and welfare reform legislation in over thirty years."

In 2004, Prince, Coe, and others would join forces again to resurrect a new Save Our State initiative.

Representative Rohrabacher to the Rescue

"I am here to express my deep concern over a dangerous trend that has agents of the federal government knocking on the doors of Americans who are participating in the democratic process. In a disturbing pattern, the Clinton administration is using the power of the federal government to intimidate individuals it does not agree with who are simply exercising their constitutional right to engage in political activities."[22]

That statement was made by Republican Congressman Dana Rohrabacher of California before the Subcommittee on the Constitution in Washington on October 19, 1995. Rohrabacher testified that the Clinton administration harassed members of the Florida-187 Committee, which is affiliated with Coe's California Coalition for Immigration Reform. He said the Florida group was issued subpoenas to appear before a U.S. Commission on Civil Rights hearing in September.

"Not only were members of this organization ordered to appear," Rohrabacher said, "the commission also demanded to have copies of the group's internal documents, including those detailing campaign strategy and other sensitive information. How many of us would feel comfortable having our campaign plans seized by the government and put on public display for our opponents to read a year in advance of our next election?"

Rohrabacher also told the subcommittee that three days before the November 1994 election in which California voters approved Proposition 187, Assistant Attorney General Deval Patrick ordered an FBI agent to Coe's home. What was Coe's crime? She distributed fliers in Orange County that stated only U.S. citizens are allowed to vote.

"Once the election was over," Rohrabacher testified, "the investigation was suddenly called off. Mrs. Coe strongly feels that incident was nothing less than an attempt by the federal government to abridge her personal freedom of expression.

"Barbara Coe and the individuals involved with the Florida-187 campaign are not anti-government conspirators. They are simply hardworking American citizens who are participating in the democratic process to promote issues they believe in. Who wouldn't be frightened to receive a federal subpoena or have the FBI question your legal political activities? I am alarmed at the use of government power by liberals in the Clinton administration to intimidate and harass individuals whose beliefs they do not agree with. Because they know they cannot win the public debate on illegal immigration, these liberals are resorting to heavy-handed tactics, attempting to silence their opponent through intimidation and fear."

Coe told me she believed the fliers were necessary to fight voter fraud after hearing from Hispanic members of CCIR that non-citizens were planning to vote in the 1994 election. She said the FBI questioned her for three hours at her home after she posted fliers around polling places. She said she was careful to follow laws requiring that fliers be distributed at least one hundred feet away from any polling place. Coe did not file charges, but she did consider the questioning to be a form of intimidation.

In 1996, Coe again distributed the fliers. She said MALDEF had contacted the FBI about her fliers. MALDEF said Coe was targeting new citizens who were voting and threatened her with legal action. In a letter to Coe, MALDEF warned: "If you or any member of your organization takes action that in any way intimidates voters, you will be violating federal and state law, and we are prepared to take immediate legal action against you."[23]

But an attorney for the Individual Rights Foundation pointed out the absurdity in MALDEF's argument. "The only people who could reasonably be intimidated by these activities are those who are not legally entitled to vote in the first place," said Patrick J. Manshardt. "Threatened legal action against the members of [the coalition] for exercising their rights guaranteed by the First Amendment is the only intimidation taking place here."[24]

Interestingly, a few years later, the FBI said they could not help Coe when she told them about threatening phone calls and death threats on her after CCIR put up a billboard that labeled California as the "Illegal Immigration State."[25] (This episode is discussed later in this chapter.)

But Coe isn't the only one whose life has been threatened for taking action against illegal immigration. In January 2004, the offices of Representative Rohrabacher received dozens of threatening phone calls, including one death threat, after he authored a bill that would require hospitals to report a patient's immigration status before they could be reimbursed for treatment. The phone calls began after the bill was discussed on a New York radio station. One of the voice mails warned, "I'm coming to kill you."

"This is not just somebody I've angered and who's expressing some hostility," Rohrabacher said. "These are gruesome threats that I will be attacked and killed."[26]

On May 18, 2004, the U.S. House of Representatives voted overwhelmingly against the bill, 331 to 88. Rohrabacher said his proposal would "live to fight another day."[27] But American Border Patrol President Glenn Spencer was less optimistic. "This vote by the House sent a message that the United States of America is the world's HMO," Spencer said. "Since we are totally unable to deny anything to illegal aliens, we had better stop them at the border."

'Reconquista! The Takeover of America'

Several CCIR members volunteer their time, day and night, to help Coe educate citizens about what she says are "the actions of many corrupt Democrat and Republican officials who, for their own personal gain, defend the 'rights' of illegal aliens." Three "patriots always on the front line" are Evelyn Miller, Elaine Proko, and John Clark. But it was Miller's first big project for CCIR that has provided American citizens with some of the most powerful evidence showing there is more behind poor "immigrants" coming to the U.S. for jobs "Americans won't do" than meets the eye.

Miller joined CCIR in 1994 to assist in the passage of Proposition 187 that year. After it passed in November, many elected officials, college professors, and pro-illegal-alien activists were "furious," Miller told me. "To them it was a declaration of war."

In January 1995, Coe read about a two-day Latino Summit Response conference at the University of California, Riverside, that month where Hispanic leaders would discuss plans to stop the implementation of Proposition 187. Coe asked Miller whether she would attend the conference if CCIR paid for her mileage and motel room. Miller said yes.

The conference would be the first of several meetings Miller would attend at various Los Angeles-area locations during the next several years where she gathered information on a dangerous and growing anti-American movement inside the U.S. That movement is the liberation of Aztlan, a mythical area that includes California, Arizona, Nevada, Utah, Colorado, New Mexico, and Texas. Race activist leaders and many Mexicans living in the U.S. and in Mexico say this Southwestern territory was stolen by the U.S. and must be re-conquered ("Reconquista") and reclaimed for Mexico. In truth, the territory was lost when Mexico signed the 1848 Treaty of Guadalupe-Hidalgo at the end of the Mexican-American War. The U.S. paid $15 million for the land.[28]

One of the most effective vehicles of these radical leaders is MEChA, an acronym for Moviemiento Estudiantil Chicano de Aztlan. MEChA is the Chicano student movement founded more than thirty years ago by "Bert Corona for the purpose of infiltrating America's educational system and brainwashing students with anti-American sentiment," says Coe.

In a story published on May 24, 1982, the *Los Angeles Times* reported that Corona had "a Marxist-Leninist viewpoint" and taught part-time for many years at California State University, Los Angeles, even though he lacked a college degree.[29] He died in 2001.

The first MEChA chapter was established in 1969 at the University of California, Santa Barbara. Fueled by massive illegal immigration, MEChA has a strong and rapidly growing presence on dozens of university and high-school campuses in America.[30]

MEChA's creed is, "Por La Raza todo. Fuera de La Raza nada." Translated, it means, "Everything for the race. Everything outside the race, nothing."

A page titled El Plan de Aztlan, from the University of Oregon's MEChA Web site reads:

In the spirit of a new people that is conscious not only of its proud historical heritage but also of the brutal "gringo" invasion of our territories, we, the Chicano inhabitants and civilizers of the northern land of Aztlan from whence came our forefathers, reclaiming the land of their birth and consecrating the determination of our people of the sun, declare that the call of our blood is our power, our responsibility, and our inevitable destiny.

We are free and sovereign to determine those tasks which are justly called for by our house, our land, the sweat of our brows, and by our hearts. Aztlan belongs to those who plant the seeds, water the fields, and gather the crops and not to the foreign Europeans. We do not recognize capricious frontiers on the bronze continent.[31]

"MEChA's goals are to re-conquer all of the Southwestern states and reclaim that land for Mexico as the Nation of Aztlan," Coe explains. "Their next goal is to control our entire government and wield the power necessary for unrestricted immigration from Mexico and ensure the immigrants' needs are fully subsidized by billions of U.S. citizen tax dollars. Those goals are well defined in the plan to promote Aztlan, which was activated in January 1995 at the U.C. Riverside Latino conference."

The conference drew more than five hundred Hispanic activists, university professors, and elected officials, Miller recalls. Miller, who speaks "pretty good Spanish," had to bluff her way into the meeting. "I had to convince organizers Armando Navarro and Marianna Gonzalez that I was a socialist who didn't want borders between the U.S. and Mexico."

Once inside the meeting, Miller found Mexican Americans displaying tremendous anger over the passage of Proposition 187 and heard speeches that were incendiary, racist, and anti-American.

"These were hard-core Mexican nationalists," Miller remembers. "Militant, paramilitary soldiers of the Aztlan movement called Brown Berets stood in uniforms against the wall all around the inside of the hall to keep order. They are vicious, bad dudes. The MEChA people from many colleges were there. There were various panel discussions by professional people. There was a lawyer's panel. There was a panel of media people from Univision, Telemundo, and other Spanish language media companies."

Miller took a concealed tape recorder to the meeting to document the speeches, but upon returning to the motel room later that day, she found that the sound was "lousy." When Miller returned to the conference the next day, she "endeared" herself to the organizers, and they said she could have an audiocassette of the conference. Miller was given eleven ninety-minute cassette recordings of the speeches and panel discussions. In the following weeks, she cut and spliced the tapes to make one ninety-minute cassette that was the "best of" those tapes. Miller also made verbatim transcriptions of her composite tape. CCIR published her transcript and other material she gathered from subsequent meetings in a 1997 booklet titled "Reconquista! The Takeover of America."

I listened to the tapes for the first time in 2003. The speakers were obsessed with race. Their voices were filled with anger and hate, evoking images of Adolf Hitler.

The following statements are a sampling of what was said behind closed doors at the U.C. Riverside conference in 1995 and at private conferences organized by the Southwest Voter Registration Education Project (SVRP) in 1995, 1996, and 1997. SVRP is an organization dedicated to registering Hispanics and electing Hispanic politicians throughout the U.S. You can hear the comments and order audio copies at www.ccir.net, or call 877-NO-ILLEGALS (877-664-5534).

Armando Navarro, U.C. Riverside professor:
"We're in a state of transition. And that transformation is called the browning of America. Latinos are now becoming the majority.... It's a game; it's a game of power and who controls it.... You are like the generals that command armies. We're in a state of war. This Proposition 187 is a declaration of war against the Latino/Chicano community of this country."

Jose Angel Gutierrez, professor at the University of Texas and founder of the revolutionary La Raza Unida Party:

"The border remains a military zone. We remain a hunted people. Now you think you have a destiny to fulfill in this land that historically has been ours for 40,000 years.... This is our homeland.... We are not immigrants who came from another country to another country. We are migrants, free to travel the length and breadth of the Americas because we belong here. We need no passport. And we believed it in the Chicano movement. We believed it. So we said, 'We're gonna build Aztlan, right here.' And each one of us began in our own way. The Brown Berets, for example, the defense unit for all of us. La Raza, primero. Group ascendancy. Why, in order for us to have a homeland, we must give up our Mexican-ness and become white-like? Why? We are millions. We just have to survive. We have an aging white America. They are not making babies. They are dying. It's a matter of time. The explosion is in our population.... Se estan cagando cabrones de miedo. [They are shitting in their pants with fear]. I love it."

Gloria Romero, former U.C. professor and today a California state senator and Democrat Caucus chair:

"I thank the students for the walkouts, for the activity, for the spirit, for the organizing.... We have a dynamic movement that will not end with the passage of a stupid proposition.... I know that a classroom is just another space in which to organize.... We recognize sin fronteras (without borders), that should be our rallying point."

Art Torres, former California state senator and current chairman of the California Democratic Party:

"Que viva la causa [long live our cause]. It is an honor to be with the new leadership of the Americas.... Power is not given to you. You have to take it. Remember, 187 is the last gasp of white America in California. Understand that. And people say to me on the Senate floor when I was in the Senate, 'Why do you fight so hard for affirmative action programs?'

And I tell my white colleagues, 'Because you're going to need them.'" (Laughter.)

Henry Cisneros, former secretary of Housing and Urban Development in the Clinton administration, former president of Univision (Spanish language television), former mayor of San Antonio, who now builds homes in Hispanic markets:

"The future of our people and the future of our country is literally in your hands. Our numbers are growing dramatically.... I'm saying to you as goes the Latino population will go California, and as goes California will go the United States of America. My friends, the stakes are big; this is a fight worth making.... We should stand for the proud Latino future. We must stand for the people, now more than ever, and then be prepared to fight."

Victoria Castro, former member of the Los Angeles Board of Education:

"Que viva La Raza, que viva La Raza. I'm here to welcome all the new voters of eighteen years old that we're registering now in our schools. You're going to make a difference for Los Angeles, for San Antonio, for New York. And to the Mechistas [MEChA students] across this nation, you're going to make that difference for us too. But when we register one million more voters, I will not be the only Latina on the Board of Education of Los Angeles. And let me tell you, no one will dismantle bilingual education in the United States of America. No one will deny an education to any child, especially Latino children."

Joe Baca, former California state assemblyman and today a U.S. congressman:

"But when we look out at the audience and we see la familia, La Raza, it's a great feeling. It reminded me of a book that we all read about, Paul Revere, and when he said, 'The British are coming; the British are coming.' Well, the Latinos are coming; the Latinos are coming. And the Latinos are going to vote. So our voices will be heard. So that's what this agenda is about. It's about ensuring that we increase our numbers.... You know we're in a civil war."

Richard Alatorre, former Los Angeles city councilman:
"Because our numbers are growing, they're afraid that we're going to take over the governmental institutions and other institutions. They're right; we will take them over, and we are not going to go away. We are here to stay, and we are saying, ya basta [enough], we have had enough."

Ruben Zacarias, former superintendent of the Los Angeles Unified School District:
"I started this [citizenship preparation centers] very quietly because there are those that if they knew that we were creating a whole new cadre of brand-new citizens it would have tremendous political impact. We will change the political panorama not only of L.A., but L.A. County and the state. And if we do that, we've changed the panorama of the nation."

Although all of those statements were made at conferences held years ago, such meetings occur regularly in Los Angeles and in cities outside California, according to Evelyn Miller and others who regularly monitor Spanish-language media outlets.

In June 1997, Miller recorded Loyola Marymount professor Fernando Guerra saying the following at the SVRP conference in Los Angeles: "Don't tell anyone outside this room—the majority of non-Latinos aren't watching [Spanish-language media]. If Channel 7 [English-language television] or the *L.A. Times* would do the things they're supposed to do, there'd be some questions raised. But because they aren't watching us, they aren't raising the questions."

In March 2004, Miller and Elaine Proko, one of the other "patriots always on the front line" for Coe, traveled to Washington, D.C., to warn members of Congress about the reconquista. With a number of illegal-alien amnesties under consideration in Congress, Miller and Proko were anxious to let representatives know about this dark agenda. They gave congressional staff members copies of CCIR's newly produced CD of the tape-recorded statements Miller had compiled years ago. Several congressional staff members were stunned when they heard the short sound clips. "They were in a state of disbelief," Miller said, but other staff members showed no interest in the warnings.

Today, two Democratic politicians with a strong allegiance to Mexico are on the national scene: New Mexico Governor Bill Richardson and Los Angeles Mayor Antonio Villaraigosa. Richardson, whose mother is Mexican, was chairman of the 2004 Democratic National Convention. In a radio interview in 1996, when he was a U.S. congressman from New Mexico, Richardson said: "These are changing political times where our basic foundations and programs are being attacked, illegal and legal immigration are being unfairly attacked. We have to band together, and that means Latinos in Florida, Cuban Americans, Mexican Americans, Puerto Ricans, South Americans, we have to network better—we have to be more politically minded; we have to put aside party and think of ourselves as Latinos, as Hispanics more than we have in the past."[32]

In 2004, Villaraigosa served as national co-chairman of Senator John Kerry's presidential campaign. In 2005, he was elected mayor of Los Angeles. A firebrand Mexican nationalist, Villaraigosa is a former chairman of the reconquista Chicano organization MEChA. In May 1999, when Villaraigosa was speaker of the California State Assembly, he and Mexico's president Zedillo addressed the California legislature in Spanish, though both are fluent in English. Then Villaraigosa initiated the "Chicano handclap," a loud, rhythmic applause. The non-Hispanic legislators were mystified. During a news conference in August 1999, Villaraigosa thanked Zedillo for killing Proposition 187.[33]

Evelyn Miller told me that the people who strive for a reconquista of America are generally the ones who come to America illegally and have no desire to become Americans.

"Millions of Mexicans and other Latinos that have illegally invaded our country and settled here have no allegiance to the United States," she explained. "Many of their children are the same way. They are holding on to their language and culture and creating a Hispanic nation within our nation. Unfortunately, the illegal-alien lobby and the invasion are casting a very bad light on Latino Americans who are good American citizens."

'Attack on America'—July 4, 1996

The call for violence at the January 1995 conference at U.C. Riverside to promote Aztlan was fulfilled the next year on America's Independence Day. The scene was similar to the one at Anaheim City Hall five years later, described at the beginning of this chapter.

On the morning of July 4, 1996, at the Federal Building in west Los Angeles, about 250 patriots from Coe's CCIR and Glenn Spencer's Voice of Citizens Together were exercising their First Amendment rights by peacefully protesting illegal immigration.

The patriots carried signs that read, "Control Our Border," "Stop the Invasion Now," and "This is the United States of America, not Aztlan." There were many American flags.

Across Wilshire Boulevard from the protest, several dozen members of pro-illegal-alien groups and the Communist Progressive Labor Party had assembled. The counter-protesters had their own signs. Many were written in Spanish, but some were in English: "Death to the Racists," "Silence the Racist Voice," "Fight for Communism," and "Don't Mess with La Raza!"

That morning, the communists and other counter-demonstrators, who were mostly younger than the American patriots, crossed Wilshire Boulevard and brutally attacked them with frozen and full soft drink cans, sticks from picket signs, and fists. Some of the patriots fought back, but several were injured, some badly. CCIR had been videotaping the protest and captured the attack. Later, CCIR produced a video about it, titled "Attack on America."

KABC-TV reporter Mark Coogan gave an account from the scene about three hours later, as the protests continued but long after the violence ended.

"At ten this morning, Westwood was the scene of a violent Fourth of July clash over the issue of illegal immigration," Coogan reported. "Six people were hurt in the fight, and apparently, no arrests were made by police. It began when a conservative group opposed to illegal immigration planned a protest here, but they were confronted by counter-demonstrators who appear to be bent on violence.

"The skirmishing went on with soft drinks thrown by the communists. Some of the right-wingers waded back in with fists and their own picket signs. There were wrestling matches for flags and banners. An American flag was ripped from a conservative and trampled by a leftist. While the soft drink cans and punches flew, there wasn't a law enforcement officer in sight to break this up. Finally, one officer from the Metropolitan Transit Police got in between the combatants, but he was one man versus many."

CCIR's video captured the ugliness from the anti-American, pro-communists, including the mob chants:

> Asian, Latin, black and white, workers of the world unite. No more nations, no more war, we know what we're fighting for. Death, death, death to the fascists. Power, power, power to the people. Fight for communism, power to the workers.

One of the anti-Americans was Augustin Cebada, of the Brown Berets, the militant, paramilitary soldiers of the Aztlan movement. The Brown Berets' pledge is: "Protect, guarantee and secure the rights of the Mexican-American by any and all means necessary." Cebada said this after the violence ended:

> Go back to the Plymouth Rock, Pilgrims. Get out. We are the future. You're old and tired. We have beaten you; leave like beaten rats. You old white people, it is your duty to die. You're taking up too much space, too much air. There's over seven million Mexicans in L.A. County alone. We are the majority. And you're going to see every day more and more of it, as we manifest that our young people grow up, graduate from high school, go on to college, and start taking over this society. The vast majority of our people are under the age of fifteen years old. Right now, we're already controlling those elections, whether it's by violence or nonviolence. Through love of having children we're going to take over.

Today, Cebada broadcasts the same hateful messages on his one-hour radio show on KPFK-FM, the Los Angeles affiliate of Pacifica Radio.

Looking back on that violent day in 1996, Barbara Coe said: "We went out there on America's Independence Day to peacefully demonstrate against illegal immigration. But the hate-America, pro-illegal aliens brutally attacked us without provocation. These people preach hatred toward all loyal, law-abiding Americans of every race and ethnicity. They preach the 'takeover' of our country. And I ask, 'Where were the police?' Just like our peaceful rally at Anaheim City Hall in 2001, they were nowhere to be found."

'The Illegal Immigration State'

On May 7, 1998, Coe and CCIR tried a new approach in their ongoing fight against illegal immigration. They put up a billboard near the California-Arizona border that called California the "Illegal Immigration State." Coe said the billboard was designed to warn other states about the destruction caused by out-of-control immigration. CCIR members paid for the billboard and placed it on the side of an interstate highway near the city of Blythe in Riverside County, California. The sign, which included CCIR's office number, read:

> Welcome To California,
> The Illegal Immigration State
> Don't Let This Happen To Your State
> Call Toll Free – (877) NO ILLEGALS

Even though the sign said nothing about race, Hispanic leaders called it racist. One leader vowed to tear it down. His name is Mario Obledo, former California Health, Education and Welfare secretary and president of the California Coalition of Hispanic Organizations. Obledo said in a *Los Angeles Times* story that he planned to "deface or burn" the billboard on June 27 and he asked others to support him.[34]

"I have invited my friends, and I invite all Californians of goodwill to join me," said Obledo, co-founder of MALDEF. Obledo said he found the billboard offensive. "It is out of order, it's racist, it's divisive and creates a climate of fear among Californians." Other Hispanic leaders agreed with Obledo.

Riverside County sheriff's deputies warned they would take action if someone tried to destroy the billboard.

"If somebody purposely damages private property, we'll take a report, and if the criteria is there to make an arrest on malicious mischief, we will," said a spokesman for the Riverside County Sheriff's Department.[35]

Coe said CCIR put up the billboard to warn other states about "the devastation that has occurred in California because of illegal immigration and bilingual education." She said the sign is not racist because it does not say anything at all about race.

Obledo responded in the *L.A. Times*: "Law enforcement? That's all right. I think I'm in the right. [Coe] may argue freedom of speech. But freedom of speech has its limitations.... The message crosses the boundaries of free speech because it could incite violence, poses a danger to public safety and creates a climate of fear and mistrust among citizens of California. I'm going to deface the billboard or burn it."

On June 17, six days after he made the threats and accused Coe and CCIR members of racism, Obledo spoke on a Los Angeles radio show about how Hispanics are going to take over California.

"We're going to take over all the political institutions of California in five years," Obledo said on the Tom Leykis show. "We're going to be the majority population in this state. If people don't like Mexicans, they ought to leave. They ought to go back to Europe."[36]

On June 23, twelve days after Obledo told the *Times* he was going to "deface the billboard or burn it," the billboard's owner, Martin Media, took the sign down. "We very much believe in free speech," said a representative with Martin Media, but "our property was being threatened."

Just five months before Obledo's terrorist threats, President Clinton awarded Obledo the Presidential Medal of Freedom, our nation's highest civilian honor, for his "struggle to ensure the civil rights of America's Hispanic citizens."

CCIR received hundreds of phone calls from people supporting the billboard and hundreds of "hate calls." Coe gave me an audiocassette and transcript of the hate calls. Here's a sampling of what four people said:

> "Hi, my name is Denise. Just to let you know that if you will put that sign up one more time I guarantee it will come down again. Down with this America, this California; this belongs to Mexico, just to let you know."

"Make sure you pass this message for Mrs. Barbara Coe of Huntington Beach. She has just signed her death warrant. We know where she's gonna be, too."

"You know what, you fucking lazy white trash piece of shit? You're here in Aztlan. You European immigrants get the fuck out. We're here and we're strong, and we ain't gonna take this shit no more."

"We're gonna take over all California. Not only California, we're already getting Nevada, Arizona, Oregon, Washington; before you know it Washington, D.C., will be ours, too. Piece of fucking white trash."

Coe shared the hate calls with the Huntington Beach Police Department and the FBI, but she said neither law enforcement agency did anything.

However, Coe and the CCIR members were not going to let threats stand in the way of their ongoing campaign to spread the facts about illegal immigration. "The death threats were frightening," said Coe, "but we weren't going to back down from telling the truth and warning America."

Later in 1998, CCIR erected another billboard across the Colorado River near Blythe, California. But it met the same fate as the first sign after threats were made against the landowner.

In September 1999, the patriots chose a new location for their sign, Highway 99, one mile north of Pixley, California. The sign was mounted on a portable hay trailer, and this time the message read:

> Demand Illegal Aliens Be Deported
> The Job You Save May Be Your Own
> Call Toll-Free (877) NO ILLEGALS
> Sponsored By The California Coalition
> For Immigration Reform

But that sign was "trashed thirteen times and repaired by local ranchers thirteen times," Coe told me. "The fourteenth time the entire trailer was stolen."

On February 2, 2000, Coe and CCIR tried once more to exercise their First Amendment rights. They put up another billboard message near the Arizona border where the first one was erected. Hispanic organizations were angry again. And again, Coe told the news media that the billboard is simply a factual statement and says nothing about race.

Here is one final note about "racist" billboards in Southern California. Billboards dot the landscape along freeways in the Los Angeles area promoting a Spanish-language FM radio station, 97.9, KLAX. In big type, the billboards proclaim, "97.9, La Raza" (The Race).

Denver Post Smears Coe and CCIR

Among CCIR's many activities, it also sponsors events to support elected officials and others who fight illegal immigration. One such occasion was on November 1, 2003, in La Canada Flintridge, a Los Angeles suburb. It was a fund-raising event for the National Center for Citizenship and Immigration, a nonprofit group that Colorado Congressman Tom Tancredo formed to continue his battle against illegal immigration. Tancredo was the keynote speaker at the event.

Also sponsoring the affair was Ron Prince's Save Our State committee, the authors of Proposition 187. The event was billed as the "American Patriot Rally," and it featured many immigration reform leaders, including Glenn Spencer, Terry Anderson, George Putnam, Ezola Foster, Lupe Moreno, former California senator Dick Mountjoy, California Assemblyman Dennis Mountjoy, and others. A CCIR flier about the rally said those who support illegal immigration were targeting Representative Tancredo for replacement:

> Founder of the Congressional Immigration Reform Caucus, an organization dedicated to protecting our lives from illegal-alien criminals and terrorists, Rep. Tancredo has been demonized by Mexico, pro-illegal-alien advocates, the White House and corrupt elected officials who welcome foreign invaders into our country for their own personal gain. To suppress the patriot movement his leadership has inspired,

he is now a "target for defeat" by denial of campaign monies from the traditional business and industry PACs!

Two days before the rally, the *Denver Post* ran a story by Washington Bureau Chief Mike Soraghan about the event. Soraghan focused on Barbara Coe and CCIR and Glenn Spencer and his American Border Patrol (ABP) organization.

By every possible measurement, the article was dishonest and biased, beginning with the headline: "Anti-immigration groups to host Tancredo; Event's planners accused of hate."[37] But CCIR and ABP have never been opposed to immigration. The groups are anti-illegal immigration, as are most Americans. And why did the *Post* write in its headline that the rally's planners are "accused of hate"? The only organization named in the article condemning CCIR and ABP was the Southern Poverty Law Center (SPLC), which has been criticized even by supporters for emphasizing fundraising rather than civil rights activism.

"'We've listed them as hate groups for their loathing of Hispanics,' said Heidi Beirich of the SPLC, which made its name hounding the Ku Klux Klan," Soraghan wrote.

Later in the article, Soraghan wrote, "Beirich said neither group has a reputation for physically attacking immigrants." Correct, neither group has a reputation for physically attacking immigrants, nor have they attacked immigrants, so why put the sentence in the article? The sentence was probably included to plant the idea in the minds of readers.

If the *Denver Post* had bothered to find out, they would have learned that many Hispanic Americans and other minorities belong to both CCIR and ABP. For example, Coe's coalition has under its umbrella: Latino-Americans for Immigration Control, from Salinas, California; Asian-Americans for Border Control, located in Sylmar, California; and Black Americans for Family Values, from Venice, California.

In addition, this chapter provides striking examples where Hispanics have brutally attacked the members of CCIR and ABP without provocation. Why didn't the *Denver Post* include those true episodes in its article instead of planting false ideas in the minds of readers?

Joe Guzzardi, who is featured in this book, is familiar with the *Denver Post* and their biased coverage of immigration issues and Tancredo. In a 2002 article for www.Vdare.com, Guzzardi wrote: "The *Denver Post* is an illegal-alien propaganda machine disguised as a newspaper.... I read the *Denver Post* every day as part of NumbersUSA's ongoing Media Standards Project, evaluating fairness and balance in immigration reporting. It can be counted on for two things: correctly reporting Sunday's Denver Broncos score; and running hundreds of stories, columns, editorials and political cartoons every year touting illegals and benefits for illegals.... At its best, the *Post* is fish-wrap."[38]

What was most astounding to me was that the *Post* did not send a reporter or photographer to the Tancredo rally. They ran a hit-piece on the rally's organizers before the event, but they did not carry anything about the actual event itself. If the paper had, they would have seen what I and many other people witnessed.

Hundreds of people attended the outdoor event. That fact alone made it newsworthy—a Colorado congressman attracting that many people to an event in California. Politically savvy people at the event doubted that any California congressman could attract that many folks to a rally in the state.

People of various races and ethnicities were shaking hands, hugging, and kissing one another. Speeches from American citizens of different backgrounds expressed the urgent need for America to control our borders and enforce our immigration laws before becoming a Third-World disaster. The event was void of anger, hate, or racism.

Others attending the rally e-mailed the *Post*'s editor. One was Haydee Pavia, a naturalized citizen from South America who supports both CCIR and ABP. "We are hate groups?" she asked. "What do we hate? I think I have the answer. We hate lawlessness and corrupt politicians who are selling out the voters to private interests. We hate to see our hard earned money go for taxes to subsidize illegal-alien slave labor for businesses; our emergency rooms closing because they can no longer care for illegals who use them as free clinics; our wages and work standards lowered by illegal immigration; our schools crowded with the children of illegals and academics being lowered. We hate to see the rise in crime and our tax money go to prisons where 25 percent of inmates are illegal aliens."

Mark Mendlovitz, who was also at the rally, wrote the following to the *Post*'s editor: "The *Post*'s coverage was incredibly biased and unfair. There was no hate-mongering (unless you consider waving the Stars and Stripes hateful), and there was no racism that I could see either, because all the whites, blacks, Hispanics, Asians, and Jews that I knew and saw there were cheering wildly. That's not to mention the environmentalists, the blue-collar types, the college professors, the old folks, and the kids too!"

The *Denver Post*'s biased and dishonest story is typical of the way the mainstream press covers the people courageous enough to battle illegal immigration. But do not hold your breath for the *Post* or most media to report the truth anytime soon.

'Save Our State' Initiative Is Resurrected

In the fall of 2003, Ron Prince launched a new Save Our State (SOS) constitutional amendment ballot initiative to battle illegal immigration. The Orange County accountant, who co-sponsored Proposition 187 in 1994, believed this second attempt would fare better for several reasons. For one, Governor Gray Davis, who sabotaged Proposition 187, was recalled from office in October 2003.

"Ten years after Prop. 187 was passed by nearly 60 percent of the voters," said Prince's SOS Web site, "the qualification of this new measure for the ballot in November 2004 will finally give Californians an opportunity to fulfill the will of the people and to correct an injustice that denied them their 'day in court'.... The voters were outmaneuvered by the politicians, but the recall of the governor who committed this travesty has changed the political landscape. It's a new day in California."[39]

Another advantage with this new measure was the Internet, which was in its infancy with the public in 1994. Prince wanted to use the Internet to help collect signatures to qualify the new initiative for the ballot.

In addition, the new SOS initiative did not include Proposition 187's prohibition of public schooling for illegal aliens. It only addressed the problem of public benefits for illegals. "By leaving education out," Prince said, "we remove the issue of constitutionality for the rest of the measure. The 1996 federal welfare reform law allows us to deny public benefits to illegals."[40]

The new measure, which Prince wrote, would prohibit illegal aliens from obtaining California drivers' licenses and welfare, such as subsidized housing, food stamps, and health care. Illegals also would be prohibited from receiving in-state college tuition and free tuition at junior colleges. And California state and local agencies would be barred from accepting foreign ID cards such as Mexico's matricula consular for identification purposes.

To assist in his effort, Prince turned to the same patriots who helped him gather more than 100,000 signatures for Proposition 187 ten years earlier: Coe and CCIR. On November 26, 2003, Prince explained the new measure to CCIR members at the group's regular monthly meeting in Garden Grove, a city in Orange County. He told the patriots that a Web site was being developed for his new measure to be downloaded and distributed.

"The Internet is the primary tool that the SOS committee has," Prince explained. "We don't have any paid staff. Like you, we're all volunteers. We also don't have money to pay signature-gatherers. It remains to be seen how many Internet users will download the petition from our Web site and turn it in to the campaign."

Prince said he needed to collect 598,000 valid signatures from California registered voters by April 16, 2004, to qualify the measure for the November ballot. But he believed up to 200,000 additional signatures would be needed as margin against the inevitable invalid signatures.

Prince struck fear in the patriots' hearts when he told them that State Senator Gil Cedillo was already cooking up a new driver's license bill for illegal aliens—just weeks after his last one was repealed—and Governor Arnold Schwarzenegger was indicating support for it.

"Illegals want licenses for more than just driving," Prince warned. "They can use a driver's license to register to vote. Licenses also would make it easier for them to obtain public benefits. The implications for the future of California, with millions of illegals voting in our elections, are staggering. We must stop this before it gets started.

This new SOS constitutional amendment will supersede any deal hatched by Cedillo and Schwarzenegger. We need your help collecting signatures."

Coe and her patriots rose to the challenge. They organized people throughout the state and worked tirelessly to gather signatures at swap meets, gun shows, fairgrounds, and other locations. They provided fliers, instruction sheets, petition forms, and envelopes.

Prince traveled California speaking to civic organizations and Republican groups about the need for citizens to sign the initiative and to circulate it. He was on talk-radio shows from early morning until late at night. Other organizations and political allies in California also helped collect signatures.

However, all the hard work wasn't enough. On April 27, 2004, Prince announced that the petition failed to qualify for the November 2004 ballot. CCIR and other volunteers had collected about 500,000 signatures, a remarkable achievement, but far short of the 800,000 signatures he thought were needed to ensure success.

"You can't get an initiative on the ballot in California today without enough money to pay for signatures," Prince explained in a lengthy letter posted on the SOS Web site. The principle reason the campaign failed to garner more support was "opposition from the Republican Party establishment," he conceded. In 1994, Proposition 187's landslide victory swept conservative Republicans into statewide offices. But today's "centrist party elites" do not support populist causes.

He said the other problem was a lack of funds. Unlike 1994, none of California's Republican leaders helped financially. Their opposition discouraged other donors from funding the campaign.

"Today," Prince said, "we are back where we were at the beginning of the twentieth century. Special interests and the politicians they can buy ignore issues that are important to the people while promoting their own agendas, often in opposition to the public will and against the common good. The gap between the elites and the people has grown, and it will eventually threaten political stability if it is not reversed."

Not surprisingly, the *Los Angeles Times* was pleased with the outcome. In a May 1, 2004 editorial, the paper wrote: "It's always good news when a bad end comes to an ugly proposition.... Like Proposition 187, the new proposal would have created nothing but problems for the state. One provision would have made it a misdemeanor for state and local officials, such as police officers, not to report illegal immigrants to federal authorities. Police have good reason to resist enforcing federal laws—so that immigrant communities might report crimes and act as witnesses."[41]

Apparently, the *Times* does not understand that illegal immigration is the problem; the SOS initiative was a solution. Even worse, it is outrageous for this paper to write that police should not enforce our laws. That is anarchy. This view that illegal aliens are a "federal problem" is absurd. It is the duty of all of law enforcement to protect the citizens.

Even though Prince's initiative did not make the ballot, Californians were not giving up. In August 2004, another grassroots group, the Save Our License Committee, announced a new constitutional amendment ballot initiative designed to prevent California governments from granting drivers' licenses and other benefits to illegal aliens. Mike Spence, president of the California Republican Assembly, the oldest volunteer group within the state Republican Party, headed the effort.

"When the legislature gives benefits like drivers' licenses and in-state breaks to illegal aliens, it is sending the signal that illegal immigration is okay," said Spence. "Well, it is not okay, and the vast majority of Californians believe it is not okay."[42]

Among those backing the effort was State Assemblyman Mark Wyland. "This initiative is about empowering Californians to stand up and do what the legislature will not do," Wyland stated. "We should not be granting special tax-funded benefits to illegal aliens, period. And in this time of huge budget deficits, there is even more reason to stop the giveaway of our tax dollars."[43]

Said committee member Victor Valenzuela: "It's time to give the power to the people to once again say 'no more.'" [44]

Spence's group needed to collect 598,000 valid signatures—the same number that Prince's initiative needed—by February 21, 2005, to qualify the measure for the June 2006 ballot, or an earlier ballot, if a special statewide election were to be called.

Unlike Prince's last effort, Spence said paid signature-gatherers would be used, along with volunteers. "We are very confident of our success with this initiative," Spence said. "We start with a strong and enthusiastic base of supporters. We have financial commitments to help with the paid signature-gatherers. And the legislature is keeping the issue in front of everyone with their efforts to pass a new driver's license bill." [45]

Spence's committee distributed more than 350,000 petitions by mail. Petitions also could be downloaded at www.saveourlicense. com.

And once again, Coe and her CCIR patriots volunteered countless hours collecting signatures throughout California.

However, the Republican Party establishment again refused to participate in the campaign and the mainstream media mostly ignored it. Consequently, although polls again revealed the popularity of the cause, too few citizens were even aware that their signatures and supporting efforts were needed. Some radio talk-show hosts publicized the measure and held signature-gathering events, but a number of conservative talk-radio hosts loyal to the party establishment pretended the ballot measure didn't exist.

Several months later, Spence announced on February 18, 2005, that the Save Our License initiative had fallen short. In a letter posted on the committee's Web site, Spence thanked citizens for their "hard work" and "financial help." He said thousands of individuals collected signatures and donated almost $200,000 for paid signature-gatherers. "But the reality is that not enough petitions were returned in the last days for us to reach the number of signatures necessary. Initiatives are difficult for groups without big special interest dollars. Ours is a truly grassroots effort, and we know this initiative would pass if we can get over the logistical hurdles of qualification."

However, there was no mention in the letter about the financial commitments that were promised months earlier and counted on to put the measure over the top. On the *John and Ken* KFI-AM talk-radio show in Los Angeles, Spence said 450,000 signatures were collected, but he wouldn't go into specifics or name who failed to follow through on their financial pledges.

A couple weeks later, Coe told me she was disappointed that Spence's initiative failed, especially so soon after Prince's measure was unsuccessful. But Coe said she and CCIR would never give up the battle.

We Will Die on Our Feet

Since the founding of the California Coalition for Immigration Reform in 1992, Coe and her patriots have been through many battles in the fight to save the nation from the illegal-alien invasion—from the victory and fraudulent "mediation" of Proposition 187, to destroyed billboards, to bloody attacks in the streets by anarchists, communists, and reconquistas, to government investigations, to newspaper smears, to the ballot initiatives in 2004 and 2005. I asked Coe why she sacrificed so much of her life fighting illegal immigration.

"I subscribe to our CCIR philosophy that was stated in 1992," said the former police department manager. "Until the U.S. controls immigration, all else is a moot point, as it will no longer matter. Illegal immigration affects every aspect of our daily lives in America, from the loss of jobs, to overcrowded substandard schools, to billions of our tax dollars used for welfare and medical benefits. What we're faced with right now is losing our very lives and the lives of our loved ones because our country is drowning in illegal-alien terrorists, smugglers, murderers, rapists, pedophiles, and drug dealers."

Coe pointed the finger at greedy politicians for America's immigration crisis. "We the people have been betrayed by many of our elected officials who are willing to sacrifice the rights of citizens for cheap labor and the power of the immigrant vote," she said. "It is up to American citizens to take action to save our country. One person can make a difference. Patriot people power can topple tyrants and save our sovereignty from the new world order globalists."

I asked CCIR's leader if she thought the illegal-alien invasion would lead to civil war in America, as a growing number of people believe. "I really see it coming to that unless this direction is reversed," she warned. "If any of these so-called guest-worker programs, which are nothing but amnesties, are approved, and we start seeing an increase in people coming in to our country, that will be the straw that breaks the camel's back. That's because we will start to see millions more Americans losing their jobs and more illegal-alien crimes. I would say that would be the flashpoint. Loyal, law-abiding American patriots of every race and ethnicity will die on their feet before we submit on our knees to traitorous politicians and illegal-alien criminals."

8 | Joe Guzzardi

"Virtually every aspect of our lives is affected by illegal immigration."
—Joe Guzzardi, teacher and columnist

When Joe Guzzardi moved to the central California city of Lodi in 1988 to start a new career as an instructor at the adult school there, he didn't know anything about immigration. He was a banker with a background in finance and economics.

"If someone had asked, I would have wagered that like most federal programs, immigration was a mess," says Guzzardi. "But I didn't have any firsthand knowledge because immigration policy wasn't part of my world." That all changed at the Lodi Adult School, where *he* ended up getting the education instead of the students.

The first class Guzzardi taught was English as a second language to Southeast Asian refugees on welfare who came to America legally. Attendance was high in his class—no, not because the immigrants wanted to learn English, but to ensure that they received their welfare check. However, students could get exemptions from attending class for reasons such as doctors' excuses, sick children, transportation problems, compelling personal necessity, and holidays like Vietnamese, Cambodian or Hmong New Years.

"What a circus that class was," says Guzzardi. "When a student wanted out—and sooner or later most of them did—he would go to his doctor to ask for a note. Typically, a Vietnamese student would go to a Vietnamese doctor, Cambodian students to Cambodian doctors, and so on. The next day, the student appeared with a note saying, 'Please excuse Mr. Tran for ninety days. He has headaches.'" Guzzardi wondered how the doctor knew his patient would have the same headache ninety days later.[1]

Guzzardi was extremely frustrated by the excessive use of the medical excuse because taxpayers got socked with all the costs but the students learned nothing or practically nothing about English. Taxpayers paid for the class, books, teacher, instructional assistants, and doctor visits. But the costs to taxpayers did not end there. Most of the students had half a dozen children and they were all fully covered by Medi-Cal.

Guzzardi the teacher was getting quite an education on the workings of the generous American welfare system. The more he learned from his immigrant students, who were coached by the Catholic Church and other special interest groups, the more curious he became. So one day Guzzardi, the finance expert, did some calculations, and here is what he discovered.

Some families that arrived in America in the early 1980s and stayed on welfare until it ended in 1996 took in between $500,000 and $1 million in cash and benefits. Guzzardi's typical student had six children. The husband and wife collected a flat rate for themselves and additional monies and food stamps for each child. That amounted to around $30,000 a year. Everyone in the family received full medical insurance. Students also received major medical, and children were covered from the day they were born until they reached twenty-one. And, Guzzardi found, a common way of getting medical attention was taking an ambulance to the emergency room. "Ambulances were, like everything else, completely covered."

He says that with cash, food stamps, unlimited medical care, subsidized housing, the Women and Infant Children (WIC) program, and many other sources of welfare, these immigrant students were not even interested in finding employment. But the best prize of all was Supplemental Security Benefits Income (SSI), which offered even better benefits.

"I could never fault the students for the advantages they took," Guzzardi explains. "What did they know? They came to America, got a check, food stamps, and a Medi-Cal card. And heaven knows that they were in the U.S. because of circumstances beyond their control.

"As for teaching English, I never made too much progress. I had aides fluent in the Asian languages. But I could never convey to my students that America was their new home and learning English would be their path out of poverty."

Writing About Immigration

Guzzardi found the subject of immigration so fascinating and troublesome that two years after moving to Lodi in 1988 he began writing about it and related social issues. All the while, he was gathering material as he continued teaching English to Southeast Asian refugees, and later to migrant farm workers and immigrants from all over the world.

He first wrote editorial columns for the San Joaquin Valley's daily newspaper, the *Stockton Record*, now called *The Record*. Years later, he began writing regular columns for the California-based CalNews. com, the *Lodi News-Sentinel*, and the nationally read Vdare.com, which covers the immigration issues the mainstream media refuse to touch. Journalist Peter Brimelow, author of the 1995 book *Alien Nation*, about America's immigration disaster, launched Vdare.com. The name comes from Virginia Dare, the first English child to be born in the New World, in August 1587.

Eventually, Guzzardi's popular weekly columns for Vdare.com helped to put him on the national map as an expert on massive legal and illegal immigration, as well as the politics behind the problems. His columns are frequently syndicated in other U.S. newspapers and Web sites.

Guzzardi began working for or serving on the boards of several well-respected organizations, including the Center for Immigration Studies (CIS), the Federation for American Immigration Reform,

NumbersUSA, and Californians for Population Stabilization. Through CIS, he presented findings about illegal immigration at the National Press Club in Washington. He also spent some time as a Senior Writing Fellow for Californians for Population Stabilization.

After writing hundreds of columns over many years, Guzzardi believes he may be the most prolific immigration reform writer in America. Through his writing, he has helped awaken many Americans to the seriousness of our nation's immigration crisis.

In 2003, Guzzardi saw another way to stir people. That year, California had a staggering $38 billion deficit, more than most states' budgets. Just before the gubernatorial election in November 2002, Democratic Governor Gray Davis told voters the deficit would be about $12 billion. Republican Bill Simon, who was running against Davis, said the deficit was much higher. Davis was reelected, beating his rival by about five percentage points. Then, just three months later, Davis said the deficit was actually $34.8 billion and began drawing up plans to raise taxes. (State Senator Tom McClintock, a financial expert, said the deficit was $38 billion.) California voters were angry.[2]

On December 30, 2002, talk-show host Melanie Morgan of San Francisco's conservative KSFO radio station suggested that Davis be recalled. There was a massive caller response. Former state assemblyman Howard Kaloogian, a San Diego Republican, then formed the RecallGrayDavis.com committee.[3]

There had been thirty-one attempts to recall various California governors in past years, but none made it to the ballot.[4] The most recent attempt was in 1999, when Glenn Spencer's Voice of Citizens Together tried to oust Davis for killing Proposition 187. Spencer's effort failed largely because the media refused to write about it, according to Spencer, Guzzardi, and others in the pro-borders movement.

However, 2003 was different. Backed by $800,000 from Representative Darrell Issa, a car-alarm mogul representing the northern San Diego County area, an army of paid signature-gatherers easily collected enough signatures to put the effort on the ballot.[5]

In July, the secretary of state's office announced that the necessary 897,000 signatures had been collected to force a special recall election on October 7. Supporters of the recall turned in 1.65 million signatures, approximately 1.36 million of which were considered valid, clearly demonstrating that voters were fed up and wanted a change. A survey from the highly regarded Field Poll showed that only 23 percent of California voters approved of Davis's job performance. Davis was the first California governor ever to face such an election and the first U.S. governor to face one in more than eighty years.[6]

While the establishment media and most politicians said the recall election was about the budget deficit and the energy crisis, Guzzardi knew California's problems were much deeper. He recognized that millions of California voters were angry over the millions of illegal aliens who had invaded the state over the years and settled there. He also knew that a huge chunk of the deficit stemmed from illegal immigration. The media and most elected officials, except the last Republican governor, Pete Wilson, having served as the state's top executive from 1990 to 1998, ignored the problems created by illegal immigration.

"Illegal immigration is inexorably tied to the budget deficit," Guzzardi wrote in a June 2003 article, when he asked out loud if he should run for the "crummy job" of governor. "Californians pay nearly $10 billion annually to educate K-12 non-English speakers. Add a billion more for Medi-Cal services to illegal aliens and lo and behold you're talking about one-third of the state's deficit."[7]

As for the energy crisis, he wrote that Californians really don't understand it. "We know there was malfeasance, we know we got screwed, but we don't really know what happened. When I asked ten friends—all college graduates—to explain step by step how the energy crisis evolved, none could respond. But guess what? They all knew about and understood illegal immigration. And that subject made them hotter than the energy debacle."

Governor Davis and Mexico Kill Proposition 187

Guzzardi explained that illegal immigration has been a "festering boil" with California voters since 1999. "That's when Davis, in a smoke-filled room deal with then Mexican presidente Ernesto Zedillo, the California Latino Caucus, and the Mexican American Legal Defense Fund, killed Proposition 187."[8]

In 1994, five million Californians voted for the proposition, and it passed by a 60 to 40 margin. Legal delays prevented it from being enacted, and U.S. District Court Judge Mariana Pfaelzer ruled the proposition unconstitutional in March 1998. The next step in the legal process would have been an appeal to a higher court. Instead, Davis entered into a contrived "mediation" with Zedillo and the others to prevent 187 from going to the U.S. Supreme Court.

Following that action, attorney Dan Stein, executive director of the Federation for American Immigration Reform, stated: "In no democracy in the world are the results of an election overturned without the voters having their day in court—that is, until today. The decision to drop the appeal of Proposition 187 has absolutely nothing to do with its constitutionality. This is a capitulation by Governor Davis to pressure from an elite group of pro-illegal-immigration politicians and organizations. The implications of this are as frightening for the future of self government in our country as they are outrageous."

According to Guzzardi, no issue in California's political history has been as "poorly reported on or as shallowly analyzed as Proposition 187. For the last decade, the mainstream media has insisted, 'the anti-immigrant proposition was killed in the courts.'"[9]

Guzzardi said the media have refused to tell the truth about the matter. "Proposition 187 is not 'anti-immigrant,'" he explained. "An immigrant is a person who applies in his native country to come to the U.S. Once his paperwork is processed and approved, a visa is issued. Then, that person legally comes into the U.S. through a port of entry. What Proposition 187 would have done is deny most social services to illegal aliens. An illegal alien is not an 'immigrant.' This is an extremely important distinction that the open-borders lobby refuses to make because it does not suit its purposes."

Also, ever since the ballot measure passed in 1994, "none of the ethnic identity activists have missed a chance at slurring anyone who voted for the initiative," said Guzzardi. "Among the predictable charges are 'racist,' 'xenophobe,' 'nativist,' and 'ignorant.' The unfounded charges of racism are, of course, directed at white Californians. In a democracy, citizens are allowed to voice disapproval without becoming the target of ugly efforts to have their voices silenced. That has not been the case for Proposition 187 supporters."

Guzzardi pointed out that a *Los Angeles Times* exit poll on November 8, 1994, found that 63 percent of whites, 57 percent of Asians, 56 percent of blacks, and 30 percent of Hispanics voted "Yes" on Proposition 187. However, over the years, rarely has the mainstream media reported the breakdown.

Guzzardi said that if Proposition 187 had been enacted, one of the major causes of California's budget crisis—expensive social services to illegal aliens—would have been removed.

Hat in the Ring

On August 9, 2003, the fifty-nine-year-old Guzzardi, a Democrat, announced his candidacy for governor. He had gathered the $3,500 entry fee and found sixty-five friends to sign the necessary papers. Now he was filing documents to become one of dozens of candidates—135 were approved—who wanted to replace the enormously unpopular governor of California, Gray Davis, whose approval rating stood at just 23 percent.[10]

Guzzardi knew he didn't have a chance of becoming governor. For the past fifteen years, he had worked in obscurity as a teacher at the adult school in Lodi, a city near Sacramento, the state's capital. He was not an elected official, a millionaire, or a celebrity like some of the other candidates such as movie star and millionaire Arnold Schwarzenegger, State Senator Tom McClintock, millionaire and former gubernatorial candidate Bill Simon, State Insurance Commissioner John Garamendi, millionaire and author Arianna Huffington, and California Lieutenant Governor Cruz Bustamante. Guzzardi had never even held elective office.

However, Guzzardi did have name recognition among the thousands of people in California and across the country who were regular readers of his print and Internet columns. To most of them he was an unwavering ally of immigration reform. Since the overwhelming majority of Californians and Americans are opposed to illegal immigration, the recall election offered a platform to openly and honestly discuss the problem.

In addition to understanding the magnitude and complexity of the immigration issue, Guzzardi had years of professional experience in other areas critical to the state's current set of problems: finance, business, and education, all of which are tied to illegal immigration. California is bankrupt; businesses are leaving the state and taking jobs with them because of high taxes and workers' compensation costs; and California's schools are among the worst in the nation, plummeting from the head of the class just a few decades ago.

After graduating from the University of Pittsburgh, Guzzardi began a long career in banking and finance. Starting at an entry-level position at Banker's Trust in New York, he advanced to vice president of the Money Market Securities Department at Merrill Lynch. He also worked at the Seattle First National Bank as vice president in the Commercial Lending Division. During his Wall Street career, Guzzardi learned the importance of prudent planning and economic forecasting, which Gray Davis and many of the California legislators failed to understand, or did not care to understand.

After twenty years in banking, Guzzardi started a small venture capital firm, Private Capital Funding, to assist start-up ventures in obtaining seed financing. He worked closely with new companies to ensure their initial phases of operation were successful.

Guzzardi then worked as a consultant and fundraiser for a variety of businesses and later started and operated his own restaurants. He learned firsthand about the frustration of small business ownership—excessive taxes, oppressive workers' compensation rules, as well as federal, state, and local reporting requirements that interfered with day-to-day operations.

In 1988, Guzzardi launched a new career as a schoolteacher. Since then, he has worked as an instructor at the Lodi Adult School, teaching English as a second language to immigrants, as well as computer skills to senior citizens, driver's education to teenagers, and basic business management to entrepreneurs. With many years of experience at the Lodi Unified School District, he understands the failings of the California Department of Education and how to fix them.

Based on his credentials as an expert on immigration, education, business, and finance, Guzzardi was better qualified to serve as California governor than most of the big names in the race. Unfortunately, in American politics, money and celebrity usually win elections, not knowledge, experience, and the courage to confront the real issues.

Guzzardi understood that the real issue impacting California is uncontrolled immigration. "Virtually every aspect of our lives is affected by illegal immigration—schools, hospitals, jobs, urban sprawl, and other key areas," he told me in an interview and repeated throughout his campaign for governor. In an August 2003 article, Guzzardi wrote:

> Californians need to hear the truth about what has happened to our once golden state. And Californians must elect a governor who is not afraid to make the bold decisions to put our state back on its way to greatness. Enlightened Californians know exactly what's wrong. Every day we see evidence of how illegal immigration has changed California. But you would never know about it if you counted on Governor Gray Davis to tell you.... Californians deserve a governor they can trust. Sadly, since 1999, you have been subjected to deceit and duplicity. Governor Davis has refused to listen to your voice. But because unchecked illegal immigration is California's most pressing social issue, an open and honest debate about that "taboo" topic must take place.[11]

Davis is just one of many in a long line of politicians in California and across the nation who have been afraid to openly and honestly discuss America's immigration crisis. Other California politicians who have ducked the issue include Senators Barbara Boxer and Dianne Feinstein, defeated gubernatorial candidates Dan Lungren, Richard Riordan, and Bill Simon, and defeated Senate candidates Matt Fong, Michael Huffington, Tom Campbell, and Bill Jones.

Unfortunately, the major gubernatorial candidates in the recall election were following the same cowardly path from the very beginning of their campaigns. Republican State Senator Tom McClintock was the exception, but he only talked about immigration when asked, mostly on talk-radio programs, where he had a friendly audience. He did not make it part of his campaign platform. Virtually all of the other leading candidates promoted immigration, and some defended and encouraged illegal immigration, notably Democratic Lieutenant Governor Cruz Bustamante and Green Party candidate Peter Camejo. Schwarzenegger, an immigrant from Austria, also made it a central part of the campaign through touting his own immigrant background.

Immediately after taping the Jay Leno show at the NBC Studios in Burbank on August 6, 2003, where Republican Schwarzenegger announced his candidacy to a stunned media and public, the actor had this to say: "As you know, I'm an immigrant. I came over here as an immigrant, and what gave me the opportunities, what made me to be here today is the open arms of Americans. I have been received; I have been adopted by America. I've seen firsthand coming here with empty pockets but full of dreams, full of desire, full of will to succeed, but with the opportunities that I had, I could make it. This is why we have to get and bring California back to where it once was."

"Who drafted that pious piece of pap?" Guzzardi asked in an article titled "Establishment to California: Shut up about immigration in this election!" "Was it the National Council of La Raza, the Mexican American Legal Defense and Educational Fund, or maybe the *Los Angeles Times*' own reconquista spokesman, associate editor Frank del Olmo?"[12]

Guzzardi pointed out that on their Web sites Garamendi, McClintock, Huffington, Simon, and Bustamante did not even mention restricting immigration. "That's a tip-off that the politicians and the press will do all they can to squelch debate," Guzzardi said.

As an example, the Lodi schoolteacher pointed to the *Ventura County Star*'s "hatchet job" on nine-term U.S. Congressman Elton Gallegly, a Republican from Ventura County, California, when Gallegly indicated an interest in jumping into the recall election. In his July 31 news release, the congressman stated:

> I firmly believe that illegal immigration is at the root of California's economic problems. It's also an issue that politicians are afraid to touch. But we cannot ignore it. It depresses wages, taxes our schools and healthcare systems, and increases the burden on our criminal justice system.

California attracts about half of America's illegal immigrants because of its incentives to come here: low-cost higher education, acceptance of foreign identification cards, the possibility of a driver's license and the like.

As a rule, illegal immigrants don't have health insurance, use emergency rooms for routine medical care and don't have money to pay their bills. California hospitals incur $3.6 billion a year in uncompensated care. More than half of the state's hospitals operated in the red last year and 82 percent of California emergency rooms reported losing money in 2000. Many have been forced to close.

Our city, county and state jails and prisons are overcrowded because of the large number of incarcerated illegal immigrants. In the federal system, about 30 percent of inmates are illegal immigrants. We cannot build prisons fast enough to hold them, and it forces the early release of criminals into society.

After Gallegly issued his news release, the *Ventura County Star*, the largest newspaper in the congressman's district, carried an editorial titled "Scapegoating is no solution." Guzzardi said the editorial implied that the congressman's position against illegal immigration is tiresome and a throwback to the Governor Pete Wilson/Proposition 187 days that supposedly cost the Republican Party during the last several years. Guzzardi said the media like to perpetuate this myth, even though nearly 60 percent of California voters voted for the proposition in 1994 and even more would surely vote for it today.

Guzzardi said the *Star*'s editorial did acknowledge that "illegal immigration is a legitimate issue that deserves attention," but the paper concluded that, "California needs a governor who can take this state forward, not backward, and hit more than one note."

"Why wouldn't the *Star* praise the hometown boy and his bold stand on a controversial issue?" Guzzardi asked. He called the editorial's author, Marianne Ratcliff, to ask why. Ratcliff's reasoning: "This race is not about illegal immigration. The issue before the voters is the recall. The recall is about the budget shortfall. And the shortfall is caused by the energy crisis." Guzzardi said Ratcliff seemed to have no position on when it would be acceptable to discuss the illegal immigration crisis.

Representative Gallegly decided not to run in the recall election.

'Man on a Mission'

Guzzardi knew that the recall election would generate tremendous media coverage, not just in California, but nationally too, because history was being made. Davis was only the second governor in U.S. history to face a recall vote. And the surprise, last-minute entry into the race by one of Hollywood's leading movie stars made the election an even bigger story. Guzzardi wanted to capitalize on the attention.

For nearly three months, the Lodi schoolteacher and columnist was a self-described "man on a mission." The goal of his one-person campaign was clear: to run on a platform to end illegal immigration.

"I hoped to force the other candidates into an open and honest discussion of the impact of illegal immigration on California," he said. "Davis had been monstrously bad on immigration. He signed bills on behalf of illegal aliens authorizing the use of the Mexican ID called the matricula consular card, approved in-state college tuition for illegal aliens, and, most outrageously, granting drivers' licenses without proof of citizenship.[13]

"Under Davis, California has ceased to work. The citizens are poised on the verge of anarchy because of the endless invasion of illegal aliens and the relentless urban sprawl that is devouring California's open spaces. Throw the bum out, was my attitude, and let's be quick about it. The recall election gave me an excellent chance to take the reform immigration platform to the people. I eagerly signed up."

But Guzzardi's quest wasn't easy. He had numerous disadvantages and had to make personal sacrifices. He was not a millionaire with plenty of money to throw into his campaign, or a big celebrity easily recognizable to the media and public, or an elected official with the various advantages that come from holding public office. He also had to take time off from his jobs at the Lodi Adult School, Vdare.com, and the *Lodi News-Sentinel*, which translated into lost income. And he knew that to reach the citizens and other candidates he would have to go through the bias of the mainstream media—supporters of unrestrained immigration and open borders.

Starting with the official date to begin collecting the required sixty-five signatures to place his name on the ballot—July 21—and ending with the October 7 election, Guzzardi vanished from his "regular haunts. I was a stranger to my friends. Even my trusty dogs despaired."

Guzzardi scraped together several thousand dollars of his own money and began seeking donations from friends in California and across the country. He mostly used the Internet and talk radio to reach people and communicate his messages. Several individuals from California and other states who are active in the immigration reform movement served as volunteers, delivering moral support and marketing assistance to their man from Lodi.

The centerpiece of Guzzardi's marketing efforts was his Web site, Guzzardi4Governor.com. In addition to information about the candidate and his positions on California's many problems, the site carried numerous articles on immigration by Guzzardi, as well as articles by other journalists. When a new article or other important information was posted on the site, Guzzardi would use e-mail to alert his supporters, who in turn would alert others. He would also use e-mail to let supporters know when he would appear on radio and TV programs or to give them a recap of his print and broadcast interviews.

The Most Pressing Social Issue

In his campaign statement, Guzzardi explained how uncontrolled immigration is California's most pressing social issue. He focused on the state's two leading budget expenditures: education and healthcare.

"Governor Davis's failure to defend Proposition 187 has the predictable consequences for our K-12 school system," Guzzardi said. "Shortly after being elected for his first term, Davis promised to make education his 'first, second, and third priority.' Now, on the eve of his recall, the high-school exit exam—touted as the barometer of California's projected new education standards—has been postponed until 2006. As a teacher, I know there are only two types of exams possible. For students to pass, the test would have to be watered down to junior-high-school level. If the test were meaningful, the percentages of failures would be so high that shock waves would reverberate all over California."

Guzzardi explained that one of the main reasons many kids are failing is that "teachers are so absorbed dealing with the 1.5 million non-English speaking students in the California K-12 system that they cannot focus on their main task: teaching. The reason your public school kids don't know anything is because learning isn't number one on the K-12 agenda. Academics are subordinate to English language development, ethnic awareness, and diversity."

And what does it cost California taxpayers to school those 1.5 million K-12 students who do not speak English? According to Guzzardi, the price tag is about $10 billion a year.

"Because of our nonsensical immigration laws," he said in his statement, "some of those non-English speakers are U.S. citizens, some are legal immigrants, and the rest are illegal aliens. But whether they are legal, illegal, or U.S. citizens, the $10 billion you spend to educate them is directly related to immigration."

Unrestrained immigration has also devastated the healthcare system in California, Guzzardi's campaign statement pointed out. According to the California Medical Association white paper titled "California's Emergency Services—A System in Crisis," 80 percent of the hospital emergency rooms lost money in fiscal 1999. That year, more than nine million patients were treated in emergency rooms at an average loss of $46 per visit. Hospitals lost $317 million in their emergency departments, and emergency physicians provided an additional $100 million in uncompensated care.

"Since this report was issued," Guzzardi said, "conditions have gotten worse. Add to this millions of dollars in payments for child delivery services and assistance for women illegally in California and you begin to understand why the state is sinking in red ink."

How did Guzzardi propose to fix California's most pressing social issue, rampant immigration? He listed eight actions he would take as governor:

- If possible, return Proposition 187 to the courts for review and encourage Proposition 187-type legislation to end subsidies to illegal aliens for all but emergency medical care. This was the original and true intention of the 1994 voter initiative. And enforce the section of Proposition 187 that Judge Pfaelzer said was within the purview of the State of California, which calls for stronger state penalties on manufacture, sale, and use of fraudulent identification.

- Tolerate no further delays in the high-school exit exam.

- Immediately send the National Guard to patrol the border.

- Demand a hearing on the constitutionality of Senate Bill 60, the bill to grant drivers' licenses to illegal aliens.

- Mount an immediate legal challenge to revoke the bill that gives in-state university tuition to illegal aliens.

- Take immediate steps to invalidate the acceptance of the Mexican matricula consular ID card currently accepted at government and business offices throughout California. All such cards issued by any government would no longer be permitted in the state.

- Promote a photo voter identification card to eliminate the growing problem of voter fraud taking place in California. Initiate legislation that requires mandatory purging of voter rolls every four years. Purging is the most effective way of making sure only registered voters cast ballots.

- Demand that the government of Mexico extradite violent felons who have committed capital crimes on California soil. Until those criminals are returned to the proper law enforcement authorities, no Mexican government officials will be welcome at the California governor's mansion.

Just weeks after the October 7, 2003, special election, the bill to grant drivers' licenses to illegal aliens was repealed by the California legislature. The state's new governor, Arnold Schwarzenegger, signed the repeal. The bill was revoked just two months after it had been signed into law by former governor Davis in a desperate attempt to win Hispanic support in the recall election. The bill had been approved by the legislature just three months before.

The *Los Angeles Times* said the law was repealed because Schwarzenegger "demanded" it. But the truth is that it was rescinded because a grassroots campaign called "Save Our License" had gathered 400,000 voter signatures in just two months—enough signatures to put a referendum on the March 2004 ballot that would have allowed voters to repeal it.

"Does anyone believe [the liberal Democrat-controlled legislature] would have done this without the threat of a referendum?" asked Mike Spence, president of the California Republican Assembly volunteer group and head of the Save Our License initiative.[14]

'Your Democratic Rights'

In his conversations with the media and in meetings with various groups throughout the state during the campaign, Guzzardi talked about other immigration issues, in addition to education and health care. One was "your democratic rights."

He said that although immigration is frequently considered to be an issue of the federal government, state governments during the past several years have become more active in legislation designed to provide benefits for illegal aliens.

"One of the most insidious results of mass illegal immigration is the expanded power and influence of California's Latino Caucus," he explained. "This group does not work for the common good of California or even for California's Latino citizens. Rather, it lobbies primarily on behalf of the narrow interests of illegal aliens and of increasing its own power."

Guzzardi said bills that affect either your personal safety and/or your pocketbook—in-state college tuition for illegal-alien children, acceptance of foreign ID cards held by illegal aliens, drivers' licenses for illegal aliens—should be voted on in a general election. However, they are not.

"Bills drafted to exclusively cater to the illegal-alien population in California are muscled through the Assembly and presented to Governor Davis for his signature or veto," Guzzardi said. "This procedure represents an erosion of the democratic process and silences your voice in California's future."

During his campaign swing, Guzzardi also discussed how unrestrained immigration drives urban sprawl, not only in California but also across the country.

"I am deeply saddened by the daily loss of prime agricultural land to development," he said. "The reality is that California's population increases by about 1,500 new people daily. And that increase is despite a net exodus of Californians to other states."

A report by Californians for Population Stabilization (CAPS) on the state's population explosion between 1990 and 2002 found that 57 percent of the increase is from immigration while 41 percent comes from births to foreign-born women. This shows that 98 percent of the growth is directly tied to immigration, not internal growth.[15]

Census Bureau figures show that California's population grew from 29.8 million in 1990 to more than 34 million in 2000, an increase of more than four million people in one decade.

If out-of-control immigration continues, according to CAPS, California will add another 16 million people by 2025, bringing the state's population to more than 50 million people.

"We are in the midst of a population crisis that is already affecting virtually every aspect of life in our state and which is only going to get worse," warned Diana Hull, Ph.D. and CAPS president. "Stop immigration and we'll be on the way to saving our quality of life. Do nothing and we will soon reach the limits of livability."[16]

Guzzardi said his hometown of Lodi is just one of many California cities and towns that is becoming unlivable.

"I'm surrounded by earthmovers, swirling dust and development," he wrote in an article. "And with Lowe's and the Wal-Mart Super Stores certainty, I wonder when the last square mile of open space in Lodi will be paved over. Less than a half-mile north of my home, the Tienda Place housing development nears completion. That will add 150 new houses to what our town fathers like to call 'Loveable, Livable Lodi.' That label may have been appropriate at one time but no longer."[17]

Guzzardi emphasized that this immigration-driven sprawl isn't just happening all over California; it also is occurring in other Southwestern states and in much of the rest of America. And he raised some serious questions.

If massive immigration continues, "Where will the money to build schools and provide social services come from?" he wrote. "Will there be water and electricity? How will we cope with the congestion? Does quality of life mean anything? What the future holds for the Southwest is unclear. But the picture doesn't look pretty. The current rate of population growth is not sustainable."

Each year, Guzzardi receives thousands of e-mails from people across the country who read his articles. Many of his readers also are concerned about urban sprawl, including Fred M. from Illinois.

"Joe, if you think Lodi is changing, Illinois is even worse," Fred M. wrote. "I have lived in Illinois for more than sixty years. The urban sprawl around Chicago is amazing. Almost everything is filled in from the Wisconsin border to the Indiana state line, and anywhere from fifteen to thirty-five miles wide. I moved more than seventy miles from the city and suburban area ten years ago for some space. Now, even the land between where I live and the crowded suburban areas are starting to be filled in with homes, shopping areas and offices."

The man from Illinois painted a frightening picture of America if Congress continues its agenda of unrestrained immigration.

"In the end," Fred M. warned, "America will be a country with no borders, millions unemployed, laws being ignored, civil unrest occurring all over the country, crime out of control, millions of immigrants coming and going at will, politicians unable to accomplish anything, even the possibility of civil war or this country breaking up into several new nations. This is not the America I would like to see, but this is what will happen if this country does not get its act together."

Charges of Racism

When Guzzardi entered the California recall election as a symbolic immigration reform candidate, he knew he would be smeared by the news media. Over the years he had read literally thousands of "lousy, unprofessional" newspaper articles about immigration and had made hundreds of "fruitless" calls to reporters and editors. So when *Modesto Bee* reporter Eric Stern interviewed him during the campaign, Guzzardi knew what to expect.

In the opening paragraph of Stern's article, "Candidate draws fire on immigration stand," the reporter wrote that the Democratic Party was "not paying much attention" to Guzzardi, that he had been "called a white nationalist" on an Internet site, and that the Southern Poverty Law Center was "keeping an eye" on the candidate. Stern pointed out that the SPLC "monitors hate groups."[18]

(Newspaper reporters frequently turn to the SPLC to smear leaders in the immigration reform movement. As discussed in chapter seven, for example, a writer for the *Denver Post* used this tactic on Barbara Coe.)

The *Modesto Bee* reporter also quoted two people from Lodi, Julio Hernandez and Rosa Maria Casillas, calling Guzzardi a "racist." Stern also quoted Bob Mulholland, a California Democratic Party spokesman, calling Guzzardi a "racist."

Guzzardi said he had "provided Stern with the names of several colleagues as character references. Stern spoke with them, and they were universally supportive." In addition, Stern used anonymous Internet postings from organizations not connected to Guzzardi or with anyone he knows, a typical tactic used on Americans fighting open borders.

After the story ran, the candidate spoke with the *Bee*'s executive editor to seek ways to make sure his positions were correctly expressed. The paper agreed to carry an op-ed by Guzzardi one month later.

"Although Stern interviewed me for two hours, he missed—perhaps purposely—why I chose to run," Guzzardi's op-ed read. "Simply stated, my immigration 'stand' is that it is time for California's politicians to talk about illegal immigration's impact openly and honestly. To ignore illegal immigration by pretending that it doesn't exist is politics at its most venal.

"But heads obviously remain in the sand. On Sept. 24, the California Broadcasters Association debate allowed the five leading candidates (Arnold Schwarzenegger, Cruz Bustamante, Tom McClintock, Arianna Huffington, and Peter Camejo) two minutes to summarize the most pressing problems facing California. Not one mentioned how California can continue to absorb tens of thousands of illegal immigrants annually.... The *Modesto Bee* had a chance to move the illegal immigration debate forward. But Stern's first paragraph falsely suggested that I am a poster boy for White Nationalists."

While the *Modesto Bee* smeared Guzzardi and a couple other news organizations ignored him when they heard about his platform, Lieutenant Governor Bustamante was getting plenty of favorable media attention, even though he may have been the real racist running for governor.

In February 2001, while addressing a group of black trade union leaders, Bustamante referred to blacks as "niggers."[19] And during his college days at Fresno State, Bustamante was a member of MEChA (Movimiento Estudiantil Chicano de Aztlan). As well as supporting "reconquista" of the American Southwest, MEChA also believes that brown-skinned people should run California. The preamble to MEChA's Constitution states: "Chicano and Chicana students of Aztlan must take upon themselves the responsibilities to promote Chicanismo within the community, politicizing our Raza [race] with an emphasis on indigenous consciousness to continue the struggle for the self-determination of the Chicano people for the purpose of liberating Aztlan."

Despite being directly asked to repudiate the racism of MEChA, Lieutenant Governor Bustamante refused to renounce the organization.

"In the minds of most reasonable voters," Guzzardi said, "Bustamante's use of racial slurs and his association with a racist, separatist group like MEChA should have been enough to disqualify him as a viable candidate for governor."

Despite his use of racial slurs and ties to MEChA, Bustamante received mostly favorable media coverage, especially from the *Los Angeles Times*. He also received 31.5 percent of the votes, or more than 2.7 million, placing him behind the winner, Schwarzenegger, who had 48.6 percent and more than 4.2 million votes. McClintock placed third, with 13.5 percent of the total and 1.16 million votes.[20]

An Overwhelming Success

After the votes had been counted, Guzzardi said many good things came out of the recall election and his mission in it. "Schwarzenegger kicked some serious butt in the election. Actually, he kicked two butts—those belonging to the pathetic Gray Davis and the monumentally inept Cruz Bustamante. In fact, even though Bustamante will finish his term, Schwarzenegger booted them both out of politics for good."[21]

Guzzardi had a few more words for the former governor. "Davis got what he deserved. For five years, he consistently promoted illegal-alien measures. Although I am glad to see him gone, I'm saddened about what Davis has allowed to happen to California. He had to take the fall."

As for McClintock, Guzzardi said the conservative Republican state senator "spoke about the immigration issue convincingly on talk radio but not to the tough audiences. My view is that he'll never be strong enough on immigration to take himself over the top."

About the new governor, Guzzardi wrote: "Schwarzenegger says he wants to balance the state budget, but ignoring the fiscal impact of illegal immigration is not an option. So let's keep our fingers crossed."

About two years after the October 2003 recall election, Guzzardi said this to me about Schwarzenegger: "He has finally started to come around about illegal immigration. He has spoken openly in support of the Minuteman Project and the importance of defending our borders. I hope he will incorporate that message in his official addresses and policy statements. I suspect Schwarzenegger realizes that the status quo cannot continue in California without completely bankrupting the state. Since Arizona's governor Janet Napolitano, formerly an avowed open-borders advocate, has made demands on the federal government to fund the costs of illegal immigration, she and Schwarzenegger could make a powerful team in lobbying Washington to patrol the borders. Let's hope they work together to bring sanity to an otherwise insane situation."

Regarding his personal mission in the election, Guzzardi declared it "an overwhelming success. My goal was to get the message out about the importance of immigration reform to the most number of people for the least amount of money."

Not including the $3,500 filing fee, he spent less than $7,000. In exchange, he was able to communicate his key messages to many people in California and across the country through big and small print and broadcast media outlets. "Putting modesty aside," he said, "I don't think anyone can do more with $7,000."

As for votes, he received 1,226, spread across the state. "I'm a nice guy," Guzzardi explained, "but I don't have that many friends. And anyway, many of my friends didn't vote for me, which was unfortunate. People must understand the nature of the protest candidacy. The protest candidate is not going to win, but he or she is going to spread our message."

In addition to booting Davis and Bustamante "out of politics for good," Guzzardi said other good things came out of the election. "Among them, for the first time, the press wrote critically about the racist, separatist group called MEChA," he explained. "And the illegal-alien driver's license bill, which Davis so foolishly counted on to save his hash, instead drove the final nail into his coffin.

"On the other hand, while the newspapers insisted that immigration issues 'dominated' the race, I disagree. That Schwarzenegger voted yes on Proposition 187 ten years ago or that Bustamante was in MEChA at Fresno State thirty years ago gives us clues about their feelings. But it doesn't get us close to the answer about what California is going to do—starting tomorrow—about illegal immigration. The status quo cannot continue without inflicting even greater chaos on the state's already dysfunctional condition."

In late 2005, Guzzardi told me he is "convinced that those who are committed to immigration reform must seek public office" at the local, state, and federal levels. "Those who share that commitment must vote for these candidates and support them in every other way. I still feel that running for public office is the best way to bring attention to the issue," he emphasized. "I am convinced that immigration sanity will soon be the single issue that will persuade people to vote for that candidate."

The year 2004 saw an increase in the number of pro-borders candidates running for Congress in several states, including some beyond the border region. The candidates included both experienced politicians and first-timers: Utah's Matt Throckmorton, North Carolina's Vernon Robinson and Fern Shubert, Kansas' Kris Kobach, Arizona's Randy Graf, and California's Cynthia Matthews and Paul Whitehead. None were elected, but several made impressive showings.

An even larger number of pro-borders candidates are expected in the 2006 election. This time, however, several are predicted to win, because the public outcry over the immigration crisis will be even greater.

As for his own plans, Guzzardi is "entertaining the idea" of running either for Congress or the California State Assembly.

The schoolteacher and columnist also encouraged citizens, especially those parents concerned about their kids' futures, to "get active." He said it is important for people to phone their representatives and senators regularly in Washington and tell them how they feel about immigration.

And what about the Southeast Asian refugees who came to America legally and were Guzzardi's first English-language students, excusing themselves from class, when he moved to Lodi in 1988?

"From time to time, I bump into them in the neighborhood," he says. "Their lives are unchanged from the first days they came to America. They still don't know any more English, and some are still on some type of federal or state assistance."

9 | Tom Tancredo

"Massive legal and illegal immigration combined with multiculturalism represents the greatest danger this country has ever faced."

—Congressman Tom Tancredo

At a luncheon meeting with editors and reporters at the *Washington Times* on April 18, 2002, Republican Congressman Tom Tancredo, in only his second term, criticized President George W. Bush for his open-door immigration policy and said the president was risking further terrorist attacks against the United States. Tancredo warned that if America suffers another attack comparable to 9/11 because our borders have not been secured, the deaths would be on the hands of Congress and the White House.

"What we have not done is to protect our borders, ignoring our own national security," the Colorado congressman exclaimed. "The president is not on our side. He believes in open borders. Unless we do something significant to control our borders, we're going to have another event with someone waltzing across the borders. Then the blood of the people killed will be on this administration and this congress."[1]

The newspaper reported the remarks the next day. That morning, as Tancredo was pulling out of his driveway en route to the Capitol, his cell phone rang. The caller was Bush's top political advisor Karl Rove. During the call, Rove attacked Tancredo for his comments. Rove screamed at him for more than twenty minutes, Tancredo recalled, accusing him of being a traitor to the Republican Party and to the president.[2]

"He told me never to darken the doorstep of the White House," Tancredo said. "I told him I don't remember a welcome mat ever being out, and second, it's not your house."[3]

Two months later, Homeland Security Secretary Tom Ridge was giving a briefing to several lawmakers and was asked why he was not employing the military to help defend our porous borders. Ridge responded that the White House opposed stationing troops on the borders for "cultural and historical" reasons.[4]

Tancredo responded: "I want an explanation of these cultural and historical reasons why we can't protect our nation's borders. It's time to authorize the deployment of troops on our borders."[5]

Two years later Tancredo called for the Republican National Committee to add several "common sense" immigration amendments, including no amnesty for illegal aliens, to the party's platform, but his request was denied. The RNC supported the president's call for an amnesty and added it to the platform.

Tancredo struck back. The RNC's platform "goes against everything the American people believe should happen with our immigration policy," he responded to the media. "Amnesty is not an option. Leaving our borders open is not an option."[6]

The Republican congressman's willingness to stand up to a Republican White House against unrestrained immigration is just one of many reasons Tancredo is beloved by people across America. He is not afraid to put principles above politics.

In his seven years in Congress, Tancredo has done more than anyone else in the House or Senate to fight mass immigration. He readily notes that other House members fought the problem before his arrival on Capitol Hill.

Tancredo's outspoken courage and leadership have made him a symbol of the growing immigration reform movement sweeping the nation. The Colorado maverick has stood up to the:

- Democratic Party, which looks at massive legal and illegal immigration as a source of voters;

- Republican Party, which looks at massive legal and illegal immigration as a source of cheap labor;

- socialists, elitists, and globalists seeking to eliminate America's sovereignty; and

- mainstream media and immigration advocacy groups who call this grandson of Italian immigrants an ideologue, racist, and xenophobe.

Since he came to Congress in 1999, Tancredo has spent nearly every day exposing the consequences of our government's immigration policies. He has repeatedly warned that if these policies are not changed, they will threaten the very existence of America.

The congressman says the government and the media have failed to confront mass immigration's negative impact on our national security, labor, crime, health, culture, and environment. Tancredo explains:

- Countless U.S. jobs have been taken over by legal immigrants and illegal aliens, displacing American workers.

- A war on our southern border is sponsored by the Mexican government and aided and abetted by the U.S. government.

- The continuing encroachment of Mexico in the affairs of the U.S. is a threat to security and sovereignty.

- Congress has shirked its primary responsibility: to defend the nation and protect sovereignty.

- Many in Congress, because of the politics of cheap labor, have chosen to represent special interests, foreign nationals, and governments, rather than the American people.

- Illegal immigration should be stopped, and the border should be properly funded, with help from the military until it is correctly financed.

- Legal immigration should be put on hold until the U.S. gets workable, practical reforms in place and the recent immigrants have assimilated.

Week after week, Tancredo has used the floor of the House of Representatives for hour-long speeches after the finish of daily business to educate the C-SPAN audience on cable TV. He pleads for common sense and recounts horror stories of Americans who have suffered because the federal government has chosen not to protect them from an illegal-alien invasion.

He has led the fight against several attempts by the White House to grant amnesty to illegal aliens.

He has led efforts—so far unsuccessful—to cut off federal funding for so-called sanctuary cities and states that harbor illegal aliens and refuse to cooperate with federal law enforcement and immigration authorities.

He has fought the Bush administration's agreement with Mexico to provide Social Security payments to illegal aliens.

And he has inspired other lawmakers and led his bi-partisan ninety-two-member Congressional Immigration Reform Caucus in the fight to save the nation from uncontrolled immigration.

'Tancredo for President!'

Admired for straight talk, courage, and resolve in the immigration crisis, Tancredo is a hero to many Americans.

Just days after Bush unveiled his amnesty proposal in January 2004, Tancredo supporters across the country began pushing a write-in campaign for him to run for president in November.

One organization, "Tennesseans for Tancredo," sought to draft the congressman as a protest candidate in the Republican presidential primary. "We need to make noise, collect signatures, build a grassroots movement that attracts citizens from all walks of life and all political parties," the organization said. "Bush might come to understand that the base he took for granted deserted him because of his traitorous—yes, traitorous—positions on immigration."[7]

Indicative of the thousands of angry letters, e-mails, and phone calls Tancredo's office received following Bush's amnesty speech was one from Southern California defense industry worker and immigration reform activist Bob Tecau:

"In the year 2000, as a loyal member of the GOP, I was one of many who voted for our current el presidente. However, I will not repeat that same mistake in 2004. President George W. Bush is no Republican, and he is certainly not a true conservative. Bush has betrayed America, as have many other so-called 'Republicans' such as Senator John McCain and Representatives Jeff Flake and Jim Kolbe. I will not mention one word about the Democrats, for their record is even worse.

"Rep. Tancredo, I am begging you, for the good of our country and for the good of those citizens who feel so utterly powerless as we watch our once great nation being ruined, day by day, please listen to those voices, the voices of people who do care. Quit the Republican Party and run for president as an Independent."

Comments posted on the Web site for Team America (www.teamamericapac.org), a political action committee founded by Tancredo and conservative activist Bay Buchanan to support candidates committed to fighting mass immigration, also show how much the congressman is respected.

"Tom Tancredo got my vote a long time ago," wrote Laila S., a researcher from Oregon. "I greatly admire his courage and tenacity for this most important cause."

B.J.K., an Arizona rancher, wrote: "We are losing our country to millions of illegal invaders. The American people need to stand together and invite our pandering politicians to another Boston Tea Party if this lunacy doesn't cease. God bless you, Honorable Tom."

Also from Arizona, Judy O. said: "I too am totally disgusted and will only vote for those who oppose the illegal-alien invasion. The borders here are wide open. Thousands come across every week. Do not believe there are 8–10 million illegals in the U.S. There are more than that here in Arizona. Tom Tancredo for President!"

Even Americans as far away as Maine support the Colorado congressman. "We the people of the United States of America must take back our government," wrote Marie S. "Time to clean house and vote for congressmen like Tom Tancredo, who is working for the good of our country."

In 2004, Tancredo said he was flattered that a number of voters indicated they would write in his name for president that year. He said voters were frustrated at how the candidates were handling the issue of immigration. "It only goes to show you how incredibly important this issue is to most people, because, frankly, a lot of those folks that are writing me in, they just know a name connected to an issue," he said. "They don't know much more about me. But that's how important the issue is."[8]

In March 2005, however, after he defeated three candidates in three online presidential straw polls that month, among them Senator John McCain, Tancredo said he would run for president in 2008 if no other Republican candidate takes the border issue seriously. "I'll tell you what," he said, "if no one else does it, I will do it."[9]

This congressman from a district near Denver has attracted a huge following across the nation because of his strong and vocal stand against the invasion. Concerned and angry citizens hold large rallies to voice their frustration and to honor their hero. One was held on November 1, 2003, in La Canada Flintridge, a Los Angeles suburb. The California Coalition for Immigration Reform and the Save Our State Committee sponsored the "Patriot Rally," which drew hundreds of jubilant Tancredo supporters. Longtime Los Angeles-area newsman-broadcaster George Putnam, who began talking about the problem of illegal immigration in the 1960s and often refers to Tancredo as "our own Paul Revere," introduced the congressman:

> "Today we are honoring this magnificent man. He's got more guts than all of us. What a man. His momma and daddy raised him, and he grew up and learned what American patriotism

and love of country are all about.... But, my friends, if we're going to continue to give this country over to foreigners, we are going to give away the greatest dream in the history of mankind—the greatest dream that was ever put forth under God. Well, we're not going to let it happen, because we're going to back people like Tom Tancredo. We're not going to stand by and let this happen to America, not as long as we draw breath. I'll be ninety years of age next July. I've been a broadcaster for seventy years. I've backed a lot of causes in my time. There is no more important cause than the one we face today. No finer leader of that cause than the man we honor today, Congressman Tom Tancredo."[10]

As Tancredo took the stage, Americans of all backgrounds rose to their feet and gave their champion a thunderous welcome.

The 'Cult of Multiculturalism'

At the Patriot Rally near Los Angeles, the fifty-eight-year-old Tancredo told the crowd about his immigrant grandparents and about "the dagger pointed at the heart of America."[11]

All four of his grandparents came from Italy and ended up in Colorado. The "oddest story" of the four of them was his father's father, Joe Tancredo, whose parents died in Italy in 1894 when Joe was a boy. Joe lived for a few months with an aunt, but she could not afford to keep him. However, she knew some people in Iowa, so she pinned a note on his lapel with his name and a request to send Joe to the people in Iowa. The aunt put him on a boat and sent him to America. (It was a time when approximately 75 million people lived in America, compared with almost 300 million in 2005.)

When Joe got off the boat at Ellis Island, there was no one there to meet him and he could not speak English. The authorities asked him where his parents were, and he told them they were dead. They decided to send him back to Italy but first put him in quarantine. There he met a lady and her family. Joe explained his plight to them, and the lady signed for him, which allowed Joe to proceed to New York City.

Joe was nine years old. He spent a few months working for an Italian grocer in the city when he met someone who was going west. Joe joined him and started walking west, but Joe never made it to Iowa.

"I asked my grandfather, 'What happened to Iowa?'" Tom Tancredo told the gathering at the Patriot Rally. His grandfather said, "I got here to Colorado and took one look at the Rocky Mountains and said, 'If Iowa's past that, the hell with it.'" The crowd laughed and Tom said, "I don't know if my grandfather was just joking, or if he missed Iowa entirely, or if he went there and didn't like it and kept moving. When I was a boy, I'd go to my grandfather's house on Sunday afternoons, and we talked about things like that. My grandfather didn't come to the United States of America with the Federalist Papers under his arm. He did not understand at nine years old what America was all about. But he became acquainted with what America was all about as he became older."

Tom said his mother's parents came to America when they were a little older than his grandfather Joe. His mother's parents were seeking economic opportunity in the U.S. and wanted to separate themselves from Italy. "They wanted to connect with a new world, with a new land, and with a new set of ideas that in their mind spelled America," Tom explained. "They were not politicians, they were not political scientists, but they knew there was something good, different, and exciting about this land."

Tom recalled that his family would take his mother's parents to the local Dairy Queen on Sunday afternoons. His grandparents would argue over his grandfather speaking Italian. "My grandmother would say, 'Speak American and be Americanized.' It was a word we'd use—Americanize. It meant connecting with this country."

The congressman shared the stories about his grandparents with the crowd at the Patriot Rally to help explain why he spends so much time and energy on immigration. He pointed out that his grandparents and millions of other immigrants from earlier in the twentieth century came to America for economic opportunities and to become Americans.

While most people come to the U.S. today for those same economic opportunities, he said, many of them demonstrate no desire to disconnect from their places of origin. They come to America but maintain loyalty to their mother countries.

In the past several decades, Tancredo explained, America's schools, the popular media, and even the churches have said there is nothing of value in Western Civilization or America. They have preached the doctrine of "radical multiculturalism." He is not referring to the idea that Americans should accept and appreciate the many different cultures that enrich our lives and our nation. Tancredo is referring to what he calls the "cult of multiculturalism," which has as its goal the elimination of the concept of America as a nation state.

He said the multiculturalists also encourage immigrants to refrain from integrating into the American mainstream. Instead, immigrants are urged to retain their native languages and cultures and even their political connections to their countries of origin.

"This is what's worrisome," he told the gathering and tells people wherever he goes. "I believe that massive legal and illegal immigration combined with multiculturalism represents the greatest danger this country has ever faced. It will eventually determine not just what kind of a nation we are in the future; it will determine whether we will be a nation at all. This is the dagger pointed at the heart of America."

From Teaching to Politics

Tancredo grew up in Denver and graduated from the University of Northern Colorado with a degree in political science. He first began to understand the issues of mass immigration and multiculturalism thirty years ago.

In 1975, while he was a civics teacher at Drake Junior High School in Jefferson County, Colorado, Tancredo attended a rally on bilingual education. Leading the rally on the steps of the capitol in Denver was a man with long black hair. He wore a bandanna and ripped jeans and shouted into a megaphone. Among the materials handed out at the rally was one titled "Return to Aztlan."[12]

Aztlan is a mythical area that includes California, Arizona, Nevada, Utah, Colorado, New Mexico, and Texas. Race activist leaders and many Mexicans say this Southwestern territory was stolen by the U.S. and must be re-conquered and reclaimed for Mexico.

The leaflet gave a series of steps to be taken to re-establish Aztlan. The first step read, "Be sure the mother tongue is retained in the school system."

Interestingly, the man holding the rally on the steps of the state house was Frederick Pena, who later went on to become minority leader in the Colorado House of Representatives, mayor of Denver, and Secretary of Transportation and Secretary of Energy under President Clinton.

Around the time of the rally in the mid 1970s, Colorado began requiring bilingual education for non-English speakers. Tancredo saw what this did to the children in the school where he was teaching and to kids in other schools, but initially he did not connect it to massive immigration.

In an interview in his Capitol Hill office in July 2004, Tancredo told me that children were taken out of his class where they were learning English and placed in bilingual classrooms where they were taught in Spanish. The children were not doing well academically, and Tancredo could not understand why anyone would want to hurt a child's ability to learn. *What is the purpose of bilingual education?* he wondered.

"The more I looked into it," Tancredo said, "the more it became apparent that bilingual education wasn't an education issue; it was a political issue, but why? Well, among other things, mass immigration creates this constituency, and the pressures for bilingual education magnify. Then you begin to understand the whole issue of multiculturalism. It's the same thing. It's a cult of multiculturalism that permeates this society and is designed to split us up into these balkanized groups around the country. Then you begin to realize that immigration is directly connected to this because it exacerbates the problem."

Tancredo's understanding that bilingual education was more of a political idea than an educational one caused him to become concerned about the rising numbers of immigrants.

Today there are several million English learners across the U.S. and most are Spanish-speaking. K.C. McAlpin, executive director of ProEnglish (www.ProEnglish.org), an organization educating Americans about the need to protect English as our common language and make it the official language of the U.S., says:

America's linguistic unity, which has enabled it to become the most successful multi-ethnic nation in modern history, is under attack as never before. Record numbers of non-English speaking immigrants threaten to overwhelm our assimilation process. And in a stark reversal of the past, our government has embarked on a policy of accommodating a growing number of foreign tongues in the name of "diversity." The result is "linguistic apartheid," in which an expanding underclass is being balkanized into linguistic ghettos, and whose members find it almost impossible to achieve the American Dream. Today almost one in five Americans speaks a language other than English at home. Alarmed by these developments, 26 states have enacted laws making English their official language, often through citizens initiatives passed by margins as high as nine to one.[13]

In 1976, Tancredo left his teaching job to run for the Colorado legislature and won. He repeatedly and unsuccessfully tried to repeal the bilingual program. The debates were so heated that his tires were slashed and hate notes were left on his car windshield.[14] He also tackled issues such as tax reform, school choice, and parental rights.

In 1981, Tancredo resigned his seat in the legislature to accept an appointment in President Reagan's administration. He served as the Secretary of Education's regional representative and was re-appointed to the position by President George H.W. Bush.

In 1993, Tancredo started a conservative public policy think tank in Colorado called the Independence Institute, where one of his first initiatives was to commission a study on the impact of immigration. The 1995 report, titled "Compassion vs. Compulsion," found that mass immigration's impact was mostly negative. The report helped him to arrive at his views on the issue. Here is an excerpt about illegal immigration:

In the U.S., taxes must be paid before one can buy food, shelter or anything else for oneself or one's children. This means that requiring American taxpayers to provide for people who have no right to be in the United States forces them to buy food, shelter, education and health care for illegal immigrants before they buy it for their own families. Such policies treat productive American workers as legally indentured servants whose labor is owned by anyone managing to cross the border. To cloak such a preposterous idea in the mantle of compassion and human rights is an affront to all who take American citizenship seriously. It is also a measure of just how far some people's notions of compassion and responsibility have strayed from reality.[15]

In 1996, Tancredo began exploring a run for Congress and found that immigration was a subject that most lawmakers did not want to discuss. However, this grandson of immigrants was not deterred.

In 1998, Tancredo won a five-way race in the Republican Primary for the Sixth Congressional District of Colorado. He then went on to defeat his Democrat opponent in the general election.

The Congressional Immigration Reform Caucus

In January 1999, Tancredo was sworn into office as a member of the 106th Congress. He wasted no time making an impact in Washington on the immigration issue. Just four months later, the freshman legislator established the Congressional Immigration Reform Caucus to review current immigration policy, initiate new immigration policy, and to create a forum in Congress to address both the positive and negative consequences of immigration. Initially the caucus had about a dozen members. But after the terrorist attacks on September 11, 2001, membership jumped. By 2004, the group had grown to seventy, with sixty-seven Republicans and three Democrats. As of December 2005, membership had climbed to ninety-two.

During the first two years of the caucus (1999 and 2000), the group focused mostly on H-1B visa legislation and potential amnesty provisions. The H-1B is a non-immigrant classification used by an alien who will be employed temporarily in a specialty occupation.

During the first session of the 107th Congress in 2001, the caucus concentrated on three primary issues: addressing the explosive growth in illegal immigration, reversing the growth in legal immigration, and stopping a further extension of Section 245(i) of the Immigration and Nationality Act, which is a mini-amnesty program. Under Section 245(i), when persons illegally in the U.S. without current status are not immediately deported, they are awarded the benefit of an amnesty. The act allows aliens who have no legal status in the U.S. to avoid deportations as long as they file a visa petition through a spouse, parent, child, brother, or sister prior to a certain date.

Following 9/11, the caucus continued to establish and emphasize the link between open borders, unregulated immigration, and the potential for terrorism. In addition, the group pushed legislative proposals to secure America's borders and reform the outdated U.S. immigration system.

'A Lonely Struggle'

In 1999, his first year in Congress, Tancredo began talking about immigration on the floor of the House during Special Order Speeches at night when the chamber was vacant. The speeches were aired on the C-SPAN cable network. Because he was not a committee chair and most of the other members of Congress wanted to avoid the issue, this was about the only time Tancredo could share his concerns with the public.

"I would come to the House floor night after night to bring my concerns to the body and to those people who were listening, but it was a lonely struggle," Tancredo said in early 2004. "I am happy to say that things do appear to be changing, that American voices are being heard."[16]

Tancredo understands that elected officials and other Americans can be uncomfortable discussing immigration. But he also knows the issue cannot be ignored.

"These issues are tough to talk about," he said at the Patriot Rally near Los Angeles in November 2003. "They make many of my colleagues very uncomfortable. They make many people in the country uncomfortable, I suppose. But just because they're

uncomfortable doesn't mean the issues should not be discussed....
But please understand this. This is not a racial issue. It is not for
me, and it should not be for anybody here. Don't let anybody make
it that way. This is what they do to try and marginalize anybody on
our side. Anytime you bring up these questions, it always turns into
this racial issue. He's a racist. She's a racist. It's my experience that
when people start throwing terms like that around is when they have
run out of all intellectual argument. And then they start looking for
these epithets to throw at you, hoping they will marginalize you and
thereby marginalize your issue."[17]

Over the years, Tancredo has made dozens of Special Order
Speeches about unrestrained immigration's impact on Americans
and America. He focuses on subjects such as labor, crime, national
security, culture, the environment, and the media. And he is not
afraid to tell it like it is and name names. Here are some excerpts:

- On national security, March 4, 2003: "The world in
  which we live, the kind of world we have lived in this
  United States for a couple of hundred years where we
  felt so secure from the problems of other countries, the
  oceans protected us, and that we could defend ourselves
  by sending armies to other countries, that world is gone.
  It no longer really exists. Our nation is at risk because
  our borders are porous, and no matter how many times
  somebody stands on the floor of this House or in front of
  the cameras at press briefings and says something like we
  are doing everything possible to defend the people of this
  country, no matter how many times they say it, it simply
  is not true. It is not true."

- On the environment, March 4, 2003: "It is, in fact,
  hordes of people, thousands of people coming across the
  [southern] border, destroying the fences, depositing litter
  throughout the land and in areas that were heretofore
  pristine in nature.... There is so much trash that a person
  literally has to be careful as they walk through there
  because of what they might step on or what they might
  touch. I mean thousands and thousands and thousands

of water bottles and trash and plastic bags because people are told they must discard everything. They must discard their backpacks, jackets, coats, shirts, whatever, get into whatever kind of transportation is made available to them with as little as possible because they need more room.... The land is devastated. If this happened anywhere else in the United States, the Sierra Club would be going crazy. We would be hearing from them on the floor of this House every single day. Somebody would be getting sued. I guarantee my colleagues that. The cameras from ABC, NBC, and CBS would be there every night saying, look what these people are doing to our land; they are destroying this property. Yet, I really have not seen that kind of exposure of this particular problem."

- On border security, March 31, 2003: "There is a report from the Tucson sector from the U.S. Border Patrol that said that as early as November of last year they apprehended in just one sector 23,000 illegal aliens, but they also said that at least for every one they get, five get by them. So in the month of November, according to the Border Patrol, 100,000 people came across just the Tucson sector into the United States. They got 23,000 of them, turned them back, and of course those people very soon just came across the border as soon as somebody was not looking."

- On crime, July 16, 2003: "Right now, there are approximately 400,000 people who have been ordered to be deported; that is to say, they have somehow gotten themselves afoul of the law. They have gotten into the criminal justice system, and they have been found guilty. Usually, this is an immigration court, and they have been ordered deported. Now they are supposed to leave from the courtroom and go right into the hands of the INS and be deported to their country of origin, but we do not, in fact, deport people very often, and the INS really does not pay an awful lot of attention, so that 400,000 of the millions who have gone through this process are now walking around the United States. At least 80,000 of those are violent criminals, felons, rapists, murderers, robbers, walking around our streets because the INS failed to do their job."

- On jobs, February 24, 2004: "The jobs that we see being developed are jobs that by and large are not going to Americans.... They are going to people coming here from foreign countries, some legal, most not. Those are the people getting the jobs.... This cheap labor is a benefit to employers. Cheap labor is cheap to employers. It is not cheap to the rest of us, to the people who pay the taxes for the schools, for the highways, for the housing, for the health care, for the incarceration rates. Those all get passed on to the taxpayer so that there can be a higher profit rate."

- On the media, February 24, 2004: "How did the major media approach [immigration]? Anyone that suggested we need to look at our immigration policy was at best xenophobic, at worst racist. That is the only way the media ever looked at it, because that is the only way they could explain how someone would stand up on the floor of the House or in a state legislature anywhere in the country, a city council or anyplace else and talk about the possibility that massive immigration into this country could be problematic, and that we had to be able to control it and know who is coming into this country. We have to know how many, for what purpose, and for how long. In order to call ourselves a nation, that is a requirement, to be able to actually control your borders. But the major media would follow the lead of papers like the *Wall Street Journal* that every single year for years on the Fourth of July would write an editorial saying that borders should be eliminated, they don't matter anymore, they are insignificant, and they just impede the flow of goods and services."

- On the new world order, February 24, 2004: "I will tell my colleagues that I do believe that it is true that there are a lot of folks here even in this body, maybe even in the administration, who believe that borders are irrelevant, they are of no consequence, and they impede the flow of goods and services and, yes, people, and that soon we will be able to achieve a new world order in which there are no real borders…. It is not a world view I hold, nor one that I will accept without a lot of fighting, but it is something that a lot of people want to see, and that is why we can see this constant movement toward a world and a country in which the whole concept of citizenship is completely and totally obliterated, where it just does not matter anymore if one is a citizen of the United States, of Mexico, of Canada or anyplace else. They are just a resident of where they happen to be…. We see cities in the United States passing laws, calling themselves sanctuary cities, laws telling people that they really do not need to show us anything except perhaps a utility bill to show that they are a resident and we will let them vote…. What is the end result of this process? It is to achieve a place in which we are simply residents, we are not citizens, that citizenship does not matter, that if one comes here across our borders even without our permission, we will give them free schooling for their children. We do that. If they come here across our borders, even without our permission, we will give them access to our healthcare system. We do that. If they come here, we will give them access to our Social Security system…. We are even telling them that if they come here, even without our permission, they can vote."

In his Special Order Speeches and elsewhere, Tancredo often talks about how uncontrolled immigration has resulted in huge numbers of people failing to assimilate into our society. This, in turn, has resulted in what he calls "radical multiculturalism" in America's schools, the popular media, and churches.

In recent years, the former schoolteacher explains, some in America's public education system have turned their backs on the idea of instilling in students a sense of pride and appreciation for American history and Western Civilization. Instead, he says, many classrooms have become places "openly hostile" to these principles, with teachers and textbooks promoting "venomous and anti-American rhetoric to de-emphasize the importance of America's collective, historical accomplishments." Tancredo talked about some of these textbooks, which can be found in classrooms across the country, in his February 24, 2004, Special Order Speech:

- "In 2002, the 'New Guidelines for Teaching History' in the New Jersey public schools failed even to mention America's Founding Fathers, the Pilgrims, the Mayflower. These were the guidelines for teaching history. What history? Whose history? Not ours. Because, of course, maybe somebody who read this could not relate to the Pilgrims or the Founding Fathers."

- "In a Prentice Hall history textbook used by students in Palm Beach County High School titled *A World Conflict*, the first five pages of the World War II chapter focused almost entirely on topics such as gender roles in the Armed Forces, racial segregation and the war, internment camps, and the women in the war effort. That was World War II, okay? That was it, gender roles in the Armed Forces. Now, it maybe deserves a line, maybe a paragraph, but this is the analysis of World War II in a history textbook?"

- "In a school district in New Mexico, the introduction to a textbook called *500 Years of Chicano History in Pictures* states this is why the book was written, 'In response to the bicentennial celebration of the 1776 American Revolution and its lies.' Its stated purpose is 'to celebrate our resistance to being colonized and absorbed by racist empire builders.' The book describes defenders of the Alamo as slave owners, land speculators, and Indian killers; Davy Crockett as a cannibal; and the 1857 war on Mexico as an unprovoked U.S. invasion. The chapter headings included 'Death to the Invader,' 'U.S. Conquest and Betrayal,' 'We Are Now a U.S. Colony in Occupied America,' and 'They Stole the Lands.'"

'Homeland Heroes'

In 2003, Tancredo began a series of Special Order Speeches called "Homeland Heroes" about American families living near the southern border in Arizona. Tancredo says these citizens are on a "war front," where an illegal-alien "invasion" has been going on for years.

"These are people who have suffered mightily because the federal government has chosen to abandon them," the congressman explains. Many are citizens whose families have lived along the southern border for generations.

Tancredo says the invasion is sponsored by the Mexican government and aided and abetted by the U.S. government. The invaders include men, women, children, pregnant women, and the elderly. Thousands flood into Arizona each day. The U.S. Border Patrol only catches about one out of every four or five that sneak across. The invaders come in large groups, usually 20 to 100 per group. Some remain in Arizona while the others move on to other states.

The congressman has spent time with Americans at their homes near the border, where they tell him about the horrors they personally experience and show him the devastation caused by the invaders.

Family members, including young children, are assaulted. Home invasions are common. Family pets are killed. Fences are torn down. Water lines are cut. Roads are blockaded and vehicles are hijacked. Cattle are slaughtered and eaten. The invaders trash the land, leaving behind water bottles, plastic bags, baby diapers, syringes, backpacks, clothes, and other items. Cattle and other animals often eat the discarded items and die. The invaders leave campfires unattended that often turn into grass fires and sometimes major fires.

The families have pleaded for help from the federal government, but their cries have mostly fallen on deaf ears. They are fighting for their lives every day. The invasion is destroying their livelihood and lives and, in many cases, forcing them off their land. Some families are bankrupt. Tancredo calls the situation "intolerable."

The families say some of the illegals that are apprehended by the U.S. Border Patrol are later proven to have criminal records as felons in the U.S., with crimes ranging from child molestation to murder. But, the families say, the U.S. Border Patrol does not have nearly enough manpower to stop the invasion.

One Homeland Hero is Gary McBride, a fifty-nine-year-old rancher in Cochise County. Tancredo talked about the Arizona rancher on the floor of the House on May 15, 2003:

"Mr. McBride found trespassers in his barn where they leave garbage, feces, and lighted cigarettes. He has been run off his road by illegal drug smugglers traveling at high speeds. In his daily experience, drugs are now smuggled across his ranchlands every single day. Equipment has been stolen from his garage. Groups of illegal aliens stand in front of his yard and yell at him, demanding to use his telephone. Real-estate values in the areas have fallen dramatically as few people want to purchase a ranch and cope with the daily stresses and additional costs imposed by the constant flow of illegal trespassers."[18]

Tancredo says McBride and many other Americans are aggravated and angry that so few in government are willing to honor their oaths of office and protect the states against invasion.

"Mr. McBride is a frustrated man because he sees nothing happening about his problem," Tancredo said on the House floor. "He has every right to be frustrated. Nothing happening. People here apparently do not care. At least not enough of us care. Many of us, however, on this floor and in this body share the frustration because we see much more that can be done and could be done to secure our borders and curtail, if not stop, this invasion."

Tancredo calls for putting the U.S. military on our borders to stop the invasion. He adds that the U.S. should not let foreign governments dictate our policies in this matter.

"We could adopt a policy that the Armed Forces of the United States could conduct routine training exercises along the northern and southern borders," he said. "As a nation, by action of this Congress, we could adopt a policy that one-third of all our military training takes place within fifty miles of our borders. That would send a message that we are serious about the borders.... We could be training our military on the border, if nothing else, even if you did not want to put them there all the time because everybody is so sensitive about, oh, my God, what would the Mexicans say, what would the Canadians say about using our troops on our border? Well, I do not really give a fig what they would say.

"I could not care less about what Mexico thinks about us trying to protect our own borders, especially when Mexico does everything it possibly can to help people invade the United States. Mexico has departments of government that are designed to help people come into this country, even come in illegally. The Mexican government provides buses, bringing busloads of people to the border of the United States, where they dislodge these passengers and let them start walking across into the country, into the desert. This is the government of Mexico. This is our friend."[19]

Bush's Amnesty Plan

On January 7, 2004, President Bush ignited a firestorm of disappointment and anger across the U.S. when he announced his so-called guest-worker proposal in a speech at the White House. Some Americans called the plan dangerous, destructive, and even treasonous. Many Americans who had voted for Bush in 2000 said they would not do so in 2004 because of his proposal. However, some Americans were enthusiastic about the plan. Others even said it did not go far enough to help "immigrants."

Interestingly, only Mexican government representatives and Hispanic political organizations were invited to attend the president's speech. Among the groups were the League of Latin American Citizens (LULAC), the Mexican American Legal Defense and Educational Fund (MALDEF), and the National Council of La Raza (The Race).

Bush's plan would allow millions of illegal aliens to remain in the U.S. as guest workers for renewable three-year periods if they have jobs. These illegals could eventually apply for permanent legal residence and be put on the path to U.S. citizenship. The plan also calls for the admission of countless family members of those amnestied.

In addition, employers would be able to seek unlimited numbers of workers from other countries who are "willing" to work at whatever wages the employers determine.

Bush called his proposal a "guest-worker" plan and never mentioned the word "amnesty." He said the plan "will make America a more compassionate, more humane and stronger country."[20]

However, Americans knew it was an amnesty—a decision by a government to forgive people who have committed illegal acts.

"The White House diligently avoided using the 'A' word in its announcement," said Dan Stein, executive director of the Federation for American Immigration Reform. "But no matter how much Karl Rove wishes to torture the English language, a program that legalizes millions of people who have cheated to get into this country, who have cheated by working off the books and avoided paying taxes, and have cheated by using billions of dollars in public services is an amnesty."[21]

Expressions of outrage over Bush's proposal came immediately from the Border Patrol union, leaders in the immigration reform movement, authors, nationally syndicated talk-radio hosts, and many others.

The National Border Patrol Council, representing the nation's 10,000 border agents, called the plan a "slap in the face to anyone who has ever tried to enforce the immigration laws of the United States."[22]

Barbara Coe, president of the California Coalition for Immigration Reform, said Bush "has just put out a welcome mat to illegal aliens, violent criminals, drug smugglers, and terrorists."[23]

Lawrence Auster, author of several books on the destructive consequences of mass immigration and publisher of www. ViewFromTheRight.com, wrote in a letter to the president: "I consider your proposal on illegal aliens to be the most radical and irresponsible piece of legislation ever proposed by a U.S. president. It is a mandate for virtually open borders. It means that any person anywhere in the world who can underbid an American for a job in the U.S. gets legal status in this country. I am stunned by the destructiveness of this plan."[24]

Talk-radio host Michael Savage, whose longtime slogan is "borders, language, culture," called for the impeachment of Bush. During his January 12 broadcast, Savage called Bush a liberal and described him as part of the "enemy within" that is destroying the nation. "This [proposal] is the worst betrayal of our country in my lifetime," protested Savage, whose program is heard on hundreds of stations.[25]

Even liberal Democratic Senators Diane Feinstein and Robert Byrd said they would resist the plan on the grounds that it would encourage illegal immigration.[26]

Tancredo said Bush's proposal failed to address border security. "It is dangerous to offer additional incentives and rewards for illegal immigration while giving only lip service to border security," Tancredo warned. "The president and his advisors are totally ignoring the nation's experience with the ill-fated 1986 amnesty program, which did not deliver on its promises of border security and only encouraged a new wave of illegal immigration." Tancredo predicted Congress would reject it.[27]

Tancredo also expressed disappointment that only Mexican government representatives and Hispanic political organizations were invited to attend the president's speech.

"If this is truly a proposal to reduce illegal immigration," the congressman asked, "why didn't the White House invite the widows of Border Patrol agents who died defending our borders or the widows of police officers who have been killed by criminal illegal aliens who cross our borders with ease? I guess the president didn't think these families would be impressed by his proposal."[28]

Until 1986, the U.S. had never forgiven the act of illegal immigration in other than individual cases and had never rewarded large numbers of illegal aliens with the opportunity for U.S. citizenship.

In 1986, Congress and President Reagan passed the Immigration and Reform Control Act (IRCA), a blanket amnesty for about three million illegal aliens, mostly Mexicans. (One of the 1993 bombers of the World Trade Center was amnestied via IRCA, which was strictly for agricultural workers, even though he lived in New York City.) Although the 1986 IRCA amnesty was sold to the American people as a one-time program, Congress has subsequently passed six additional amnesties totaling more than two million illegals. In 2005, nine amnesty bills were pending in Congress.[29]

For years, poll after poll has shown that the overwhelming majority of Americans oppose rewarding illegal aliens for their misdeeds. One week after Bush's announcement, a CBS News poll showed that the president's approval rating dropped to its lowest point. More than two-thirds of Americans disagreed with his plan.[30]

While Americans voiced frustration and anger, many businesses were delighted. The U.S. Chamber of Commerce called the program "momentous." The National Restaurant Association applauded Bush for addressing the economic problem faced by its members, who employ many "immigrants."[31]

However, Hispanic separatist organizations said the plan did not go far enough in putting "immigrants" on the path to U.S. citizenship. "If the president is trying to appeal to the Latino community, we're baffled by this," complained Lisa Navarrete, a vice president of the National Council of La Raza. "This is not what the community needed."[32]

Presidential candidate and former Vermont governor Howard Dean, the Democratic front-runner at the time, said: "President Bush's decision to raise immigration at this juncture appears to be little more than a cynical gesture in an election year." [33]

Presidential candidate John Kerry, a Democratic senator from Massachusetts, stated: "Bush's policy rewards business over immigrants by providing them with a permanent pool of disenfranchised temporary workers who could easily be exploited by employers."[34]

In Republican congressional offices, lawmakers received a flood of angry letters, e-mails, and phone calls from constituents vowing they would not vote for Bush if his program were approved. Twenty-three Republican congressmen, all from Tancredo's Immigration Reform Caucus, warned the president in a letter on January 27 that he risked a backlash from voters.[35]

"It is a matter of great concern to us that these constituents— politically active American citizens—are so disillusioned by the proposal that many of them will become disenchanted with not only the administration, but with Congress as well," the letter read. "If we do not listen to our constituents on this matter, our influence and effectiveness in Congress could be jeopardized. Simply put, we cannot continue to allow our immigration laws to be violated and ignored—and illegal aliens are by definition criminals." [36]

At a news conference on Capitol Hill the next day, January 28, House Minority Leader Nancy Pelosi and other Democrats announced their own proposal for "immigrants." Their plan would give blanket amnesty and citizenship to all aliens in the U.S., while opening the door to an unlimited number of foreign workers willing to underbid American workers for their jobs. [37] Tancredo was one of many who were outraged.

"I can't believe that Pelosi and company could look American workers in the eye and tell them that this amnesty will 'promote ... economic opportunity,'" Tancredo said. "What they didn't tell them is how many Americans and legal residents will lose their jobs to illegals that are willing to work for less. This economic mugging will force American working families into bankruptcy, while fattening the coffers of large corporations and union bosses. The Democrats could have summed up their proposals by simply saying that in America, borders, citizenship, and the rule of law are no longer relevant concepts." [38]

The next day, January 29, at a Republican retreat in Philadelphia, House lawmakers directed their anger at Bush's political strategist Karl Rove during his talk to them.

"They were all over Karl on immigration and spending," said Tancredo. "This is the first time I didn't even have to raise the immigration issue myself. Everyone else did." [39]

Many of the 218 Republicans at the meeting said immigration and overspending had emerged as the top two issues in their home districts.

Not surprisingly, illegal immigration from Mexico immediately shot up following Bush's January 7 announcement and continued to climb for several months, as hundreds of thousands of people rushed across the border in hopes of getting work visas under his scheme. During the first three months of 2004, the number of illegal aliens apprehended on the southwestern border by the U.S. Border Patrol had climbed 25 percent over the same period in 2003. In Tucson, the busiest sector, nearly 250,000 illegals were apprehended from January 1 through April 14, representing a 53 percent jump from the year before.[40]

"It doesn't take a rocket scientist to tell you the president's speech was the catalyst for lots of folks to make their way north and try to get into this country in order to get what they accurately believe to be amnesty," Tancredo said.[41]

Illegal immigration also shot up after the IRCA amnesty was announced in 1986.[42]

Tancredo pointed out that if apprehensions are increasing, so is the number of illegals making it across the border freely because, according to the Border Patrol, for every one person caught, several more make it across without being apprehended.

However, one immigration expert, Juan Mann, said amnesty critics have ignored stealth amnesty for years. In an August 2004 article for Vdare.com, Mann, a lawyer and proprietor of www.DeportAliens. com, wrote: "As long as the idea of a one-time amnesty free-for-all remains overwhelmingly unpopular with the American people—as it should be—the federal immigration bureaucracy look for ways to give more legal status to more illegal aliens more often ... all behind closed doors."[43]

"The threat of amnesty is not something that can be blocked just by defeating one 'heinous bill' in Congress," Mann explained, "because amnesty is already underway in many forms," including:

- allowing illegal aliens in the country;

- tolerating illegals who can adjust status through family or employment petitioning in the future;

- giving green cards (permanent resident status) to illegals already in the U.S.;

- handing out green cards abroad, at ports of entry, and at Department of Homeland Security service centers through the refugee and asylum process;

- continuing the visa lottery; and

- allowing convicted criminal aliens to keep their green cards (or even get new green cards) in spite of being deportable for their crimes.

For several months following Bush's January 2004 speech, the administration was silent about its so-called guest-worker program, except when it was communicating with a particular group of people.

Visitors to the "En Espanol" link on the reelection Web site for Bush and Vice President Dick Cheney were taken to the campaign's Spanish-language site, where a Mexican flag was prominently displayed on the home page. The American flag was significantly smaller.

Near the top of a page, on the Spanish-language site listing translations of the president's speeches, was a link to Bush's amnesty speech. The speech was not listed on the English-language site.

ProjectUSA Director Craig Nelsen commented: "Call me a cultural nativist, but there is something very wrong with an American president asking voters to entrust him with another four years as the nation's leader, while dividing the nation's voters into two groups and appealing to one under the flag of some other nation."[44]

Recruiting Patriotic Candidates

Fighting amnesty proposals are just some of the many battles Tancredo and the members of his Immigration Reform Caucus have fought in recent years. In 2004 alone, they worked to involve state and local police in enforcing immigration laws, protect Social Security from illegal aliens, ban acceptance of foreign-issued consular ID cards, and prevent voting by illegal aliens. They also worked to reduce uncontrolled legal immigration by abolishing the Diversity Visa Program, which awards green cards to people winning a lottery. The program is designed to increase diversity in America and includes lucky winners from states that sponsor terrorism.

While Tancredo has done more than anyone else in Congress to restrict immigration, there were congressmen fighting these battles before he was elected to the House in 1998.

"We had a loose-knit organization till Tom came," said Representative Nathan Deal, a Republican who has seen years of massive immigration strain his Georgia district's schools and healthcare services.[45]

"I just happened to be in Congress at the time 9/11 occurred," Tancredo says. His caucus had about a dozen members before terrorists struck that day, but membership jumped after those immigration-driven catastrophes.

However, even though the caucus has grown to a fairly significant size with ninety-two members, Congress continues to vote down commonsense bills that would protect Americans and America.

Two such cases occurred in June 2004. One was an amendment designed to make the U.S. safer from terrorism. The other would have helped clamp down on skyrocketing healthcare costs.

Tancredo had introduced an amendment to the Department of Homeland Security's Appropriations Act, H.R. 4567, to prohibit federal funding for states or cities that violate existing law by allowing sanctuary to illegal aliens.

In 1996, Congress passed legislation that prohibited state and local governments from granting sanctuary. Under sanctuary, public officials, including police officers, are not allowed to inquire about an individual's immigration status. Even if an individual is applying for public benefits or is suspected of a criminal offense, their resident status cannot be questioned.

Although such policies violate federal laws, Los Angeles, San Francisco, Denver, Houston, Chicago, and New York have enacted sanctuary policies. So has the entire state of Maine.

The Tancredo amendment would have created financial incentives for cities to revoke their sanctuary policies. At the same time, the amendment would have provided additional protection to citizens, since illegal aliens and terrorists congregate in places where they know their residency status will not be questioned.

The proposed amendment was called "racist" and "mean-spirited," and it failed by a vote of 148-259. By rejecting the Tancredo amendment, Congress voted to ignore existing federal law.

Also in June 2004, Congress rejected H.R. 3722, the Undocumented Alien Emergency Medical Assistance Amendment introduced by Representative Rohrabacher.

The Rohrabacher amendment required that anyone applying for emergency medical services would need to provide information regarding citizenship and actual place of residence. Also required would be an indication of financial responsibility (insurance) and some tangible form of identification such as a passport or fingerprint. American citizens follow the same procedure in emergency rooms where ID and proof of insurance are shown.

The amendment did not deny medical treatment. However, it did say that healthcare to illegal aliens should be given only to protect U.S. citizens, to save the life of an alien in a life-threatening medical emergency, or to stabilize that individual until he or she can be sent back to his or her native country for medical care.

In January 2004, the offices of Rohrabacher received dozens of threatening phone calls, including one death threat, after he authored the bill.[46]

The Rohrabacher bill was defeated, 88-331.

Tancredo told me that in most cases he could count on about 125 to 150 congressional members to stand with him on immigration and represent the American people. "That's what I would call our core group," he explained. "We probably have enough [members] to stop [the open-borders lobby] from doing what they want to do, but I do not have enough to do what I want to do. I need a couple hundred."

In January 2004, just after Bush's amnesty speech, Tancredo and conservative activist Bay Buchanan launched the Team America political action committee to "identify, recruit, and help elect to public office individual patriots who agree with our motto, 'The Defense of a Nation Begins at its Borders.'" To qualify, candidates have to agree to:

1. Oppose any sort of amnesty,

2. Support a "time out" on immigration until serious reforms can be enacted,

3. Support the use of American military forces on the border until the Border Patrol is at full strength, and

4. Join the Congressional Immigration Reform Caucus.

In a statement on the Team America Web site at www. teamamericapac.org, Tancredo explains the central role of Congress and the main reason America's borders are still open:

> What does the Constitution say about congressional responsibility to defend America? It's clear and unambiguous. It is our primary role. It is the one thing we are supposed to do: defend the Nation.
>
> We shirk our primary responsibility when we refuse to defend our own borders because of the politics of cheap labor. And that is the reason we do not defend our borders. That is it. As ugly and as uncomfortable as that is to deal with, here, years after the most devastating attack on our shores we have ever experienced, we still do not defend our own borders and enforce them because of that fear, the fear that we would stop cheap labor. It is politics. It is unacceptable.

Bay Buchanan, president of The American Cause, an educational foundation devoted to advancing traditional conservative issues, called Bush's amnesty proposal and guest-worker program "the final chapter of the sellout of America." Buchanan has been involved in politics for many years, working for Ronald Reagan's presidential campaigns and chairing her brother, Pat Buchanan's, runs for the White House. In a letter on the Team America site, Bay Buchanan says:

> The arrogance of those in power today is as great as it has ever been. Knowing full well that an unprotected border threatens our national security, increases the violence in our cities and schools, burdens our hospitals, suppresses our wages, bankrupts our governments, and balkanizes our nation, our so-called representatives do nothing to enforce the laws of this land.
>
> "We, the People" has been replaced as the driving force in this nation by "We, the Corporations," a group that doesn't give a rat's tail about our workers, our communities, or our national sovereignty for that matter! But these corporations

are calling the shots in Congress and open borders means cheap labor. That is good for them and they could care less about the consequences to the nation.

Buchanan called the situation "urgent" and said "unless we move now it may be too late…. We must take charge of our future or there will be none! Congressman Tancredo can lead the battle, but he needs troops behind him to win."

Leading up to the 2004 primaries and general election, thousands of Americans joined Team America. Many also signed Team America's letter to Congress stating that they pledge to only give their votes and financial support to candidates who defend U.S. borders, enforce immigration laws, and protect Americans against cheap foreign labor. Many who signed the letter had some strong words for politicians.

Gerard W., an electronics engineer from Nevada, wrote: "We will take back the House of Reps one step at a time, one open-borders cheap-labor bagboy at a time. A tough fight, this will require sustained effort. The only way to take our country back is to burn down the political careers of those who seek to undermine our immigration laws."

California resident Janice S., a food and beverage manager, said: "I think this is the most important issue facing us today. I have thought long and hard about working to defeat Bush over this issue. The party I have belonged to my whole life has deserted us on this issue…. I am mad as hell."

Information technology worker Jerry V. from Ohio wrote: "I have said it all, continuously, to both my Ohio senators and my representative … only to be simply ignored. My vote and my family's votes will be directed over the next few election cycles to elect real patriots! I think it's important for me to note that I am a conservative ex-Republican!"

Mike A., a mechanic in Connecticut, said: "Hello Congress! There's a new sheriff in town. It's the American people. We are awake, fed up, and ready to run you out of town if you don't do your duty to protect the USA."

After only a few months in business, Team America was proving to have some positive effect, helping two congressional candidates clinch primary wins in Georgia and Kansas. The PAC also was involved in two other primaries that resulted in tight runoff elections. But some of the immigration reform candidates supported by Team America lost.

"It is so hard to beat an entrenched congressman," explained Buchanan. "They have the money of their corporate friends and the endorsements of the party establishment. But our candidates are better and they're running stronger than ever before. And the voice of those demanding our borders be closed grows louder every day. We are gaining enormous strength, despite the occasional setback."

Fighting Amnesty at the GOP Convention

At the Republican National Convention (RNC) in New York in August 2004, Tancredo worked with delegates to add an immigration plank to the party's platform condemning amnesty for illegal aliens, a direct challenge to Bush's guest-worker amnesty proposal. But party bosses were trying to keep any controversial discussion on immigration from being considered. The congressman vowed to "raise as much hell as possible" if he was thwarted.[47]

Tancredo called for the Republican National Committee to add several commonsense immigration amendments to the party's platform: no amnesty for illegal aliens; no drivers' licenses for illegal aliens; and no totalization agreement with Mexico on access to Social Security. (Earlier in the year, the Bush administration had quietly signed an agreement with Mexico to provide Social Security payments to illegal aliens. The agreement is projected to drain $350 billion from the Social Security Trust Fund during the next decade.[48]) Tancredo also had plank proposals that called for supplementing the Border Patrol with military troops and for involving state and local police in enforcing immigration laws.

However, all of Tancredo's amendments were denied.

The RNC supported the president's call for a massive guest-worker amnesty and added it to the platform. The platform said: "This new program would allow workers who currently hold jobs to come out of the shadows and to participate legally in America's economy," and "would allow men and women who enter the program to apply for citizenship in the same manner as those who apply from outside the United States." The word "illegal" did not appear in the platform, explained Mark Krikorian, executive director of the Center for Immigration Studies, in an article titled "Splintered plank: The White House spins and misses on immigration."[49]

At the same time, the RNC contradicted itself by renouncing amnesty for illegal aliens.

The platform represented a major departure from the 1992, 1996, and 2000 GOP conventions, when the party had strong language against illegal immigration.

This time the RNC shut Tancredo out of the platform process and warned Republican congressmen and other party officials not to discuss immigration. The major media also avoided any talk about illegal immigration.

But Tancredo was not going to be silenced.

"The Republican Party platform on immigration smacks of doublespeak and goes against everything the American people believe should happen with our immigration policy," Tancredo said. "Amnesty is not an option."[50]

During the convention speeches, speaker after speaker stressed the importance of fighting the war on terror, but no one addressed Bush's open-borders policy and the millions of illegal aliens in the country, including those from terrorist-sponsoring nations.

There was a total absence of any reference to borders and immigration during the entire convention. And the Republican platform on immigration was nearly identical to the platform the Democrats adopted at their party's national convention in Boston in July. It supported offering citizenship to illegal aliens in the U.S. who pass background checks.[51]

On August 30, the first day of the GOP convention, Tancredo and others held a news conference at a restaurant in New York. Joining him were Michael Cutler, a former Immigration and Naturalization Service senior special agent who testified before the Presidential Commission on the Terrorist Attacks of September 11; Bruce DeCell, a member of the board for 9/11 Families For A Secure America who lost his son-in-law in the attacks; and Matthew Reindl, who owns and operates a carpentry shop on Long Island.

At the news conference, Tancredo said the president's open-border policy panders to businesses that simply want cheap labor. "There are a billion willing workers," he said, "all of them willing to work for less than [an American] already employed."[52]

Reindl said he provides his workers with good wages, health insurance, and workers' compensation coverage, but his competitors who hire illegal aliens do none of those things. As a result, his labor costs are more than 60 percent higher than their costs.

DeCell warned that the president's offer of amnesty might increase the risk of terrorism. "I just think they are trying to put their spin on what they have done to benefit the country as of 9/11," DeCell said. "I really don't think that they have done their job correctly. I disagree with what they're saying, that they're making the country safer. I just don't agree with that."[53]

Tancredo's Enemies

Tancredo demands that America's borders and sovereignty be defended. He demands the protection of American jobs. He believes that the rights of U.S. citizens come first. He believes that all current immigration and visa laws and regulations should be vigorously enforced. He has done more than anyone else in Congress in recent years to fight unrestrained immigration. And he has become the name and face of the growing pro-borders movement. As a result, this new hero of Americans has become the enemy of many powerful forces who want open borders and, thus, want Tancredo out of office.

Who are his enemies? Among others, they include corporate special interests, the Mexican-American lobby, the congressional leadership, the White House, the establishment media, and immigration lawyers.

Immigration advocacy groups and the mainstream press routinely attack Tancredo and call him an ideologue, racist, and xenophobe. In August 2002, for example, the *Denver Post* ran a front-page victim story urging that an illegal alien named Jesus Apodaca get in-state university tuition. Tancredo called the Immigration and Naturalization Service and suggested an inquiry into the man's status.

"As soon as Tancredo spoke out, the *Post* launched an old-fashioned vendetta against him," columnist Joe Guzzardi wrote. "More than 30 *Post* stories appeared. All the *Post*'s columnists lined up to take their shots, some more than once."[54]

Interestingly, Guzzardi wrote, Tancredo found that the Mexican Consulate in Denver was "spoon-feeding sob stories to the *Post* about how cruel it was that the illegal alien Apodaca could not attend the University of Colorado at the in-state rate."

In a March 2004 column attacking Tancredo, *Denver Post* columnist Cindy Rodriquez included the following: "'[Congressman Tancredo] makes Pat Buchanan look like Pat Schroeder,' said Michael Huttner, executive director of the Rocky Mountain Progressive Network. 'If you do a Google search using the terms Tancredo and racist, you'll get something like 800 websites.'"[55]

Commenting on the article, ProjectUSA Director Craig Nelsen said: "Rodriguez, who disagrees with Tancredo on immigration policy, has used the *Denver Post* to make the congressman a frequent target. Many of her attacks are attempts to smear Tancredo as a racist, even though, ironically, it is she who openly argues her side of the immigration debate from a racial perspective, while the congressman does not."

Nelsen explained how Rodriguez violated journalistic ethical and professional standards through distortion and misrepresentation: "While it's true that a Google search using the terms 'Tancredo' and 'racist' will yield 800 hits, if you search 'Rodriguez' and 'racist,' you'll get 14,900 hits—over 18 times as many as 'Tancredo' produces. 'Bush' and 'racist,' incidentally, will return 304,000 hits, and even 'Jesus' and 'racist' will give you 129,000 hits."[56]

During the 2004 GOP convention, the *New York Times* carried an editorial calling Tancredo an "ideologue" because he "not only opposed easing rules for undocumented workers but has even favored a 'time out' on legal immigration."[57]

According to elite media like the *New York Times*, immigration law enforcement and common sense are subjects that interest only the most extreme conservatives. However, polls consistently show that the majority of Americans across the political spectrum want immigration to be legal, controlled, and reduced.[58]

While Tancredo's enemies attack and smear him, they also want him out of office. In 2004, Denver-based First Data Corp. started a Political Action Committee to defeat Tancredo and others who fight illegal immigration and defend U.S. borders. The company also began hosting a series of around-the-nation seminars to promote open borders.[59]

The company is the world's largest provider of money transfers through its Western Union subsidiary. Western Union wires annually transmit tens of billions of dollars in remittances by illegal aliens living in the U.S. to Mexico and other countries, generating enormous profits for First Data and a huge cash package for Chairman Charles T. Fote. In 2003, First Data's revenues were $8 billion and Fote's cash compensation totaled $4.8 million.[60]

First Data tried to replace Tancredo with an open-borders pro-amnesty zealot, Joanna Conti, a "moderate Democrat" and former Republican who made big money with her own commercial food-science company.

Conti's campaign included cruel attacks against Tancredo, according to the congressman. "I am being viciously attacked because I want to stop illegal immigration and secure our borders!" Tancredo said in a letter to concerned Americans. "My opponent and a so-called 527 group funded by three open-border millionaires, are calling me a bigot, racist and other names." (Congress created the 527 classification to exempt organizations that engage in political activities from taxation.)

However, despite strong opposition from big money interests and Colorado newspapers, Tancredo won 60 percent of the vote in November 2004. It was his fourth consecutive congressional win.[61]

In addition, every member of Tancredo's Immigration Reform Caucus seeking reelection won, and several more lawmakers joined the group.

I asked Tancredo about his powerful enemies and about the impact his battle to save the nation from unrestrained immigration has on him and his family. He replied: "Thank God I'm healthy and my family is well. We take a great deal of abuse, and that comes with the territory. I pray to God for his blessing."

'No Matter What It Takes'

At the Patriot Rally outside Los Angeles in November 2003, Tancredo talked about what inspires him in the immigration struggle and his reasons for becoming a member of Congress.[62]

"What motivates me in this endeavor has got nothing to do with race," he explained. "It's got everything to do with America, made up of all races of people who love the same thing, who love those ideals and principles" on which America was founded.

"I didn't come to the Congress of the United States to be a pain in the you-know-what. I really didn't. I came to serve my country. I didn't come to be obstreperous. I did not come to get in an argument with the president of the United States, my own party's president. I did not want to be ostracized in my community or among my colleagues.

"But I'll tell you this, when I stand on the floor of the House of Representatives, if I am lucky enough to be reelected, this little Italian kid, I stand there and I put up my hand and I take an oath. And that oath is not to the party, and it's not to the president; it is to the Constitution of the United States of America. That is what I follow. That is the path I am on. That is what motivates me, and seeing so many wonderful people all over America."

Tancredo told the crowd he has met young Hispanic men at a Colorado Rockies baseball game, Hispanic Border Patrol agents on the border with Mexico, and people living in his congressional district whose families have lived there for many generations, and they all understand the immigration crisis facing the U.S.

"They know exactly what's happening to America," Tancredo said. "They want to save America just like you and I want to save America. And that's why it is so foolish for people in my party to keep telling me and others, don't address this issue, don't talk about this issue, we'll lose the Hispanic vote. And I tell them to look at my mail, look at the response everywhere I go."

The congressman also said the immigration reform movement is growing and urged Americans not to give up the fight, no matter the cost.

"I assure you this," he said, "don't lose heart. There's a very wise old statement: 'There is nothing more powerful than an idea whose time has come.' And I'm telling you immigration reform, the idea is now, the time is now. It's happening, it really is. We're seeing a movement all across this country. Everywhere I go large crowds appear. It's amazing to me. It's wonderful to me.

"I know we are going to be heard. But we have no other choice, do we? No matter what it looks like, no matter how overwhelming. [Long-time newsman-broadcaster] George Putnam must have thought a million times in the years he's been [talking about this crisis], that this is overwhelming. But he doesn't stop, and you know why? He can't stop. There is no alternative to doing everything we can do. I don't care what your lot in life is. I don't care what you're doing or what your job is. You have a role to play with your neighbors, with your friends, with letters to the editor, with ways you can influence your constituency. I have the same role to play. We all have to do it, no matter what it takes and no matter how challenging."

10 | Jim Gilchrist, Chris Simcox, and the Minutemen

"If our own elected officials will not defend our nation's border, American citizens will."

—Jim Gilchrist, Minuteman Project founder

Jim Gilchrist, a retired certified public accountant and decorated Vietnam War veteran from Orange County, California, was fed up with the illegal-alien invasion of America. He heard people complaining about the crisis but saw few people doing anything. He decided to do something.

In the fall of 2004, Gilchrist began sending out e-mails across the country inviting civilian volunteers to join him in a month-long combination of border watch and protest in southeast Arizona in April 2005. But he didn't have a name for the project.

"I had struggled for an appropriate title," the fifty-six-year-old Gilchrist told me. "One day as I sat in my car waiting at a traffic light, I thought about how I was requesting volunteers from every state in the country to come to the aid of Arizona. It reminded me of Paul Revere and the Minutemen, patriotic civilians of several New England colonies who in the period before the American Revolution volunteered to fight the British at a minute's notice. I realized my project had the theme of the original Minutemen."

In one October 2004 e-mail to about two dozen citizens, Gilchrist announced:

> To warriors of Democracy of the Republic of the United States of America: Anyone interested in spending up to 30 days manning the Arizona border as a blocking force against entry into the U.S. by illegal aliens early next spring? I invite you to join me in Tombstone, Arizona in early spring of 2005 to protect our country from a 40-year-long invasion across our southern border with Mexico. Chris Simcox of Civil Homeland Defense, and the publisher of the *Tombstone Tumbleweed* newspaper in Tombstone, Arizona has been doing this with only a handful of patriotic volunteers, and it is time we provided him with reinforcements.
>
> I am recruiting volunteers to converge on the southern border of Arizona for the purpose of aiding the U.S. Border Patrol in "spotting" intruders entering the U.S. illegally. This is strictly a volunteer project, and no financial subsidies are available. And, you will probably need a tent. You will be responsible for all costs associated with your participation.
>
> Currently, about 5,000 illegal aliens enter the U.S./Arizona border DAILY. Another 5,000 invade the U.S. from the Texas, California and New Mexico borders … DAILY. That's 10,000 per day. 300,000 per month. Over 3,000,000 (three million) per year!
>
> … I hope to bring serious media attention to this event, which will tune the American people into the shameful fact that 21st century minutemen have to secure U.S. borders because the U.S. government REFUSES to do so.[1]

By March 2005, four weeks before the operation was to begin, about one thousand patriotic men and women from all fifty states had signed up through the MinutemanProject.com Web site to join Gilchrist and co-organizer Simcox to defend our nation and make a statement. They were from all occupations, age groups, and backgrounds.

"We are, variously, of European, Jewish, American Indian, Hispanic, African, and other backgrounds," Gilchrist stated. "Consequently, we are multi-racial and multi-ethnic. Eight of our participants are married to immigrants, and sixteen are themselves immigrants."

The citizen volunteers included retired servicemen and law enforcement personnel, teachers, bankers, factory workers, and store clerks, among many other professions.

Gilchrist and Simcox gave the volunteers explicit rules to follow when on the border, stressing non-violence: "We will seal the border by our presence, but will not violate anyone's civil rights, and will not abuse anyone from any country. By legal means we will observe illegal aliens on trails heading north. We will alert border patrol to the location of illegals and wait for the U.S. Border Patrol to come and pick them up."

Minutemen Maligned

Many media, Hispanic activists and university professors, the American Civil Liberties Union, high-ranking government officials including President Bush, and the president of Mexico maligned the American patriots seeking to protect our homeland and sovereignty.

A number of newspaper editorial boards condemned the Minutemen, while reporters in "news" stories planted the idea in readers' minds that the Minutemen were "racist gun-toting vigilantes."

Los Angeles Times columnist Steve Lopez thought the idea of American citizens wanting to protect their country from an invasion was a joke: "If you happen to be in the area, give wide berth to anyone who looks like a cast member from 'F-Troop,' and do not wear a straw hat or carry a jug of water, because you could be shot dead."[2]

Gilchrist and Simcox were neutral on the issue of firearms. "We encourage everyone to obey the laws of the state of Arizona, including open carry laws regarding firearms," they told project participants.

Hispanic open-borders extremists protested and threatened the Minutemen. One was Armando Navarro, a University of California professor and a fierce advocate of Aztlan separatism. At a news conference in San Bernardino, California, on March 18, Navarro called Minuteman members "terrorists" and predicted that they would treat border-crossers violently during the patrols. Navarro said his coalition, the National Alliance for Human Rights, would warn people at the border about the Minutemen and would confine themselves to nonviolent tactics.[3]

"We will adjust to the situation," Navarro said, "and obviously some of us have experience in the military.... So there will be maybe some elements of surprises in terms of activities, and that is a warning to the militias."

The next day, March 19, Navarro and a group of UC students harassed Gilchrist and his family personally by demonstrating outside their Orange County home.

Navarro co-organized the Latino Summit Response conference at UC Riverside in 1995, as discussed in chapter seven, where hundreds of Hispanics, including U.S. government officials, discussed plans to stop the implementation of Proposition 187. At the conference, Navarro proclaimed:

> We're in a state of transition. And that transformation is called the browning of America. Latinos are now becoming the majority.... It's a game; it's a game of power and who controls it.... You are like the generals that command armies. We're in a state of war. This Proposition 187 is a declaration of war against the Latino/Chicano community of this country.[4]

On March 10, just three weeks before the Minuteman patrols were to begin, Secretary of State Condoleezza Rice was in Mexico City discussing with her counterpart, Luis Ernesto Derbez, the "integration" of the United States with the other nations in the Western Hemisphere.

In Mexico City, Rice made the following comment about the citizen border group: "And then finally, I think it's well known that the United States has a federal system, but obviously the United States government would not condone any extralegal means to deal with immigration issues. That should be dealt with by immigration officials, and we work very closely with our Mexican counterparts.

We try and make sure that our borders are safe and secure as possible and that it is very important that the laws of the United States be respected."[5]

On March 16, Mexican President Vicente Fox told a Mexico City press conference: "We totally reject the idea of these migrant-hunting groups. We will use the law, international law, and even U.S. law to make sure these types of groups, which are a minority, will not have any opportunity to progress."[6]

On March 23, President Bush met with Fox and Canadian Prime Minister Paul Martin in Waco, Texas, where they reached an agreement on the establishment of the "Security and Prosperity Partnership of North America." (Later it was revealed that they agreed to merge the U.S., Mexico, and Canada. This is the subject of chapter twelve.) Following the closed-door meeting, Bush told a news conference: "I'm against vigilantes in the United States of America. I'm for enforcing law in a rational way. That's why you got a Border Patrol, and they ought to be in charge of enforcing the border."[7]

The *Washington Times* carried an editorial about Bush's comment. In part, it read:

> We've reached a very strange moment in the immigration debate. On Wednesday President Bush condemned a group of good American citizens worried about the breaking of U.S. immigration law. He condemned the organizers of Project Minuteman as "vigilantes" even though they have broken no law and pledge not to do so. An hour or two later, Mr. Bush welcomed to his Texas ranch a man who insults the United States for its immigration policy and leads a government that routinely flouts U.S. immigration law.
>
> Mr. Bush's description of the Minutemen as vigilantes is a misreading of American history. The vigilantes were a lynch mob. The Minutemen are an expanded version of the Neighborhood Watch programs popular in many American cities. It's sad to see an American president roll out a royal welcome to a foreign dignitary so openly contemptuous of U.S. law, while simultaneously condemning Americans who are trying to help dully constituted authorities enforce the law.[8]

The American Civil Liberties Union (ACLU), aggressive advocates of open borders, said it would follow and monitor the activities of the Minuteman volunteers. In April, it sent dozens of ACLU lawyers and observers to the border, hoping to find infractions upon which they could file civil cases against the American citizen participants.[9]

ACLU of Arizona spokesman Ray Ybarra described the American patriots as "vigilantes" who will "attempt to take out their frustrations on a group of individuals who are simply in search of a better life." He said they could "come to our state as 'vigilantes' and end up leaving as 'defendants.'"[10]

But the Minutemen said they simply wanted to exercise their constitutionally protected freedom of speech, freedom of assembly, and freedom to petition the government for a redress of grievances.

"We are American citizens who want to freely assemble under the First Amendment to express our displeasure with federal, state, and local appointees who have been charged with U.S. immigration laws and have left us wide open for another terrorist attack," Gilchrist declared.[11]

On March 30, an Arizona TV station reported that the Mexican government had deployed about 1,000 soldiers to the border, across from the stretch of land where the Minutemen would be assembled. There was no comment from the White House about foreign troops massing just miles from American communities.[12]

In addition, several news organizations reported that the violent Latin American gang Mara Salvatrucha (MS-13), which has thousands of members throughout the U.S., planned to "teach the Minuteman vigilantes a lesson they will never forget."[13]

Around the time of those reports, the Department of Homeland Security announced 103 arrests of MS-13 members in six U.S. cities, the beginning of an operation to rein in the vicious criminal organization.[14]

Patriots Persevere

But despite the threats from university professors, gangsters, and the Mexican army, plus criticism from the news media and high-ranking government officials, the hundreds of brave American patriots pushed ahead with their campaign, knowing that millions of Americans were behind their cause.

On April 1, an orientation for volunteers and a major news conference featuring Congressman Tom Tancredo and Team America Chairman Bay Buchanan were held in Tombstone, the town famous for the O.K. Corral gunfight of 1881. Tombstone is about twenty-five miles from the twenty-three-mile stretch of the Arizona-Mexico border where the patrols would take place.

In front of Schiefflin Hall, where volunteers registered, "immigrant rights" advocates and faux Aztecs were dancing, beating drums, wearing feather headdresses, and carrying signs. One sign read: "No borders, no racists."

Noting that there is much more to illegal immigration than people looking for work, American Border Patrol President Glenn Spencer explained: "I find it instructive that, once again, protestors underline the claim that the American Southwest is really Aztlan, the so-called mystical homeland of the Aztecs. If our government had an intelligence service worth its salt, it would have warned the president that the United States is being invaded by a hostile force."[15]

Inside Schiefflin Hall, Tancredo, Buchanan, Gilchrist, and Simcox spoke to a packed room of peaceful Minuteman volunteers and the media. The Colorado congressman gave the keynote speech. Here are excerpts:

> I am here today to say thank you on behalf of millions of Americans who can't be here with you today. You have the courage to say to the government of the United States, 'Do your duty! Protect our borders! Protect our communities! Protect our families! Protect our jobs!' You are good citizens who ask only that our laws be enforced. When did that become a radical idea? If the federal government were doing its job, if our elected officials were fulfilling their constitutional duties, you wouldn't be here.
>
> Two days ago the government announced that 500 additional agents will be added to the ranks of the Border Patrol in Arizona. A year ago they came down here and held a big press conference on the air force base at Tucson and bragged that they were adding 250 new agents and new

aircraft. What they didn't tell you was that most of those new resources were temporary, and on September 30th they evaporated. We need to tell those people that when the border region is bleeding to death, it needs a tourniquet, not band-aids!

Some people say that we are hypocrites when we protest the open borders because people are coming for jobs and we should ask for a crackdown on the employers who hire illegal aliens. There is no hypocrisy here. We need both! We will support any new proposal for stiffer penalties and more effective law enforcement against employers of illegal aliens. The only hypocrisy in this national debate comes from those who offer amnesty to illegal aliens in the name of better law enforcement and border security. That is a Clintonesque way of simply redefining the problem. Who honestly believes that the next amnesty will be the 'last amnesty'? Who can ask the American people with a straight face to accept it as the solution?

You are here as a kind of neighborhood watch program to help the Border Patrol spot illegal aliens as they enter our country. A year ago in the month of April, in only one month, over 64,000 illegal aliens were apprehended here in the Tucson sector. But you are not here to help the Border Patrol apprehend them. You must not try to stop these interlopers if the Border Patrol does not come to get them. The media are here to observe and report, so let them tell the story of how many trespassers are not caught.

Obey the rules the organizers have set down for you. Observe and report what you see, but do not chase anyone, and do not try to apprehend anyone. Your job is that of a witness, a witness to the truth, a truth that can no longer be hidden from the American people. Our borders are wide open. That must be changed. You are here to hasten that change. May God bless you for your courage, and when you finish the job here, bring this same message to Washington. Together we can awaken America and secure our borders![16]

Margaret Talev, Washington bureau correspondent for the *Star Tribune* in Minneapolis/St. Paul, reported that the Minutemen on that first day "chatted in small clusters, generally talking calmly about their concerns for America's long-term economic prospects, free trade policy, overcrowding in public schools, the burden undocumented workers who lack insurance place on hospitals and local government resources, and their fears that Islamic terrorists are slipping unchecked into the United States across an insufficiently protected border. Many were sensitive to accusations that they are vigilantes or racists."[17]

"I'm not even mad at the immigrants; I'm mad at the [U.S. and Mexican] governments, both of them," said Tim Donnelly, a thirty-eight-year-old plastics supplier and father of five from Twin Peaks, California. "They've got to seal the border and get serious about it. And I want them to crack down on employers who are tax cheats. You've got big business exploiting people," he said. "I see these people as economic refugees, not as criminals."

Greg Sheehan, forty-three, of Altoona, Pennsylvania, said the idea that employers can't find Americans to do certain jobs is bogus. As the owner of two hotels, he said, "All my employees are native-born Americans. We do background checks."

Talev reported that a sixty-five-year-old government worker and retired marine from Oceanside, California, who asked to be identified only by his first name, Len, said he is concerned that a lack of sufficient patrolling and barriers along the U.S.-Mexico border is an invitation to terrorists.

"Why are American forces defending the borders of Iraq and not the borders of the U.S.?" he asked. "There's a bigger threat to our security through the southern border in terms of a direct attack on our infrastructure than from Syria or Lebanon. It just hasn't materialized yet."

The next two days, April 2 and 3, massive rallies were held at the Naco and Douglas Border Patrol stations in southeastern Arizona in support of America's border agents and dissatisfaction with our government's open-borders policy. Citizen activists participating in the rallies and the Minuteman Project represented almost every state in the Union. They carried signs reading: "Terrorists love open borders," "Put U.S. troops on our borders," "Pres. Bush—Do your job," "Coyotes hide behind a Bush," and "Impeach Bush."

On April 4, hundreds of Minuteman volunteers began monitoring the border. Using cell phones and two-way radios, they reported illegal aliens to the Border Patrol. Earlier, an illegal alien from Guatemala stumbled into the Miracle Valley Bible College camp where the volunteers were operating. "He inadvertently wandered into the hornets' nest, but it turned out to be his lucky day," organizers reported. "He was tired and dehydrated, and volunteers gave him medical attention, food, and drink before the Border Patrol was able to arrive."

"We all know this is a 'moment in history' in our ongoing effort to halt the illegal-alien invasion of our country," reported Barbara Coe, head of the California Coalition for Immigration Reform (CCIR) and one of the volunteers during the first week of operations, in her CCIR newsletter. "It was a thrilling experience to be there with so many truly loyal American patriots.[18]

"Rest assured, this is no 'walk in the park' for the Minutemen. After pulling 8–12-hour shifts, they catch a few hours' sleep in either tents or at the bible college dorms, grab a bit to eat, and are 'back on the job.' They face Mexican President Fox's 1,000-plus military in their Humvees armed with 50-caliber machine guns and carrying AK-47s. These are the Mexican troops that Border Patrol has repeatedly reported guard the truckloads of drugs the smugglers bring into the U.S."

'Mission Accomplished!'

After the first week of activity, the Minuteman Project was already drawing national attention to the invasion with its effectiveness in stopping illegal-alien traffic where the citizen volunteers patrolled.

On April 11, Tancredo declared the Minuteman Project a success. He invited co-founders Gilchrist and Simcox to Washington later that month to tell members of his Congressional Immigration Reform Caucus the story of the Project and what it had accomplished.

"Congratulations on your immensely successful Minuteman Project!" the Colorado congressman wrote in a letter to the two patriots. "By all reports you have accomplished your primary mission, which was to draw public attention to the deplorable and unacceptable conditions on our borders. You have demonstrated that a physical presence on the border will deter illegal crossings, and the world can now see this."[19]

By the Border Patrol's count, Tancredo wrote, apprehensions had fallen 50 percent so far that month. Mexican military units had diverted migrants east and west away from the area where the Minutemen were patrolling, "showing that the Mexican government can control the exits if it chooses to do so."

"Congratulations on a job well done!" Tancredo enthused. "Mission accomplished! Please convey my congratulations and admiration to all your Minutemen volunteers."[20]

On April 18, the Minuteman Project announced that because of the "tremendous success" of its effort in just seventeen days of operations, its involvement in border monitoring in Cochise County would cease on April 20.

"We have demonstrated that ordinary citizens sitting in lawn chairs not only have the will but the means to secure our border," Gilchrist declared. "If our own elected officials will not defend our nation's border, American citizens will."[21]

Border monitoring continued through April under the direction of Civil Homeland Defense Corps. That was the civilian organization Simcox founded two and a half years earlier to monitor the border near Tombstone. His group created the tactical organizational model that provided the infrastructure for the Minuteman Project.

"We have demonstrated that ordinary American citizens can secure our border simply by maintaining a presence on the border and that thousands of citizens are ready, willing, and able to do the job our president and Congress will not do," said Simcox, a former Los Angeles schoolteacher. "We are determined to assist the U.S. Border Patrol in becoming an effective arm of the Department of Homeland Security in spite of the lack of support and funding from Congress and our president. There is no compromise—we will continue to exercise our civic duty until relieved by the National Guard and the U.S. military."

Congressmen Applaud Minutemen

On April 27, Gilchrist, Simcox, and about two dozen other Minutemen and women met with ten members of the Immigration Reform Caucus on Capitol Hill to discuss the project and direction of the organization. The two Minutemen leaders promised to expand the patrol to other states along the Mexican border and to states on the Canadian border. They also said they would begin pressuring employers of illegal aliens.

The ten congressmen, all Republicans, congratulated the Minutemen and said much more needs to be done to protect the nation. Caucus chairman Tancredo repeated some of the remarks he made in his speech in Tombstone's Schiefflin Hall on April 1. Other caucus members offered these words:

> John T. Doolittle of California: "Our outdated immigration laws are no longer enough to secure our homeland in a post-9-11 world…. Congress must immediately secure our borders by passing tough, updated immigration legislation."

> Lamar Smith of Texas: "When the federal government fails to do its job, we should not be surprised when law-abiding citizens want to protect their property and our borders."

> Scott Garrett of New Jersey: "[The Minuteman Project] is helping to keep national attention focused on the need for effective border security and immigration reforms."

> J.D. Hayworth of Arizona: "[I]t is up to every American to get involved in this critical struggle to preserve our security and our sovereignty by demanding that this administration and this Congress stop thinking about amnesty and start enforcing our immigration laws."

> Phil Gingrey of Georgia: "The Minuteman Project is a shining example of how community initiative and involvement can help make America a safer, better place to live. These brave men and women are standing up for our security, defending America from the illegal immigrants who are crossing our

borders by the millions. I encourage other citizens to support this cause and defend our nation."

Congressman Virgil Goode of Virginia: "I salute the Minutemen for assisting in a task which the government should be doing.... I hope the president and a majority of the House and Senate will recognize that border security should be a top priority. I hope they will support the legislation to authorize the use of U.S. troops on our border in peacetime to help with border security as needed."

Walter Jones of North Carolina: "It is time the federal government steps up to the plate to defend our borders so that private citizens like those here today don't have to."

Tom Price of Georgia: "The Minutemen truly are the nation's most successful neighborhood watch program. American is fortunate that so many citizens are willing to dedicate their time and energy to this effort. Their work should serve as a wakeup call to all those in Washington who've opposed our effort to strengthen our immigration and border policies and enforcement."

J. Gresham Barrett of South Carolina: "I hope the Minuteman Project has raised awareness around the country for the need to reform our seriously flawed immigration system. Illegal immigration adversely impacts our job market, our education system, and healthcare costs. Hardworking American taxpayers are being forced to shoulder that burden placed on society.... And let's be clear, illegal immigration exposes us on a daily basis to an increased risk of another terrorist attack."[22]

The Minutemen Song

At the end of April, Minutemen and women returned to their homes across America after hard and dangerous work monitoring the border in Cochise County. One was Gianluca Zanna, a business owner, musician, and legal immigrant from Italy who was about to become an American citizen.

The border patrols inspired Zanna to compose a song during his trip back to Southern California. Here are some verses from "The Minutemen":

We're the Minutemen, we're gonna stand
For our country; we'll fight till the end

We're the Minutemen, we're common people
We're just women and men
But our borders we'll defend

Against invaders
Against the traitors
Against Vicente the Mexican dictator

Dear Presidente,
I am not a vigilante
But we'll say to Mr. Fox
That we'll stand hard like rocks

Under the sun
Of the desert
In the darkness of the night
All we want is to defend
Our country, our rights

"The Minutemen" was one of twenty-three patriotic songs Zanna wrote, produced, and arranged in 2004 and 2005 for a CD he released in May 2005 titled *Wake Up America*. Among the other songs are "Remember the Alamo," "The Second Amendment," and "The Enemies Within." Other musicians performed the music. Some radio stations and at least one TV station, the CBS affiliate in El Paso, have aired "The Minutemen," according to Zanna.[23] The song also is played at pro-borders meetings.

On April 29 in Los Angeles, after returning from the border patrols, Zanna took the oath of citizenship. He renounced allegiance to his former country and swore to "support and defend the Constitution and laws of the United States of America against all enemies, foreign and domestic ... so help me God."

"My dear fellows Americans, I've achieved the dream of my life. I am officially an American Citizen!" he declared on his Web site, WakeUpAmerica.US. "Technically I was born in Rome, Italy, my accent and my English is not exactly what you can call perfect, and yes, I love pasta, but in my heart, in my blood and in my spirit, I've always felt as an American. It took me almost 7 years since I came legally to this Country to become an American citizen, following the rules and the laws of the Land!"

In addition to the oath of citizenship, Zanna proclaimed on the Web site that he'd taken a personal oath to join in the "historical struggle" against the illegal-alien invasion:

> So, my dear Illegal invaders that come to America with the object to conquer, divide, and suck our Tax Dollars, Dear corrupted politicians on the payroll of Foreign Countries like Mexico, Dear Racist organizations with reconquista's dreams like la Raza, dear Communists and Trojan horses on America soil that are trying to destroy our Constitution, creeds and our way of life like the ACLU ... Today you have a new enemy ... and that's me. I may be just an average person, but I remind you, dear enemies, that average men and women made this Country Free and Great! So watch it!

Minutemen Expand Battle

Many in the press believed the Minuteman Project was nothing more than a publicity stunt and one-time event. But they were wrong. Newspaper headlines, the phenomenal success of the patrols in Arizona, and support from many congressmen gave the group tremendous momentum. The illegal immigration crisis was now on the national stage.

"It was time to take [the Minuteman Project] to the next level," the forty-five-year-old Simcox told me in an interview.[24]

After the patrols in April 2005, the group hired lawyers, reorganized into separate corporations, filed to legally protect the name "Minuteman Project," hired a consultant, and started a fund-raising campaign.

Gilchrist, a retired certified public accountant, decided to focus on violations of immigration, tax, and employment laws. The effort was called "Operation Spotlight." His group became the Minuteman Project, Inc.

Simcox's Civil Homeland Defense Corps was now the Minuteman Civil Defense Corps, Inc. The new group would continue to organize, train, and sanction other border watches. They also would continue to rescue illegal aliens lost in the desert with no food or water, and help clean up ranches and private property destroyed by illegals.

MinutemanHQ.com became the dual Internet portal for the two organizations.

Simcox's group recruited citizen volunteers and formed chapters in other states in preparation for a thirty-day operation in October along the southern and northern borders and for other maneuvers. By July, there were chapters in twenty-one states, with anywhere from six to hundreds of members in each chapter.[25]

During October, thousands of volunteers patrolled borders from California to Texas and in eight northern states to report illegal crossings.[26]

One of the volunteers was Greg Thompson, a retired businessman from Oklahoma, who spent October guarding the border at a south Texas ranch. He also participated in the first Minuteman patrols in April.

Later in 2005, Thompson began organizing Minuteman chapters in Oklahoma. He said the local groups would focus on projects such as photographing and videotaping locations where employers hire day laborers.[27]

Also targeting employers was software engineer and former naval officer Greg Taplin. In October, he founded the Minuteman chapter in

Herndon, Virginia. The chapter planned to crack down on landlords and city officials who illegally aid aliens.

"Our weapons are our cameras," said Taplin. "Our weapons are our common sense. Our real weapons are that we're following the law."[28]

In December, Taplin submitted to the Internal Revenue Service and other government authorities the names of sixteen contracting companies that he believed were in violation of various laws.[29]

Anarchists Attack

In the summer and fall of 2005, mobs of self-described anarchists, communists, and reconquistas confronted Minutemen at border locations and at rallies. CNN correspondent Casey Wian reported from one such location, Campo, California, on *Lou Dobbs Tonight* on July 18:

> Wian: "About two dozen volunteers from the California Minuteman Project began patrolling a twenty-five-mile stretch of the border east of San Diego this weekend.... Though there are fewer illegal aliens crossing the border here, it's a popular route for violent drug smugglers."
>
> Mike Lefeve, California Minuteman: "We want to get support for these Border Patrol agents. They're understaffed, they're overworked, and they're doing an unbelievable job out here."
>
> Unidentified group: "Racists go home! Racists go home!"
>
> Wian: "Outnumbering the Minutemen, a group of aggressive protesters who tried to drive the civilian volunteers away. They included anarchists, communists, and advocates of returning the Southwest to Mexico."
>
> Unidentified male: "It was stolen by the United States government, and we're going to take it back. We're going to smash the border."
>
> Wian: "This local rancher had to be rescued by sheriff's deputies after protesters surrounded his motorcycle. One Minuteman did leave his post, but most others stood their

ground. This state senator was also harassed by the mob while touring the Minuteman outposts."

Bill Morrow, California State Senate: "I would respectfully disagree with my president's characterization using the word 'vigilante.' It's not taking the law into your own hands when you're simply being a good citizen and reporting what is a crime."

On October 15 in Arlington Heights, Illinois, about one hundred Minuteman supporters from that state and others attended the first summit of the Chicago Minuteman Project. They heard speakers discuss securing the borders and reducing legal immigration.[30]

Hundreds of protesters rallied outside the school where the meeting was held. One demonstrator's sign read: "The Minutemen Used to Wear White Sheets."

A "small but belligerent group of self-described anarchists" blocked the entrance to the school, the *Chicago Tribune* reported.[31] Five protestors were arrested for assaulting police officers.

Rosanna Pulido, co-founder of the Chicago Minuteman Project and the granddaughter of Mexican immigrants, said several attendees did not enter the building because they feared for their safety.

"It's disappointing that people here could not exercise their First Amendment rights," Pulido said.

On October 30, the California Minuteman chapter held a "Secure Our Borders" rally on the steps of the state capitol building in Sacramento. The rally drew about two hundred supporters and an estimated six hundred counter-demonstrators from "immigrant-rights groups."[32]

Among the speakers were Jim Gilchrist; Tim Donnelly, leader of the California Minuteman chapter; Lupe Moreno, president of Latino Americans for Immigration Reform; and Frank George, a naturalized Cuban immigrant and spokesman for the Texas Minutemen.

Counter-protestors included Nativo Lopez, president of the Mexican American Political Association, and Peter Camejo, former Green Party candidate for California governor.

"We believe in no borders," said counter-demonstrator Tomas Alejo. "A lot of humans are migrating not because they want to, but because they need to. We deny what the Minutemen are about."

Three counter-demonstrators were arrested, including one for kicking a California Highway Patrol officer in the stomach, then attacking a city officer with pepper spray.

"Their intent is to trample our Constitution," Gilchrist declared. "Their goal is not our domestic tranquility, it is our destruction. If it's a war the anarchists want, then damn it, it will start here."

In December 2005, California Minuteman leader Tim Donnelly said support for the organization was growing among political groups, especially Republican women's organizations.

"They're so angry at the president and his shenanigans [in endorsing a guest-worker program] that they're celebrating people like myself and Chris Simcox and Jim Gilchrist," Donnelly explained. "They see our movement as perhaps their only and last bastion of hope."[33]

As of January 2006, there were forty-one Minuteman chapters and 6,000 volunteers nationwide, Simcox told me. Their goal is to have chapters in all 435 congressional districts in the country.

Gilchrist Runs for Congress

On June 2, 2005, President Bush nominated Republican Congressman Christopher Cox to head the Securities and Exchange Commission. The Forty-eighth Congressional District in Orange County, California, would soon be vacant due to the appointment.

A primary election was scheduled for October 4. If none of the candidates received more than 50 percent of the votes, there would be a runoff election on December 6.

Political observers claimed that Bush and the Republican establishment had already chosen the candidate they wanted in Cox's seat: Republican State Senator John Campbell. As a California lawmaker, the fifty-year-old Campbell had a long record of supporting illegal immigration.

Jim Gilchrist lived in the forty-eighth district in Aliso Viejo. In June and July, the Minuteman Project founder was launching "Operation Spotlight" to focus on violations of immigration, tax, and employment laws.

Friends and supporters were encouraging Gilchrist to enter the contest to succeed Cox. Gilchrist had never held political office, but they believed his notoriety as a border enforcer could help him win the congressional seat.

Minuteman Corps leader Simcox wrote an e-mail to supporters across the nation urging them to financially support Gilchrist's possible run.

"Jim is seriously considering running for this seat," Simcox said. "And, if he wins, he'll take the fight to protect our borders straight to the president with *real* border security legislation![35]

"If ever there were a time to support a fellow Minuteman, it is now! We cannot afford to have another congressman in D.C. who is willing to sell out our country's national security for party gain!"

Campaign contributions flowed in from across the U.S.

On August 19, Gilchrist told an enthusiastic group of supporters in a hotel ballroom in Ontario, California, that he had decided to enter the race. The announcement was made on KFI radio's popular *John and Ken Show*, broadcast live from the ballroom. State Senator Campbell and other lawmakers attended the event, a kickoff of the campaign to put the "California Border Police" initiative on the 2006 ballot. Here's the portion of Gilchrist's statement that addressed illegal immigration:

> I'm here today because, like you, I have grown weary and frustrated with the decades-long refusal of federal, state, and local government to simply enforce U.S. immigration laws.[36]
>
> My friends, our enemies love to try and portray us as "single issue" radicals, but they are misinformed and misguided, at best.
>
> The truth is, this "single issue" veils a number of threats to the domestic tranquility of our nation—the floundering public schools, bankrupt hospitals, an ever-increasing tax burden, traffic gridlock, runaway housing prices, and much more.
>
> Because of the failure of our elected leaders to enforce the law, we are facing a great threat to the security and safety of our families. We are seeing the infusion of criminal gangs like the MS-13 El Salvadoran gang into our communities,

and, most seriously of all, the continuing risk of terrorist infiltration and attacks against U.S. territory and citizens by international saboteurs.

Simple enforcement of U.S. immigration laws is not too much to ask.

The fulfillment of our elected leaders' primary duty, which is to protect the lives and the property of the American people, is not too much to ask.

Gilchrist also mentioned a broad range of other issues including undisciplined federal spending, tax reform, "out-of-control liberal judges," property rights, energy policy, and "local control" of education.

Gilchrist proclaimed that on those "or any of a thousand other important issues" he will be "on the side of the traditions and the fundamental principles that have made this country great for the last two centuries, and which are enshrined in the basic law of our land—that being the United States Constitution and our beloved Bill of Rights."

Scores of supporters in the audience cheered Gilchrist. Fewer people were in the audience when Campbell appeared on the radio show, the *Orange County Register* reported. But the senator received "lots of applause" when he stated what he had done to fight illegal immigration.[37]

Political consultants believed that the combination of Gilchrist's candidacy and a probable field of more than a dozen candidates would make it hard for anyone to receive the majority of votes necessary in the primary election on October 4 to avoid a December 6 runoff.[38]

Running as the only American Independent Party candidate, Gilchrist was assured a spot in the December 6 election if no one won the primary. In California, the American Independent Party is an affiliate of the Constitution Party.

Gilchrist wanted to use the title "Minuteman Project Founder" to identify himself on the ballot, but California Secretary of State Bruce McPherson claimed the designation did not meet the definition of an appropriate title so he prohibited it.

"I'm known more by 'the Minuteman,' the word 'Minuteman,' than I am by my own name," Gilchrist said on the *John and Ken Show* on August 31. "I continually have people tap me on the shoulder in stores or at Starbucks or gas stations, and they ask me, 'Are you that Minuteman guy?' And then I tell them my name, and they vaguely remember the name. But I ought to change my name legally to Jim Minuteman Gilchrist."[39]

Gilchrist's lawyers fought the government ruling in court but lost. The Minuteman left his title blank on the ballot and predicted the ruling would cost him many votes.

While Gilchrist was battling the government to simply show the voters he was the Minuteman Project founder, Campbell used the media, campaign literature, and his Web site to portray himself as tough on illegal immigration and border security.

For example, in a September 29 interview with www.townhall. com, Campbell declared he was "very anti-illegal immigration." He said his plan for border security would be to erect "a complete physical barrier across the entire border with Mexico. And then to put federal officers all along that border so we secure that border. And then to enforce the immigration laws on this side of the border both with employers and by requiring not just allowing local and state police turn over illegal immigrants that are here."[40]

Asked in the interview about drivers' licenses for illegal aliens, Campbell stated, "I hate it. I voted against it six times." The state senator added, "I've voted against it every year, including this year."

However, Campbell's voting record and earlier statements to the media told a far different story about his position on illegal immigration. Just three days after the terrorist attacks on September 11, 2001, California Assemblyman Campbell refused to vote on a bill giving drivers' licenses to illegal aliens, according to government records. Also that day, he voted for a bill that would allow illegal aliens to pay discounted in-state tuition at state universities. These rates are subsidized by state taxpayers and not available to American citizens from other states.[41]

On August 30, 2002, Assemblyman Campbell voted for a bill that would allow illegal aliens to use the Mexican matricula consular as a legal form of identification in California.[42]

The August 19, 2005 edition of the *Orange County Register* reported that in one of its March 2000 editions Assemblyman

Campbell "says illegal immigrants should be given the same benefits as everyone else."[43]

In that same townhall.com interview on September 29, 2005, State Senator Campbell said America needed more legal immigration. "I believe we need more legal immigration than we have now.... There are a lot of high-technology companies in California trying to get H1 visas. They want to get highly educated, highly paid visas for these people. And they can't get visas for these people to work here where there are just not enough Americans of this education and expertise."

Apparently, one million legal immigrants arriving in the U.S. each year—far more than accepted by all other nations combined—is not enough for Campbell.

Perhaps Campbell should have asked any of the many thousands of high-tech American workers who have lost jobs to guest workers on non-immigrant visas if the U.S. needs more foreign workers. In reality, shortages don't exist. Greedy corporate executives only claim there are insufficient numbers of Americans with the right skills so they can get sellout politicians such as Campbell to vote for more cheap foreign workers. In turn, the politicians receive massive campaign contributions and get to keep their power.

One week before the October 4 primary election, Gilchrist received the endorsement of Congressman Tancredo, who broke Republican Party ranks to support the American Independent candidate.

"I need Jim Gilchrist with me in Congress," Tancredo stated. "Together, Jim and I can fight to stop illegal immigration.... [H]e's the real deal, he's a real leader."[44]

California Congressman Darrell Issa called for Tancredo to resign from the Republican Party for backing a third-party candidate against a Republican. "I would ask the state of Colorado to strip him of his party membership," Issa stated.[45] Shouldn't Issa be more concerned about the good of the nation than trying to boot Tancredo out of the party?

Gilchrist Surprises Experts

The October 4 primary election results astonished political observers. "The biggest surprise wasn't Campbell, who won 46 percent of Tuesday's vote—short of an outright victory, but enough to secure the Republican nomination for a December 6 showdown among top party vote-getters," reported Jean O. Pasco in the *Los Angeles Times*.[46]

"More striking was that Gilchrist—a political unknown a year ago—grabbed more votes than the top Democrat, Steve Young. [Young is an attorney from Newport Beach.] He also came within shouting distance of the second-place finisher, former assemblywoman Marilyn C. Brewer of Newport Beach, a Republican who represented much of the district for six years."

Political consultant Scott Hart, who wasn't associated with any of the seventeen candidates on the ballot, commented: "This is the first time I've seen a third-party candidate with such a strong showing."[47]

Times reporter Pasco also reported: "Gilchrist will force Campbell—a millionaire former car dealer—to continue talking about illegal immigration, said Mark Petracca, a political science professor at UC Irvine and a Democrat."

"It's not popular with his country club friends, and that's because illegal immigrants are out there cutting the country club lawn," Petracca said.

The race, now down to five candidates, was receiving national attention. Gilchrist was drawing the spotlight with his campaign for securing America's borders and enforcing immigration laws.

On November 19, Tancredo and Simcox joined Gilchrist and hundreds of supporters for several campaign events in Orange County.

Declared Gilchrist: "There are special interests out there, like the Hollywood media elite, the open-borders lobby, and radical left-wing globalists who are trying to stop this movement, but they are getting nowhere. They can't put out this fire because its flames are fed by the right-minded concerns of Americans of every race, creed, color, and ethnicity who are sick and tired of their government neglecting the crisis at our borders and in our communities.... The politicians in

Washington, D.C. are starting to feel the heat, but too few have seen the light!"[48]

Financial contributions continued to roll in to the Gilchrist campaign from across the nation. By December, the campaign had raised more than $600,000, an astounding figure for a political novice running on a third-party ticket.[49]

But Campbell, with the Republican establishment behind him, had raised more money than the other candidates combined.[50]

Gilchrist said Campbell was using his war chest to portray himself in mailings and campaign commercials as being tough on illegal immigration.

"John Campbell's claims that he is tough on illegal immigration are laughable to anyone who knows his true record," stated Gilchrist. "But because he has so much money to spend on his campaign, he clearly hopes that he can 'fool all of the people, some of the time.' The 'some of the time,' as far as John Campbell is concerned, is the period between now and the election this Tuesday."[51]

On December 1, Republican National Committee Chairman Ken Mehlman warned against the rise of "anti-immigrant" sentiment.

"Throughout our history, there have always been Americans who believed that coming to these shores was a right reserved only for them and their ancestors, but not for others," Mehlman declared before the Republican Governor's Association in Carlsbad, California. "Ladies and gentlemen, that was wrong then and those who argue that now are wrong today."[52]

Gilchrist shot back. "Chairman Mehlman's remarks are false, patently offensive, and represent demagoguery in its worst form. He knows we are pro-immigrant—but under the rule of law. Mehlman and the political establishment know very well that this is not an anti-immigrant movement. In fact, legal immigrants and naturalized citizens are a major part of the vanguard of this battle."[53]

The day before the December 6 special election, T. J. Bonner, president of the National Border Patrol Council, with more than 10,000 agents and employees, endorsed Gilchrist during a live remote broadcast of the *John and Ken Show* in Orange County before a crowd of cheering Gilchrist supporters.

Campbell won the election but received just 44.6 percent of the vote in the heavily Republican district. Democrat Steve Young placed second with 27.7 percent. American Independent Gilchrist was third with 25.3 percent, even though his party represents just 2 percent of the registered voters in the district. Only 25 percent of the registered voters cast votes.[54]

But Gilchrist beat his rivals on election day, with 35.3 percent of the vote. Young had 32.2 percent and Campbell 30.3 percent. Campbell won the election with absentee votes.

Gilchrist believed he lost many votes because the government would not allow him to use the title "Minuteman Project Founder" on the ballot.

"That ruling cost me several thousand votes, since many voters who otherwise would have voted for me did not know I was the Minuteman founder," Gilchrist explained.[55]

Nevertheless, he and Simcox declared victory. Simcox proclaimed: "Jim Gilchrist got the national attention of the mainstream media and politicians in both major parties when he astonished the pundits, winning the election day polling with over 35 percent of the vote, and—outspent 2 to 1—garnered 25.5 percent of the total vote despite having to run outside both major parties. Make no mistake, this is a big win for Minutemen, border security, and real enforcement of our immigration laws."[56]

Said Gilchrist: "My race was astoundingly victorious. I sucked away 25.5 percent of the voters in a district that had only 2 percent of them registered as Independent Party members. So, that is proof enough that not all party minions vote the official party line. Now, I just have to get more Republicans and Democrats to come my way and vote for their country rather than for their party.... This election was round one. Even Rocky Balboa never won a fight in the first round."[57]

11 | Thousands of Patriots Across America

"How will we know when we have enough illegal aliens in our country, and how will we stop them then?"

—D. A. King, founder of The American
Resistance Foundation

While the twin drugs of television and consumerism mesmerize many Americans, a growing army of angry and determined citizens is actively fighting to save our nation from immigration anarchy.

This grassroots legion numbers in the tens of thousands, and new troops are coming onboard daily, as more Americans are waking up and wondering where their country went. Many citizens have reached the boiling point over their deteriorating quality of life due to the invasion and colonization of America.

Many of the patriots in this army belong to the dozens of immigration-reduction organizations across the country that help to empower citizens at the grassroots level. There are national groups such as Federation of Americans for Immigration Reform, NumbersUSA, and ProjectUSA. There are regional groups such as the Midwest Coalition to Reduce Immigration. There are statewide organizations such as Connecticut Citizens for Immigration Control,

Mississippi Federation for Immigration Reform and Enforcement, Colorado Alliance for Immigration Reform, and Oregonians for Immigration Reform. And there are many other groups based in cities across the nation, including 9/11 Families for a Secure America, Veterans for Secure Borders, Secured Borders U.S.A., Friends of the Border Patrol, and Mothers Against Illegal Aliens, to name just a few.

These Americans come from all walks of life, from every race and ethnicity, and from across the political spectrum. Many have been active in the struggle for years. Many others joined the fight after the terrorist attacks of September 11, 2001. And many more came onboard after President Bush announced his "guest-worker" amnesty proposal in January 2004. Still others simply looked at their crumbling schools, hospitals, and neighborhoods, and disappearing culture, language, and open space, deciding enough is enough. No matter when they entered the fray, these Americans wonder what happened to their U.S. citizenship, representative government, and way of life. They question whether many of their government officials have any common sense or have literally lost their minds. And they wonder what happened to their swearing-in pledge to "preserve, protect and defend the Constitution of the United States," particularly the part that guarantees against invasion (Article IV, Section 4).

Most of these activists spend at least a portion of their day battling the crisis in some way. Some spend several hours a day in the fight. Many are retirees and military veterans seething about what has become of our beloved country. And a few are so concerned that they left their jobs to work on the problem day and night. All have come to understand that it is up to average Americans like themselves to rescue the nation because so many of our elected and appointed officials are working against the interests of the American people and breaking the laws they are sworn to uphold.

These activists start local organizations; organize rallies; publish Web sites, newspapers, and newsletters; write letters to newspaper editors; fax and phone government officials; launch ballot measures; buy billboard space; produce videos; form border patrols; and try just about anything they can think of to get the attention of the government, media, and citizens. Average people are increasingly running for elected office for the first time in their lives in hopes of winning races so they can do the job present government officials won't.

This rising citizen revolt is against the few but powerful elites from big business, organized labor, the establishment media, well-financed ethnic lobbies, large foundations, academia, major religious groups, and the Republican and Democratic parties' leaderships. All these elites support—in deed, if not in word—mass immigration with its open-borders agenda and elimination of America's sovereignty.

Citizens Fight Back

Illegal immigration angers citizens the most, but an increasing number also are voicing their frustration about the one million legal immigrants entering our country each year when millions of Americans are out of work and our cash-strapped communities are already crowded. Americans across the nation are fed up and taking action. Here are just a few examples.

Since founding SaveOurState.org in 2004, Joseph Turner has organized several successful rallies in Southern California to protest the hiring of illegal aliens. One was on the morning of March 12, 2005, when his organization became the first in the nation to protest Home Depot's support and sponsorship of day-labor centers and its partnership with the National Council of La Raza to recruit Spanish-speaking employees.[1] "Our goal was to transfer economic pain to Home Depot for supporting racist, anti-American organizations like La Raza and for aiding and abetting illegal aliens through their sponsorship of day-labor centers," proclaimed the twenty-seven-year-old Turner. "To accomplish this, we essentially locked down their Rancho Cucamonga store [in Southern California] by filling it with customers attempting to purchase small items. This consumed valuable time and discouraged other customers from staying to purchase. Ultimately, this hurt their bottom line sales and profits for the day." About seventy-five citizen activists participated in this legal and peaceful protest, while Home Depot staffed the store with about two hundred employees, far more than normal. Lou Dobbs carried the story on his popular CNN news program, giving the unique protest national attention. "With a little more manpower and replication," declared Turner, "we can drop Home Depot to its knees and force them to honor our demands."[2]

In Washington County, Utah, residents formed the Citizens Council on Illegal Immigration (www.cciiwc.com) in September 2004. "Many of us have observed the disastrous consequences of uncontrolled illegal immigration in other areas of the United States and the ever-increasing number of incidents and problems coming into our own county," stated Council Chair Phyllis Sears, a retired math teacher. She said illegal aliens in Utah are taking jobs away from Americans, murdering citizens, guarding marijuana fields with guns, and committing other crimes.[3] Utah has become home to about 65,000 illegal aliens as of February 2003, a fourfold increase since 1996, and most are from Mexico.[4] Elected officials in Utah encourage illegal immigration by offering illegal aliens drivers' licenses and in-state college tuition. The Utah organization documents problems caused by illegal immigration and proposes solutions that can be implemented by the community, law enforcement personnel, and public officials. They also recognize local business owners with a "Utah Business Patriot" stamp of approval if the owners can prove they only hire U.S. citizens or legal workers. "We recognize that any group that stands up to right these situations risks being labeled a 'hate group,' 'racists,' 'xenophobes,' or 'bigots,'" said Sears. "Those hurling those labels hope to stop discussions and even paralyze thinking.... It is time for citizens all over the country to form councils such as ours and demand that we find solutions to these problems."[5]

Citizens in Riverside County, California, created a registry of businesses that follow legal hiring practices and don't employ illegal aliens. In April 2004, publisher Nancy Knight and resident Rick Reiss began making public a list of businesses on *The Bugle* Web site (www.thebugle.com) that pledge not to hire illegal aliens. *The Bugle* publishes community newspapers in the county. Knight and Reiss named their group the Southwest California Business Alliance. Their Web site reads: "When the government refuses to enforce our employment laws, the only alternative is a self-enforcement by the consumer." Dozens of Southern California businesses are listed in the alliance directory.[6]

The family of U.S. Park Ranger Kris Eggle has been raising public awareness about the illegal-alien invasion ever since a Mexican drug smuggler murdered Eggle in 2002 at Organ Pipe Cactus National Monument in southern Arizona. "We are trying to increase funding and support for border security, in particular for National Park Service areas," Bonnie Eggle, Kris's mother, of Cadillac, Michigan, told me.[7] "We have sought to spread the word about the sad state of our border areas, in particular the Arizona-Mexico border. We are shocked and appalled by the unwillingness of authorities to crack down on illegal immigration." The Eggles created a newsletter and a Web site (www.kriseggle.org) to educate Americans about the crisis. They have written numerous letters to editors, participated in news conferences, appeared on various news programs, and traveled to several states for speaking engagements. "Our primary goal is to help alert Americans about the illegal invasion, the devastation of our lands and natural beauties, and the lack of law enforcement to really protect our borders. More citizens must get involved and realize these problems won't go away when apathy reigns. Our country is too important to let fall over the cliff, which is what's happening each day." In October 2003, the first annual Kris Eggle Award was presented in Washington, D.C., to the U.S. Border Patrol men and women killed in the line of duty between 1919 and 2002. The next month, the visitor center at Organ Pipe Cactus National Monument was renamed after Eggle. Representative Tom Tancredo was instrumental in both efforts.

Hispanic Americans spoke out against illegal immigration in May 2004 when the Hispanic Citizens for Secure Borders (www.hispanics4secureborders.org), with members in several states, adopted a "statement of principles" calling for America's immigration laws to be enforced. "Millions of Hispanic citizens and legal Hispanic immigrants suffer lost job opportunities and lower wages because of the flood of illegal workers," the organization says. "Hispanic communities suffer from the impact of crimes committed by felons among the illegal population as well as overcrowding in many public schools." The organization asked other American citizens of Hispanic heritage to write President Bush and tell him to oppose any amnesty for people who entered the U.S. illegally. "Your first priority," the group told Bush, "should be to make our borders secure—north and south."[8] Lupe Moreno, a charter member of Hispanic Citizens for Secure Borders and president of Latino Americans for Immigration Reform, has stronger words for elected officials. "When the men and women we send to Washington have no sense of what is right and wrong, we have to change the leadership in this nation," says Moreno. "As for illegal aliens, I am tired of the mess. I say deport them."[9]

In Marietta, Georgia, D.A. King left his insurance agency of twenty-six years in January 2004 to work full-time fighting illegal immigration and start The American Resistance Foundation (www. theamericanresistance.com). Since 1990, Georgia has experienced a frightening 300 percent increase in immigration, mostly from Mexico. King declares on his home page that he formed the foundation "to confront the powers that would destroy our Republic and our way of life. It is our intention to bring together and focus the power of the millions of angry citizens and the many small groups who will no longer be silenced." He told me his goal is to have "full-time, salaried workers in offices in most states. I want to have a lobby feared and heard as much or more than the treasonous Ford Foundation."[10] King has become a prominent figure in the immigration reform movement. He writes often about illegal immigration for newspapers and Web sites. He's made several trips to the U.S.-Mexico border to see the invasion with his own eyes. He has organized a number of successful rallies in Georgia and Washington, D.C., including one across from the White House in April 2005, to protest immigration anarchy. "How will we know when we have enough illegal aliens in our country and how will we stop them then?" the former marine asks. "Our nation is being invaded and colonized. As is our duty, we the people will resist. As American patriots, we are joining to take back an America that has lost the rule of law on which it was founded—a nation that is nearly unrecognizable from only a generation ago. We raise our voices in our common language to demand that our borders be secured, our laws be enforced, and that our Constitution be honored."[11]

In North Carolina, which also has experienced an alarming 300 percent increase in immigration since 1990, again primarily from Mexico, businessman Randy Lewis started a grassroots group called "Stop the Invasion!" After living in California for thirty-five years, Lewis left the state and his construction company because of unrestrained immigration. "I saw it go from the best state to the worst." He moved to North Carolina in 1998. After the attacks on 9/11, he launched his group to protest the invasion. "I found it unbelievable that we had done nothing about the borders," he said. "The problem is, we can't let everyone in, and if we do, it won't be America." Lewis has organized several successful rallies in North Carolina to protest the federal government's pro-illegal-immigration policies. Lewis also is angry about massive legal immigration and warns our nation will become a Third-World country if all immigration isn't brought under control very soon.[12]

In Los Angeles, business trial lawyer Walter Moore took an unpaid leave of absence from his law firm in July 2004 to campaign full-time for L.A. mayor. He ran on a strong pro-borders platform. "Illegal immigration is, in essence, an invasion of our country," Moore stated. "It is bankrupting our government, shutting down our emergency rooms, overcrowding our schools and jails, and destroying our American culture. Illegal aliens have no right to welfare, free medical care, free education for their children, drivers' licenses, in-state college tuition, etc." He promised to do everything legally possible to eliminate the city's Special Order 40 sanctuary policy and "deport every single illegal alien as quickly as possible…. While our city, alone, cannot stop them from coming into the country at the border, we can certainly make our city the least attractive destination in America for lawbreakers."[13] Moore was the lone Republican in a large field of liberal Democrats running for mayor and the only candidate who said he would fight illegal immigration. Due to a near total blackout on Moore's candidacy by the mainstream media and being "stabbed in the back" by the Republican Party, he was defeated in the March 2005 election.

In Escondido, California, Barbara Vickroy leads a group of about two dozen patriots across the nation who bombard editors of news organizations with literally thousands of letters each year. This grandmother launched her Internet writing circle in 2002 but began her activist fight in the 1990s during the battle over California's Proposition 187. Before Vickroy had a computer, she used a typewriter and copier. "I made up a postcard out of green card stock and sent it to 600 people throughout the state. The cards said something about, 'Here is your unofficial fake green card, which gives you free schooling, medical care, and other services.'" Later, she met other "warriors" such as Barbara Coe. Vickroy, a passionate environmentalist, says a forty-year flood of legal and illegal immigration is destroying the country. "It's the sheer numbers of people."[14]

One of the most dedicated and productive activists is Paul Westrum of Albert Lea, Minnesota. He played for the famous U.S. Olympic hockey team having won the Gold against the Russians in 1960 and later played pro for the Los Angeles Kings. In the mid-1990s, Westrum began noticing mass immigration's effects during vacations with his wife in Minnesota. The state has been flooded with Mexican recruits to the meatpacking industry and the relatives of Southeast Asian and African refugees from previous decades. The number of foreign-born residents in Minnesota jumped 130 percent in the '90s. Westrum began writing letters to the editor about the "numbers of people" coming to America. He hand-delivered letters to newspaper editors in Minnesota and neighboring states. Then, working as a team with friends and armed with Roy Beck's videotape "Immigration by the Numbers," he began making presentations to local service clubs, church groups, and high schools in Minnesota. Eventually he inspired many of his contacts to start local immigration-reduction groups. Teaming with Beck and his NumbersUSA staff, Westrum convinced his congressman, Gil Gutknecht, to join Representative Tancredo's Immigration Reform Caucus. Then he persuaded Representative John Kline from an adjacent district to become a member. Westrum's letters have been published in two hundred newspapers in Minnesota and other Midwestern states. His efforts and those of his contacts have been responsible for the founding of thirty-one groups in Minnesota and three in Iowa totaling hundreds of members.[15]

Another patriot in the fight is Craig Nelsen, director of ProjectUSA (www.projectusa.org) in Washington, D.C. Nelsen is a former open-borders advocate who says his "eyes were opened to the severe problems associated with overpopulation and the dangerous naiveté of Western universalists during a two-year stint living in China." Today he advocates ending illegal immigration and reducing legal immigration to traditional, sustainable levels. He also supports "a ten-year time-out on legal immigration while the U.S. reassesses immigration in terms of the long-term consequences of present policy." In 2004, Nelsen launched a billboard campaign in key congressional districts in Iowa, Kansas, New York, North Dakota, and Utah to let voters know how they are being represented. In Utah, for example, the billboards read, "Congressman Chris Cannon wants amnesty for illegal aliens. Do you?" The billboards helped to expose the four-term Republican's agenda and forced him into a primary he struggled to win. Nelsen declares, "Control over U.S. immigration policy must be returned to those whose country it is in the first place: the American people."[16]

In the Rocky Mountain state, citizens with Defend Colorado Now launched a ballot initiative for 2006 to restrict state services to illegal aliens, similar to the Protect Arizona Now measure that passed in November 2004. The illegal-alien population in Colorado is estimated at 200,000 to 250,000. The group said their "pro-citizen, pro-legal-immigration initiative would amend the Colorado constitution to prevent people unlawfully in the state from receiving publicly funded services that are not required by federal law." If the organization's supporters successfully collect the required number of voter-registered signatures, the proposed amendment would be placed on the ballot for voter approval in November 2006.[17]

The Day of Reckoning

Although tens of thousands Americans are fighting to save our nation and increasing numbers are hearing the wakeup call, not enough Americans have yet joined the cause. True, numerous polls for years show most Americans want immigration legal, controlled, and reduced, but not enough are taking action to bring the situation under control.

Many Americans are afraid to take a stand for fear of being called a "racist," "xenophobe," "nativist," or some other name. In today's America, the press, racial groups, and others say you are anti-immigrant if you're opposed to illegal immigration. But illegal aliens are not immigrants, and racism means discriminating based on race.

There is nothing racist about enforcing immigration laws and an immigration ceiling. The U.S. already allows more legal immigrants each year than all other nations combined. Like any other country, the U.S. is entitled to control its borders and limit the number of people it allows.

Still, many Americans refuse to acknowledge the destruction that is taking place. They are living in a state of denial. Many see the unlivable communities around them and don't like it, but uneasiness breeds apathy. Many are waiting for Washington to fix the mess. Still others think they need only leave their crumbling American city to escape the nightmare. Many Americans don't care because the crisis hasn't touched their city or community, but it is coming soon.

We cannot sustain the endless importation of poverty. Eventually it will become irreversible. You need to get angry about this problem in a controlled way. Let your local, state, and federal officials know how you feel and that you want something done now. Otherwise, they will do nothing, or very little, because in reality most don't care about you or America. They care only about control, power, and reelection through massive campaign donations from corporations and others profiting from mass immigration.

We must only elect people with common sense, the courage to enforce our laws, and the wisdom to uphold the Constitution. We must stop voting for politicians who are voting for more immigration while pandering to illegal aliens, foreign governments, and the sweatshop lobby.

Demand that your newspapers, TV, and radio news programs report the harm to American citizens. If they refuse to cover this immigration issue truthfully, then drop your subscription. Switch to another channel. Better yet, go to the Internet, where there is no censorship. Hold the mainstream media accountable for refusing to tell Americans the truth. The job of the news media is to inform the public and keep a watch on our government, not advocate lawlessness.

If the media were doing their job, they would tell Americans the government's refusal to seriously guard our borders, deport illegal aliens, reduce massive legal immigration, and stop developing so-called "free trade" agreements is part of the agenda to erase America's national independence and create a one-world socialist system.

Let's momentarily reflect upon the scene on the steps of Los Angeles City Hall in September 2003 at the end of chapter one:

> After Mayor Hahn and other city officials spoke, Hispanic organizers screamed into the microphone in Spanish, calling for "rights" for the "immigrants" and open borders. The hundreds of invaders fervently chanted back in Spanish while pumping their fists into the air. The noise was thunderous. It resembled a Hollywood portrayal of a South American revolution. But this pro-communist revolutionary activity was real and happening in the United States.

A revolution has begun. Illegal aliens from California to Georgia are marching in the streets and demanding all the rights held by American citizens—and more. They are stealing millions of American jobs and bleeding our taxpayer funds dry. They are ruining our schools, bankrupting our hospitals, and taking over communities and cities with violent criminal gangs. They are bringing in diseases that were eradicated in America decades ago. So many of them have invaded the U.S. that they are changing our culture, replacing our language, and dividing our country.

I do not believe the American people are going to continue to stand by and watch our great nation be invaded and colonized by millions of foreigners. I do not believe the American people are going to continue allowing our government to import millions of legal immigrants to take jobs away from Americans and further crowd our cities, towns, and communities.

I believe this issue will build to a critical mass where it can no longer be denied as the most important issue of our time. The illegal aliens are not going to leave the U.S. when they can comfortably stay here for jobs and free services, knowing our government won't enforce our laws. And the rising tide of angry American citizens is not going to give up their country and continue allowing the government to stand idly—or complicitly—by. Something has to give. Will we summon the wisdom to responsibly address the issue as reasonable people before it's resolved "on the streets"?

The immigration reform movement must become massive.

Pandering, open-borders politicians must be thrown out of office and replaced with candidates ensuring laws are enforced, upholding the Constitution, and putting America first.

We must enforce immigration laws and deport illegal aliens, particularly through workplace enforcement and removal of day laborers, whose presence on street corners is a constant reminder of how our legal system is broken to the core. When we enforce labor laws, illegal jobs will dry up as employers raise wages to attract legal workers. Illegal-alien workers will gradually self-deport.

We must take taxpayer-funded services away from the invaders. This will lead to voluntary deportations.

We must eliminate automatic citizenship by birth for any baby born in the U.S. to non-citizens or non-resident aliens.

We must secure our borders through one or more of the following organizations: Border Patrol agents; the National Guard; state militia units; or regular, active-duty military forces.

Legal immigration must be put on hold so commonsense reforms can be implemented and immigrants can assimilate.

But the day of reckoning will only come if we collectively rise in controlled anger and demand an end to the anarchy. You need to become an American patriot or your city will end up like Los Angeles, with fewer jobs for Americans, bankrupt hospitals, surging gang crime, jam-packed schools that are Spanish speaking and dysfunctional, resurgent deadly diseases, balkanized ethnic groups, the decline of English as our standard language, more sprawl and congestion, and higher taxes for a lower standard of living.

You need to take action or there will be no more America as we have known it. USA will just become an address. You will not be a citizen, merely a resident. And your surroundings will become a Third-World gutter of poverty, crime, and anarchy.

Join the battle to save our nation, before it is too late.

12 | Bush and Other Elites Merging U.S., Mexico, and Canada

"Have our political elites gone mad?"

— CNN anchor Lou Dobbs

For many years, Americans have demanded our federal officials do their job and defend against a foreign invasion entering through our nation's open borders, the seriousness of which was intensified a thousand-fold with the terrorist attacks on September 11, 2001.

Throughout the accelerating process, Americans have been dumbfounded that our government won't police our borders. Why, why, why? has been the question in a million patriot minds.

Now we know the answer, which became perfectly clear in the spring of 2005, except most Americans don't know about it. Open borders and illegal immigration are part of a larger scheme to discard American sovereignty in favor of a regional government, a plan to which President Bush has already agreed privately, but with little explanation of what's really happening.

In March 2005, an Independent Task Force sponsored by the Council on Foreign Relations (CFR) wrote a report titled *Creating a North American Community*.

For decades, the CFR has advocated the elimination of national identities and boundaries and centralizing government power into a single global authority. The CFR includes globalist elites from banking, industry, government, academia, and the corporate media. Knowledgeable critics call it America's shadow or hidden government.[1]

The CFR report began: "When the leaders of Canada, Mexico and the United States meet in Texas on March 23, they will be representing countries whose futures are shared as never before."

The report went on to say: "To build on the advances of the past decade [in reference to the North American Free Trade Agreement, or NAFTA, pursued by Republican President George H.W. Bush and passed by Democratic President Bill Clinton] and to craft an agenda for the future, we propose the creation by 2010 of a community to enhance security, prosperity, and opportunity for all North Americans."

Among other radical measures, the CFR task force called for the free movement of people between the U.S., Mexico, and Canada.

On March 10, just three weeks before the Minuteman border-watch patrols were to begin in Arizona, Secretary of State Condoleezza Rice, a CFR member, was in Mexico City meeting with Mexico's Foreign Secretary Luis Ernesto Derbez. The U.S. Department of State transcript shows that Rice and Derbez discussed the "integration" of the United States with other nations in the Western Hemisphere.[2]

The mainstream media, including "conservative" media such as Fox News, which is owned by CFR member Rupert Murdoch, never told Americans about Rice working to merge the U.S. with other countries.

In response to the Minutemen, Rice said at the meeting in Mexico City that it is the U.S. government's job to protect America's borders. "We work very closely" with Mexico to "try and make sure that our borders are safe and secure as possible," she stated.

If that is the case, why did T.J. Bonner, head of the union representing U.S. border agents, state at a conference of immigration experts in December 2004 that 10,000 people illegally cross America's border every day?[3] Why do Americans tell us that the U.S.-Mexico border is a war zone? Why didn't the media question Rice about her obviously untrue statement and report the facts?

One week later, on March 16, Mexican President Vicente Fox declared that his government would stop the Minutemen and women from defending America from foreign invasion. "We totally reject the idea of these migrant-hunting groups," he proclaimed at a news conference in Mexico City. "We will use the law, international law, and even U.S. law to make sure these types of groups, which are a minority, will not have any opportunity to progress."[4]

The Mexican government doesn't allow unrestricted immigration across its southern border. Why should the U.S.? Why didn't Bush, Rice, or anyone else from the Bush administration respond to Fox's outrageous comment and interference in American sovereignty?

Elites Establish 'Security and Prosperity Partnership of North America'

On March 23, 2005, one week after Fox vowed to stop Americans from defending their nation's borders, Bush welcomed the Mexican president and Canadian Prime Minister Paul Martin to a special North American summit at Baylor University in Waco, Texas. The three leaders met for an hour and reached an agreement on the establishment of the "Security and Prosperity Partnership of North America." They assigned "working groups" to fill in the details of the partnership.

In the media handouts and in the news conference immediately following the closed-door meeting, the three leaders repeatedly talked about broad goals of improving "security" and "prosperity" in North America, or as Bush put it, "this neighborhood of ours." But little detail was provided about the partnership. Here are some excerpts from the White House transcript of the news conference:

> Bush: "We had a good discussion about prosperity and security. And it turns out the two go hand in hand. It's important for us to work to make sure our countries are safe and secure, in order that our people can live in peace, as well as our economies can grow."

Fox: "This is why my government is working toward a true coordination with our partners in North America. We are seeking an objective balance between the concerns that have to do with security and those that have to do with having a good and agile flow of goods and people across the borders."

Martin: "In terms of security, we understand that protecting our borders is a crucial checkpoint on the road to our collective prosperity. Our safe borders secure our people not only against terrorism, but they make possible a speedy flow of goods, services, and people and information among our three nations."

Later in the news conference, Bush said, "I know the people of Mexico are proud of their democracy. I'm proud of the democratic traditions upheld by Vicente Fox." If the Mexican people are "proud" of their government, then why are millions escaping to the U.S.? No reporter asked that natural and logical question.

Bush also talked about an increasingly favorite theme since he announced his amnesty/guest-worker plan in January 2004: matching any "willing employer" in the U.S. with any "willing worker" from another country.

"And the basis of the policy is that if there is a job opening which an American won't do, in other words—and there's a willing worker and willing employer, that job ought to be filled on a legal basis, no matter where the person comes from," Bush declared at the news conference in Waco. "But there's a better way to enforce our border. And one way is to be compassionate and decent about the workers who are coming here to the United States." No reporter asked whether this policy might harm citizen workers.

What the president of the United States said is his administration is going to refuse to accept its responsibility to enforce immigration laws and border security so that American employers can have a never-ending supply of cheaper and cheaper Third-World labor subsidized by the rapidly shrinking American middle class. There are literally billions of people in economic need around the world, and our government wants to open America's doors to all of them. The Bush plan is the ultimate nightmare scenario of globalization.

In January 2005, Wall Street investment firm Bear Stearns published a report saying that illegal aliens hold between 12 million and 15 million jobs in the U.S., jobs once held by Americans, who are now subsidizing the illegal labor.[5]

Arms Twisted to Pass Central American Free Trade Agreement

At the news conference in Waco, Bush also talked about so-called free trade agreements: the North American Free Trade Agreement (NAFTA), which joined the U.S., Canada, and Mexico in a developing economic and political union in 1994; the Central American Free Trade Agreement (CAFTA), passed in 2005; and the proposed Free Trade Agreement of the Americas (FTAA), which would include all of the countries of the Western Hemisphere except, for now, Cuba.

"In order to make sure that the Free Trade Agreement of the Americas has a chance to succeed, it is important to show that sovereign nations in South America that trade has worked amongst the three of us," Bush proclaimed. "NAFTA has been a success. All you've got to do is go down to the border of [Texas]. If you could have gone down ten years ago and gone down today, you would have seen a marked difference of quality of life on both sides of the border. I mean, it's been a very successful program in order to lift the standard of living in Mexico and the United States."

If NAFTA was a "success," why have millions of Mexicans left their country for America since NAFTA passed in 1994? Why have millions of Americans lost jobs? Why have wages steadily declined in the U.S.? Not one reporter asked these commonsensical questions.

At the news conference, Bush said CAFTA is "an important part of the prosperity agenda throughout the hemisphere, and I asked Congress to make sure that they approve CAFTA this year." Bush got what he wanted, but just barely.

The Senate approved CAFTA on June 30, 2005, by a vote of 54-45, with one senator not voting. The House of Representatives defeated the trade pact on July 28 by a vote of 180 to 175, with dozens of members undeclared. The House leadership broke House rules by keeping the voting open so they could twist arms and make deals until they finally had enough votes to pass CAFTA just after midnight by a razor-slim margin of 217-215. "The last-minute negotiations for Republican votes resembled the wheeling and dealing on a car lot," the *Washington Post* reported. In all, 202 Republicans and fifteen Democrats voted in favor of CAFTA. Voting against the agreement were 187 Democrats, twenty-seven Republicans, and one Independent.[6]

Bush and House leaders knew the vote would be close, so the president made a rare appearance on Capitol Hill on the day of the vote to speak before a closed-door, members-only meeting of House Republicans. The president brought Vice President Dick Cheney and Secretary Rice with him. (Like Rice, Cheney also is a CFR member.) Bush sold CAFTA as a national security issue. "'Mothers and fathers in El Salvador love their children as much as we love our children here,' Bush said, stressing the need to look out for the young democracies in 'our neighborhood,' according to lawmakers," the *Washington Post* reported.[7]

Who does Bush represent: the American people or people in other countries? Or does he represent the corporations?

Soon after CAFTA was passed, American corporations began outsourcing production to low-wage nations in Central America. For example, in late 2005, the George C. Moore Co. announced that it would move most of its Edenton, North Carolina manufacturing plant to El Salvador in 2006. The plant weaves and dyes elastic materials used by the textile industry, and had been in Edenton since the 1960s. Moving the factory meant that more than two hundred American employees would lose their jobs in 2006. Edenton's town manager said the company's decision was the result of CAFTA.[8]

In a few years, will the next U.S. president proclaim CAFTA was a "success" and improved the "quality of life" and "lifted the standard of living" for Americans, as Bush said about his father's and Clinton's NAFTA?

When George H.W. Bush was president from 1988 to 1992, he stated his goal for a "new world order" in numerous venues. He didn't explain the meaning of the new world order, a seemingly innocuous term, to the American people. The phrase "new world order" has been used for generations by individuals seeking to control the world through socialism, step by step, in a deceptive and gradual process, as I painfully discovered while spending several years researching America's growing immigration crisis and the reasons behind it.

While the elder Bush certainly could not be called a socialist in the traditional sense, he is philosophically allied with today's corporate globalists who seek a world government, run by and for the benefit of big business, in which the concept of "citizen"—an active member of the nation with rights and responsibilities—has become meaningless.

CAFTA Undermines U.S. Immigration Laws

Leaders and organizations in the immigration reform movement opposed CAFTA and asked the House of Representatives to consider the negative and hidden consequences in the trade pact. One was the Federation for American Immigration Reform (FAIR). In a letter to House Majority Leader Tom Delay and Minority Leader Nancy Pelosi three weeks before the House vote on July 28, 2005, FAIR President Dan Stein wrote, in part:

> This agreement has unfortunate, unintended implications for our country because it will aggravate our already serious problem with illegal immigration, and it will likely create new pressures for increased numbers of foreign temporary workers in competition with American workers.
>
> The negative implications of the CAFTA provisions for illegal immigration to the United States are likely to be caused by the same effects that have generated increased illegal immigration from Mexico under the North American Free Trade Agreement. As the 2000 Census revealed, the number of illegal immigrants from Mexico has increased substantially since the adoption of NAFTA, with no end in sight. Illegal immigration from Central America is already too numerous without adopting trade policies that will likely displace and motivate more subsistence farmers from that region to find work illegally in our country.
>
> You must certainly realize that any action that aggravates illegal immigration across our borders not only does harm to our poorest workers and to our society at large, but it also

further exposes the public to the threat from international terrorism.[9]

In a written commentary about two weeks before the vote, Congressman Tom Tancredo said the trade pact would do more than just phase out tariffs and open new markets. It also would threaten U.S. sovereignty and allow foreigners to sidestep immigration laws. Here are excerpts from his commentary titled "CAFTA undermines U.S. immigration laws":

> Buried among its nearly 1,000 pages, the agreement contains an expansive definition of "cross-border trade in services." This definition would give people in Central American nations a de facto right to work in the United States. CAFTA is more than a trade agreement about sugar and bananas. It is a thinly disguised immigration accord.
>
> The immigration provisions are cloaked as "service agreements" in the document that have become standard fare in most trade agreements.
>
> What those provisions mean is that a foreign company would be empowered under CAFTA to challenge the validity of our immigration laws. If an international tribunal rules against us, Congress would then be forced to change our immigration laws or face international trade sanctions. These tribunals have the authority to rule that U.S. immigration limits, visa requirements, or even licensing requirements and zoning rules are "unnecessary burdens to trade" that act as "restrictions on the supply of a service."
>
> The hidden legislation to open the U.S. border is only the beginning.
>
> If CAFTA were really just about trade, the agreement would be little more than a few pages long, declaring that tariff treatment for U.S. and Central American goods will be on a reciprocal basis. But it isn't. In reality, CAFTA is about expanding a growing body of international law that supersedes our own.
>
> If CAFTA is approved, Congress' "exclusive" authority to regulate immigration policy will be subjugated to the whim of

international tribunals and trade panels—in much the same way that Congress' once supreme constitutional authority to "regulate commerce with foreign nations," has already been largely ceded to the WTO [World Trade Organization].[10]

Surprisingly, most of the members in Tancredo's Congressional Immigration Reform Caucus voted for CAFTA. One was this author's congressman, Republican Dana Rohrabacher of Southern California. The nine-term congressman and former speechwriter for President Reagan has a career grade of A+ on his immigration-reduction report card, as analyzed by NumbersUSA's BetterImmigration.com. He also has supported the Minutemen.

On August 6, 2005, just one week after the passage of CAFTA, Rohrabacher held three town hall meetings in his district. Constituents were most concerned about illegal immigration and CAFTA. At the meetings the congressman claimed that NAFTA's been a success and hasn't contributed to illegal immigration. He defended his CAFTA vote on the grounds that America must assist young democracies in Central America in danger of communist takeover and help the people there, echoing President Bush's comments at the meeting of House Republicans on the day of the CAFTA vote.

That's right. According to Representative Rohrabacher, American jobs have to be sacrificed to save Central America.

Rohrabacher also claimed that FAIR advocated a "yes" vote on CAFTA, even though FAIR clearly recommended a "no" vote.

Just after the vote, Pat Buchanan, best-selling author and former presidential candidate, said on Doug McIntyre's radio talk show on KABC in Los Angeles he was stunned Rohrabacher and other supposedly conservative Republican congressmen voted for CAFTA. Buchanan predicted a "revolt" is coming to America over the federal government's conscious export of American jobs and refusal to defend U.S. borders.

Back at the news conference in Waco on March 23, 2005, where Bush, Fox, and Martin approved the "Security and Prosperity Partnership of North America," one reporter asked Bush for his opinion about "those people who are hunting migrant people along the border."

The reporter's bias was clearly visible, because the Minuteman border patrols hadn't even started yet. When the patrols were underway along the Arizona-Mexico border, the multi-racial, multi-ethnic Minutemen and women didn't "hunt" anyone. They peacefully and lawfully observed people illegally crossing the border, then used cell phones and two-way radios to report the intruders to the U.S. Border Patrol. Here's Bush's response to the reporter's question and the epithet he pinned on the brave and patriotic Americans:

> I'm against vigilantes in the United States of America. I'm for enforcing law in a rational way. That's why you got a Border Patrol, and they ought to be in charge of enforcing the border.

Many media were more than happy to report that Bush labeled the Minutemen and women "vigilantes." The *Washington Post* went further with its "news" story, writing that the Minutemen were going to "hunt for Mexicans," planting in the reader's mind an image of armed and dangerous Americans stalking Mexicans like wild animals.

However, neither the "liberal media" nor the "conservative media" explained to citizens the important news that President Bush had announced plans that America was to be dissolved.

Building a North American Community

In May 2005, just two months after the summit in Waco, the Council on Foreign Relations Task Force on North America published a report titled *Building a North American Community*. It was written in association with the Canadian Council of Chief Executives and the Consejo Mexicano de Asuntos Internacionales.

The report in English, Spanish, and French states that Bush, Fox, and Martin "committed their governments" to building a North American community when they adopted the "Security and Prosperity Partnership of North America" in Waco and assigned "working groups" to fill in the details. Building a North American community means integrating or merging the economies, populations, and cultures of the U.S., Mexico, and Canada.

This unconstitutional agreement is going forward on the fast track. The CFR document calls for the "establishment by 2010 of a North American economic and security community" with a common "outer security perimeter." That means no more U.S. borders or sovereignty.

The plan calls for "a space in which trade, capital, and people flow freely." That means no more illegal immigration across America's borders because millions of Mexicans, Canadians, and anyone else using those regions will be able to freely enter the U.S. Imagine what will happen to the quality of life in what was once America.

Among other radical actions, the plan calls for:

- American taxpayers to provide "long-term loans in pesos" to help Mexico's economy. Isn't the U.S. more than $8 trillion in debt?

- A North American Investment Fund to send U.S. private capital to Mexico. Ditto.

- A "permanent tribunal for North American dispute resolution." That means court decisions from judges outside the U.S. and unaccountable to Americans.

- A "Social Security Totalization Agreement negotiated between the U.S. and Mexico." That means putting illegal aliens into the U.S. Social Security system, and with far less time to qualify than U.S. citizens. Didn't President Bush spend months telling Americans it was crucial that we fix the Social Security system to protect the retirement years of American citizens?

- A U.S. taxpayer fund to finance 60,000 Mexican students to study in U.S. colleges. Why are Americans supposed to fund college education for Mexicans?

- Allowing Mexican trucks "unlimited access" to the U.S., including the hauling of local loads between U.S. cities. Do we need more trucks on American highways, especially from Mexico?

- A "tested once" principle for pharmaceuticals, by which a product tested in Mexico automatically will be considered to have met U.S. standards. Are Mexican standards how we want our medicine judged?

- Combining the military and police forces of the U.S., Mexico, and Canada. Remember that Mexican police are known the world over for their corruption.

- Developing a "North American Border Pass with biometric identifiers" such as fingerprints and iris scans for people who pay a fee, submit to background checks, and "pose no risk" at border crossings, airports, and seaports. Big Brother.

To ensure that the U.S. government carries out this radical scheme so that it is "achievable" by 2010, the CFR calls for supervision by a North American Advisory Council of "eminent persons from outside government ... along the lines of the Bilderberg" conferences.

The Bilderbergers are a quasi-secret consortium of international elites who meet annually to plan world economic and political policies.

The best-known Americans who participated in the CFR's *Building a North American Community* report are President Bill Clinton's immigration chief Doris Meissner, former Massachusetts governor William Weld, and American University Professor Robert A. Pastor.

Interestingly, Pastor has been involved in Marxist activities in Latin America for many years, according to investigative journalist William F. Jasper.[11]

On June 27, 2005, a follow-up meeting was held in Ottawa, Canada, where representatives of the U.S., Canada, and Mexico discussed the implementation of the Security and Prosperity Partnership agreement launched in Waco on March 23. One of the U.S. representatives at the Ottawa meeting was Homeland Security Secretary Michael Chertoff, co-author of the Patriot Act. Chertoff told a news conference in Ottawa that "we want to facilitate the flow of traffic across our borders."[12] Isn't Homeland Security supposed to protect Americans from terrorist attacks? Instead, they are making it easier for people to enter the U.S.

Amazingly, U.S. borders are being erased under the facade of protecting Americans from terrorists. The words "secure," "security," "terrorism," and "terrorist" are used repeatedly in the *Building a North American Community* report. It's like one of the paradoxical slogans in George Orwell's political novel *Nineteen Eighty-Four*: "War equals peace." This time it's "Erased borders equals security." How are Americans going to become safer and more prosperous by merging with the socialism, corruption, poverty, and populations of Mexico and Canada?

Mass Media Ignore Merger

One would think that abolishing the USA would be front-page news. But where were the newspaper headlines screaming: "Bush Administration Agrees to Merge U.S. with Mexico and Canada"? Why didn't TV and radio newscasters bring this shocking and unbelievable news to Americans?

The plan was summarized in a widely distributed CFR news release and available on the CFR Web site. Information about the Security and Prosperity Partnership of North America can be found on several U.S. government Web sites. The report *Building a North American Community* is available for sale. Yet 99 percent of Americans don't know that the Bush administration has agreed to dissolve America's borders. However, thanks to some courageous journalists and activists, at least a few Americans are aware of this nefarious scheme.

For many years, *The New American* magazine (www.newamerican. com) has been warning its readers that our government's immigration and trade policies are being used to intentionally destroy U.S. borders and sovereignty.

On June 9, 2005, CNN anchorman Lou Dobbs, virtually the only voice in the mainstream media reporting the truth about illegal immigration and "free trade," told his viewers about the CFR's *Building a North American Community* report. "Tonight, an astonishing proposal to expand our borders to incorporate Mexico and Canada and simultaneously further diminish U.S. sovereignty," Dobbs reported. "Have our political elites gone mad?"

Renowned conservative icon Phyllis Schlafly reported the merger plan in her July 2005 Eagle Forum newsletter. "The Council on Foreign Relations has just let the cat out of the bag about what's behind our trade agreements and security partnerships with the other North American countries," Schlafly's detailed article read. "Before it's too late, we should rise up and encourage all our public officials to be very zealous defenders of American sovereignty."[13]

Joseph Farah, editor and CEO of worldnetdaily.com, wrote about the scheme in his July 20, 2005 commentary. "The shadow government—the elitists—do indeed have a plan," he explained. "And it is a plan that does not include any vestige of U.S. sovereignty or constitutional government. It is a plan for merger—a European Union-style government for North America and eventually the rest of the Americas and the world.

"It is a stunning betrayal of the will of the American people, the Constitution of the United States, the Declaration of Independence and all of our notions of limited government, self-government, freedom, sovereignty, the rule of law and justice. I don't know how else to say it: It is an open conspiracy to commit treason. It's time to fight the War of Independence all over again."[14]

Other journalists and commentators on various Web sites, in newsletters, and on some radio talk shows have reported the merger scheme, but they don't have the reach of the mass media outlets where most Americans get their news and information.

Calls for Impeachment

In late August 2005, well-known columnists Pat Buchanan and Joseph Farah called for legislation to begin the impeachment process of President Bush for refusing to defend America's borders from the human tsunami.

"Some courageous Republican," wrote Buchanan, "to get the attention of this White House, should drop into the hopper a bill of impeachment, charging George W. Bush with a conscious refusal to uphold his oath and defend the states of the Union against 'invasion.'"[15]

Wrote Farah: "President Bush has had nearly five years in office to honor his oath of office and enforce immigration laws in this country. He has not only failed, he has intentionally neglected this sworn duty, instead claiming he prefers to promote a vague immigration 'reform' plan that involved a 'guest worker' program that has served as an encouragement to the most massive influx of illegal immigration this country has ever seen."[16]

Congressman Tancredo, Capitol Hill's most vocal critic of Bush's record on border security, dismissed the calls for impeachment. In a telephone press conference on September 2, 2005, Tancredo proposed the best way to deal with the border crisis is for Congress to pass legislation with tougher regulations on employers of illegal aliens, reducing the demand for illegal workers. He predicted that millions of illegals would voluntarily return to their countries of origin if they don't have jobs in the U.S.[17]

"Right now," Tancredo said, "I'm kind of hopeful. Things are moving our way, and I don't think anything like [an impeachment bill] is necessary to keep this momentum going."

The illegal immigration issue "is reaching critical mass in this country. Something will happen ... to force this nation to come to grips with this problem."

Connecting the Dots

It is important to emphasize that on March 23, 2005, the day President Bush used the label "vigilantes" to condemn American citizens concerned about unsecured borders, he was quietly agreeing with the leaders of Mexico and Canada to erase U.S. borders and end American sovereignty after 230 years of independence.

The agreement is called the "Security and Prosperity Partnership of North America." Bush, Fox, and Martin assigned "working groups" to fill in the details of the partnership.

The agreement was reached after the CFR proposed the creation of a "North American community" and the free movement of people by 2010 to "enhance security, prosperity and opportunity for all North Americans."

In May, the CFR revealed in its *Building a North American Community* report that, in fact, Bush, Fox, and Martin had "committed their governments" to integrating the three countries when they adopted the Security and Prosperity Partnership.

Americans, Canadians, and Mexicans were never consulted on whether they approve of the political unification.

Virtually none of the print and broadcast journalists working for the giant media conglomerates, which control most of the information in the U.S., told Americans about this merger scheme that would have grave consequences on our daily lives and the lives of future generations. But the media do report countless other stories, including the most insignificant things that have no impact on our lives.

In June, representatives of the U.S., Canada, and Mexico discussed the implementation of the Security and Prosperity Partnership. One of the U.S. representatives was Homeland Security Secretary Michael Chertoff, co-author of the Patriot Act. Chertoff, who is in charge of America's border security, said "We want to facilitate the flow of traffic across our borders."

In July, Vice President Cheney and Secretary Rice, both CFR members, accompanied Bush to Capitol Hill to convince House Republicans to vote for the Central American Free Trade Agreement (CAFTA). Bush sold CAFTA as a national security issue. House leadership broke the rules by keeping the voting open so they could twist arms and make deals until they finally had just enough votes to pass CAFTA after midnight. "The last-minute negotiations for Republican votes resembled the wheeling and dealing on a car lot," the *Washington Post* reported.

Congressman Tancredo and others warned before the vote that CAFTA would threaten U.S. sovereignty and allow foreigners to sidestep immigration laws. "The hidden legislation to open the U.S. border is only the beginning," he cautioned.

Later, American corporations began outsourcing production to low-wage nations in Central America and more Americans lost jobs.

In November 2005, Bush spoke to a group of border enforcement personnel in Tucson, Arizona. He tried to sell the idea of a massive illegal-alien amnesty and admission of millions of additional foreign "guest" workers as "immigration reform." He also defended his disastrous illegal immigration record.

"Our responsibility is clear," the president proclaimed. "We are going to protect the border.... We are going to build on the progress we've made."

What progress? According to the Center for Immigration Studies, the period between January 2000 and March 2005 marked the highest five-year period of illegal immigration—and legal immigration—in American history.[18] During most of this five-year period, Bush has been president and America's been in a "war on terror." Also, the Department of Homeland Security was created. Again, what is Homeland Security securing?

However, after years of allowing the illegal immigration problem to become a national crisis, Bush declared in Tucson: "[W]e will not be able to effectively enforce our immigration laws until we create a temporary worker program."[19]

The president of the United States actually said he won't do his constitutional duty to protect the nation from a massive foreign invasion unless we amnesty millions of illegal aliens and let corporations go overseas and hire foreigners to come and take American jobs.

The dots have been connected. The CFR documents explain the details of the larger agenda that has been lurking in the background for years.

Our government's immigration and trade policies are being used to bring down America's middle class, lower wages, and integrate the hemisphere, thereby erasing America's national independence. Through these methods, the U.S., Mexico, and Canada are being merged into a single economic and political block.

These policies are designed to serve the economic interests of the globalists and the multinational corporations and to centralize government power.

Now you know why the federal government won't protect our borders and enforce our immigration laws—our leaders have a different plan entirely.

If the U.S. trades its sovereignty for membership in a world government, what would become of our freedoms, as articulated in the Bill of Rights? What would become of our quality of life?

Military cemeteries are filled with Americans who fought and died to protect our freedom, independence, and sovereignty. Now many of our elected representatives, including the president, are giving away those precious rights in the service of the latest totalitarian ideology, corporate globalism. How tragic it would be for our great nation to be dismantled piecemeal through apparently innocuous trade legislation, while the attention of the public is channeled elsewhere by the media.

The merger of the U.S., Mexico, and Canada is on the fast track, probably because the new world order elites see that more Americans are awakening to the illegal-alien invasion and internationalist agenda to abolish America. The question is will enough Americans wake up in time to stop this treason and madness before it is too late?

Epilogue
My 'Vacation' with the FBI

Challenges were expected in writing this book. However, becoming the focus of a multi-state national security investigation reaching "the highest levels of government" was not one of them. Due to factors I still don't completely understand, I was questioned about letters sent to the FBI warning of possible biological and suitcase-sized nuclear weapons near the July 2004 Democratic National Convention site in Boston and in other states. You read that correctly.

Coincidental circumstances surrounding my visit with extended family in Binghamton, New York, that month somehow led to this very unpleasant ordeal. I'm recounting the experience in this book because what happened to me relates to the illegal-alien invasion, massive immigration, and the "war on terror."

For two weeks that July, I was visiting my dad, and my brother and his family at their home in Maryland. As part of the trip, I also arranged to interview two of the patriots featured in this book: Congressman Tom Tancredo at his Capitol Hill office and NumbersUSA Executive Director Roy Beck at his Virginia office. In addition, I planned a drive to Binghamton, my birthplace, to visit extended family and to possibly meet my birth mother for the first time.

On Wednesday, July 14, at my brother's home in Maryland, I read a review published that day on NewsMax.com, a popular news and commentary Web site, about a new book titled *Osama's Revenge: The Next 9/11: What the Media and the Government Haven't Told You.* The book is written by Paul L. Williams, an author of several books on terrorism and a former FBI consultant. The review was by Stewart Stogel.

In the review, Stogel wrote that Williams "claims al-Qaida not only has obtained nuclear devices, but also likely has them in the U.S. and will detonate them in the near future.... Williams claims that al-Qaida has been planning a spectacular nuclear attack using six or seven suitcase nuclear bombs that would be detonated simultaneously in U.S. cities." Stogel wrote later in the article, "And how could al-Qaida manage to transport such weapons into the U.S.? Williams points out that the borders with Mexico and Canada are still dangerously porous and not equipped to detect the smuggling of nuclear materials. U.S. seaports are even more vulnerable, he argues."[1]

The article was one of the most detailed and worrisome I had read on the subject of possible terrorist attacks in our country. It reinforced my beliefs about how our government is playing Russian roulette with open borders. I immediately told my brother and dad about the article.

Two days later, on Friday, July 16, I drove from Maryland to Binghamton, about a five-hour trip. It was my first time in Binghamton in about three years. I arrived at my aunt and uncle's home in the late afternoon, just in time for dinner with half a dozen extended family members. Like most American families, we talked about family, work, and stories in the headlines.

I told them about this book I was researching and writing at the time. At least two of them were already aware of it. I described how the quality of life has deteriorated dramatically in Southern California because of our government's insane immigration policies and that the Mexican invasion and colonization has reached states far from our southern border.

I also discussed the NewsMax.com article and said I found credible the former FBI consultant's claims that terrorists have smuggled suitcase nuclear bombs into the U.S. I criticized our government leaders for refusing to enforce our federal immigration laws and protect us from invasion.

I explained that the foreign terrorists who murdered 3,000 Americans on 9/11 had violated our immigration laws and held valid U.S. drivers' licenses, which enabled them to open bank accounts, rent cars, get flight training, and move freely within our country.

In addition, I explained that our government's open-borders policy is part of a broader scheme to permanently erase the borders.

My extended family's reaction to my words ranged from indifference to disbelief to belief. That night, one family member who has known me since I was adopted at the age of three said, "If you don't watch what you say, the FBI is going to come knocking on your door."

The next day, Saturday, I mustered the courage to meet my birth mother for the first time. At the suggestion of a family member, I drove to the neighboring Johnson City Post Office in hopes of locating her home. A postal clerk gave me directions to her home. I spent several hours with my birth mother, an amazing experience for both of us.

On Sunday, I had breakfast with two more extended family members whom I hadn't seen in about three years. Again, we talked about the usual sorts of things, and I repeated the comments I made two days earlier to the other members of my family. I drove back to Maryland a couple of hours later.

Early Monday morning, three FBI agents appeared at my brother's home and began questioning me. Their first question was, "Do you know why we're here?" "No," I replied, in disbelief as to what was happening. Their next question was, "Do you have nuclear bombs in the trunk of your car?" "No," I responded, wondering whether I had just entered the *Twilight Zone*. My eighty-nine-year-old father stood there watching this exchange, also in total disbelief, and my brother's two young sons were hiding in fear.

The agents, who were courteous and professional, asked whether I had been talking about bombs in Binghamton. I said yes and told them about the article on NewsMax.com and the book by the former FBI consultant. I know you're doing your jobs, I told them, but I haven't done anything wrong. I'm one of the good guys. I love this country. Like many Americans since 9/11, I am openly concerned about terrorist threats to U.S. security and our government's refusal to secure the borders and deport people here illegally.

In response to their many questions, I told the agents about this book and that I would be driving to Washington that week to interview Representative Tancredo and Roy Beck.

The questioning continued for an hour or so. I cooperated with the agents and answered their questions truthfully. Then they left.

My dad and I looked at each other, not believing what had just taken place. For me it was an emotional roller-coaster ride. In less than forty-eight hours, I met my birth mother for the first time and was questioned by FBI agents about nuclear bombs.

I cancelled my trip to Beck's office because I was too upset to drive to Washington that day. We rescheduled the interview for Wednesday of that week, the same day I would be interviewing Representative Tancredo.

On Wednesday, July 21, I drove to Washington, about a forty-mile journey from my brother's home. I felt strangely uncomfortable and wondered whether the government was tailing me. I felt the same way walking through giant Union Station on Capitol Hill. Ironically, there was a special display of World War II photos inside the station. Some of the photos showed Nazi troopers marching through German streets. I wondered whether similar scenes would be coming to America in the name of the war on terror.

I caught a taxi and headed across Capitol Hill to the Longworth Building, where Tancredo's office is located. I was shocked and saddened to see what had happened to our nation's capital, where I had worked as a reporter in the 1970s and 1980s. Capitol Hill was turned into an armed camp, with roadblocks, concrete barricades, torn-up streets, and police and military personnel on every street corner. There's no other way to describe it—it was a scene out of a police state. It reminded me of my trips to other countries many years ago when I often saw police and military personnel with machine guns on street corners and at airports. I always thought how lucky we Americans were to live in a country where such authoritarian scenes didn't exist. But, sadly, they do today.

Inside Tancredo's waiting room, I introduced myself to his press secretary, Carlos Espinosa, briefly told him about the FBI visit, and asked if I should tell the congressman what happened. Espinosa suggested I tell him about it later in a phone call.

Espinosa and another staffer joined me in the congressman's office. To my surprise, Tancredo greeted me coldly. He asked me several questions about my background and about this book, two subjects about which he had already been briefed. Then he invited me to go ahead with questions about his views on uncontrolled immigration. As the interview progressed, he began to relax and act more natural.

I left his office and asked one of the many uniformed officers outside the building for directions to the nearest Metro station, where I would catch a train to Beck's NumbersUSA office in Arlington.

At Beck's office, I told him about my trip to Binghamton, the FBI visit, and my interview with Tancredo. He found the story fascinating. Then I interviewed him for this book.

The next morning, Thursday, July 22, I received a phone call from a family member who attended the get-together in Binghamton. She said FBI agents questioned her and said they believed I wrote and sent letters to the FBI that warned about hidden bombs. You've got to be kidding, I told her. She said someone called the FBI on Sunday night, hours after I left Binghamton and drove back to Maryland, and said I was talking about bombs while I was in Binghamton.

Later that morning, two more FBI agents, one local and one from Binghamton, came to my brother's home. They wanted to take me to the local FBI office to show me "some things." They said I could be helpful in their investigation. I was reluctant to go. I knew that under executive branch orders and the Patriot Act—passed just forty-five days after 9/11—the government could pick up anyone it wishes and hold them as long as it desires without evidence or trial. But since I didn't have anything to hide and wanted to cooperate, I agreed. My father asked, "Am I going to see my son again?" "Yes," they replied. This was turning out to be some vacation.

During the drive to their office, the agents said they had seen my published articles about illegal immigration and thanked me for warning about the "invaders." They said I was a "good writer" and kept calling me "the patriot."

At the local FBI office, the two agents took me inside a windowless room, and the three of us sat down. They read me my rights and continued to call me "the patriot," which puzzled me.

Then they asked, Why did you write the letters? Why did you send us the letters? What letters? I replied. I didn't send you any letters. They kept repeating the questions.

Later, one agent placed on the table in front of me an article I wrote, titled "Iraq's sovereignty: What about America's sovereignty?" It was published at www.MichNews.com, a news and commentary site, just three weeks earlier. Someone had highlighted in yellow marker the first two sentences:

> "Mr. President, Iraq is sovereign." Those were the words in a note to President Bush from his national security advisor, Condoleezza Rice, on June 28, immediately following the so-called transfer of power from the U.S.-led occupational forces to the Iraqis.

Not highlighted but immediately following those sentences, I wrote:

> Bush, who was attending a NATO summit in Turkey, declared: "The Iraqi people have their country back."
>
> Mr. President, I want my country back, the United States of America! So do millions of Americans who are sick and tired of our country being invaded by hundreds of thousands of illegal aliens each year while most of our government officials do nothing about the crisis, and many work hard to facilitate the invasion.

The agents then put three letters, three maps, and two envelopes on the table in front of me. All the letters were typed and short. I read the letters and maps but barely absorbed the details because I now was in a state of shock from all that was happening. The agents said the letters were mailed from Binghamton and neighboring Johnson City to the Binghamton FBI office. They said the first two letters were postmarked Thursday, July 15, and received the next day. The FBI received the third letter on Sunday, July 19. The letters closed with the word "Patriot," which explained why the agents kept calling me "the patriot."

However, I was in Maryland all day and night on Thursday, I told them. Then the agents accused me of telling someone to mail the letters. I told them I didn't write or send any such letters. Nor did I arrange for anyone to send any such letters on my behalf. I hadn't visited the Binghamton area in almost three years and don't know anyone there outside my few family members, with whom I rarely communicate.

The maps, which the agents said were computer generated, identified places in Massachusetts and in other states, I vaguely recall, where biological and nuclear bombs were supposedly placed. There was writing and circles on the maps. They accused me of making the maps too, but I knew nothing about the maps.

The agents told me the investigation reached "the highest levels of government." Do you know how many man-hours we're spending on this investigation? one agent asked. Why don't you just tell us why you did it? I've worked in this business for twenty years, and I know when someone's lying, and you're lying.

That was it for me. I had had enough. I wanted a lawyer and refused to answer any more questions. I wanted to return to my brother's house. They handed me a subpoena from a U.S. district court in New York and said I had to provide handwriting samples immediately but had no right to an attorney while I gave them samples. They put a stack of blank white paper next to me and told me to write words and draw circles for what seemed like an eternity.

The agents drove me back to my brother's house and said they'd be in touch. I began looking through the yellow pages for a lawyer while telling my father what happened. About five minutes later, three more FBI agents were at the door, then the two who had just finished questioning me joined them. They said they wanted all of the computers in the house and had agents at my brother's place of work seeking permission from him. The five agents walked through the house and took my brother's three computers. Then they inspected my father's car parked in the driveway that I drove to Binghamton. I wondered why the first agents who interviewed me three days earlier and asked if I had nuclear bombs in the trunk of my car hadn't looked through it then. Of course, the agents didn't find anything because there was never anything to find. My eighty-nine-year-old father, who was a young man during the tyranny imposed by Joseph Stalin and Adolf Hitler, stood in the driveway wondering what had happened to his beloved United States of America. The five agents left.

I spoke on the phone with a lawyer in Baltimore who told me, "Your interview days with the government are over. Don't answer any more questions."

Later that day, I called several friends to tell them what happened and to get solace. I learned from one that I had been on the Capitol Hill Police Watch List the day before when I was meeting with Tancredo. No wonder the congressman was acting strangely when I was in his office.

I was wide awake that Thursday night, listening to each passing car in my brother's neighborhood and wondering if there would be a knock on the door, or if government agents would quietly sneak in and take me away to some secret prison.

The next day, Friday, July 23, an FBI agent returned the computers and left. The agency had copied all the files.

My dad and I thought that was the end of it. Then two Secret Service agents arrived at the door late that Friday morning. They were polite and professional, but also persistent. I told them to call my lawyer. One agent, who said he was on the detail protecting Senator John Kerry, the Democratic presidential candidate, asked, "Are you a threat to the president of the United States?" "No," I answered. "Are you a threat to Senator Kerry?" "No." The agents left shortly thereafter.

The next day, Saturday, July 24, I returned to my home in Los Angeles as scheduled, concluding a "vacation" I would never forget and wondering if the nightmare was over. I soon found out it wasn't.

Two weeks later I received a call at home from the *Binghamton Press & Sun-Bulletin*. Their reporter said the newspaper had received government documents from a Seattle newspaper about the investigation. The reporter and an editor asked me several questions and said they were carrying a story about the investigation the next day but would not name me. I had no comment. But I knew the paper wouldn't stop with this one sensational story and that once the story was published, other media outlets would be covering it.

The story appeared in the *Press & Sun-Bulletin* the next day. A second reporter called and said they were running another story the next day. This time they were going to name me and where I lived, even though I had not been charged or arrested by the government, only questioned. Since they were going to publish my name, it was obvious other media would be contacting me.

I phoned a number of friends that evening and was fortunate to find a lawyer who said she would come to my home the next morning to help me draft a statement explaining my side of the story. It was important to contain the story in this age of media madness and herd mentality when everything is reported without regard to the harm done to innocent people.

As expected, other media outlets, virtually all from the Binghamton area, contacted me. I faxed them my statement. The *Binghamton Press & Sun-Bulletin* ran two more stories, and radio and TV stations also reported on the investigation for a couple of days. The media used portions of my statement.

The Binghamton paper also reported: "The FBI notes that family members interviewed described Sheehy as a 'patriot,' and 'the relatives indicated Sheehy has radical ideas about everything, especially with respect to immigration.'"

Radical? Like most Americans, I want legal, controlled, and reduced immigration. I want our borders secured. I want government officials to do their jobs: enforce our immigration laws and protect us from foreign invasion. And it is a fact that our government is working to merge the United States with the other nations in the Western Hemisphere.

It is a sad day in America when innocent citizens are named in front-page newspaper stories concerning government investigations and described as "radicals" for being patriotic and criticizing the government for refusing to enforce our laws. If the story had become national news, what would have become of my life and those close to me? But this is how the media operate in our country today.

The Binghamton stories traumatized me so much that I discontinued work on this book, but several people encouraged me to press ahead.

As terrible as this entire ordeal was for me and for those closest to me, the FBI and Secret Service agents were doing their job. I felt that way then and still do nearly two years later. I applaud the FBI agents for their quick action and thoroughness. The government has not contacted me since agents conducted their interviews in July 2004. And I have not been arrested or charged with any crime. There is still a shred of justice left in America.

Coincidental circumstances surrounding my visit to Binghamton led to this torment. I simply told my family in Binghamton about the book I was writing and about the former FBI consultant's claims that terrorists have likely smuggled suitcase nuclear bombs into our country. And, exercising my right under the Constitution, I criticized our government. Then someone in my family apparently called the government and said I was talking about bombs. That week I was questioned by the FBI about anonymous letters they said they received around the time I was in Binghamton. Several friends described the situation as "a perfect storm."

It is important to note some of the events that took place in July 2004, the month I was questioned:

- As described in chapter four, Glenn Spencer's team successfully smuggled simulated weapons of mass destruction across the Mexican border, past the U.S. Border Patrol, and into Tucson, Arizona. Some media reported the demonstration, and Spencer videotaped the operation and made it available for viewing on his Web site. He hoped it would help convince government leaders that America's southern border remains a national security risk. Instead, President Bush later labeled as "vigilantes" American citizens peacefully patrolling the border as members of the Minuteman Project in April 2005. [2]

- Fourteen Syrians flew aboard a Northwest Airlines jet from Detroit to Los Angeles. The pilot radioed for law-enforcement assistance because the Syrians were exhibiting suspicious behavior. Thirteen of the fourteen men were found to be in the U.S. illegally, without valid visas, when authorities at Los Angeles International Airport met and interviewed them. The *Washington Times* reported that "several other pilots and marshals have come forward and confirmed that groups of men are conducting what looks like dry runs for a terrorist attack." Syria is one of seven countries designated as state sponsors of terrorism by the U.S. State Department. Asked one pilot: "They came from a country known to support terrorism and no one noticed their visas had expired?"[3]

- Twenty-five Chechen terrorists illegally entered Arizona from Mexico, according to an intelligence report supplied to the U.S. government. The Chechen group is suspected of having links to Islamist terrorists.[4]

Using the U.S. Border Patrol's own figures, 10,000 people illegally come across our border every day and only 3,000 are caught.[5] This would mean that during the five-day period when I was questioned, 35,000 people entered our nation illegally and evaded the Border Patrol. How many were carrying diseases and illegal drugs? How many were murderers, rapists, pedophiles, thieves, and vicious gang members? And were any of the invaders carrying chemical, biological, or nuclear weapons?

I'm sharing this story about my ordeal to demonstrate how our government's priorities in the war on terror are totally misplaced. I support the government's conscientious efforts to investigate all threats of terrorist activity. But why did I warrant a multi-state investigation—authorities in at least seven states were involved— reaching "the highest levels of government," when nothing is done about the thousands of people invading our country each day or the millions allowed to remain in the U.S. illegally? Our government has no idea who these people are or what they plan to do.

If the government was concerned about a possible terrorist bombing during the 2004 political conventions or prior to the election—and rightfully so—why does Congress continue with its mass immigration policy, including granting asylum to thousands of people from terrorist-sponsoring nations, when we are in a war on terror?

Whatever emergency we might be experiencing since 9/11 is due almost entirely to the idiotic and suicidal policy of unrestrained immigration our government has promoted for decades. If the government had enforced our immigration laws, then 9/11 wouldn't have happened.

In fighting the war on terror, we Americans are losing our freedoms, especially our right and expectation of privacy. But there is no clampdown on the open-borders policy causing the whole mess in the first place. Our government leaders refuse to control immigration. Instead, they control the law-abiding American citizens.

The Patriot Act has made all Americans suspected terrorists. Billions of our tax dollars have been spent on homeland security, but borders are wide open.

What happened to me could happen to almost anyone in America. This is what our government and their media puppets have created with their war on terror—citizen spies. Friends, neighbors, and relatives are reporting average American citizens to the government—Big Brother and the Police State. Our government has created a society that makes Americans, including one's own family, paranoid.

If the media told Americans about the daily invasion of our country and the government's plan to abolish our nation, perhaps my family in Binghamton would have agreed with my serious concerns and frustration, instead of contacting the government, as I suspect someone did. Instead, Americans are fed a steady diet of government propaganda disguised as news, plus "reality" TV shows, celebrity trials, and other distractions.

As for my ideas being "radical," I'll close with the following. On April 27, 2005, Congressman Tancredo told a news conference after his Immigration Reform Caucus meeting with the leaders of the Minuteman Project in Washington: "I would like to thank the

Minutemen on behalf of the millions of Americans who can't be here with you today. You have the courage to say to the government of the United States, 'Do your duty! Protect our borders! Protect our communities! Protect our families! Protect our jobs!' You are good citizens who ask only that our laws be enforced. When did that become such a radical idea?"[6]

Sources

Chapter 1: A Stranger in My Own Country

1. Leon Bouvier, Ph.D., and Dick Schneider, "California's population growth 1990-2002: Virtually all from immigration," Californians for Population Stabilization report, June 2003.
2. Ricardo Alonso-Zaldivar, "Immigration laws might have stopped Sept. 11 plot," *Los Angeles Times*, Aug. 23, 2004.
3. Bouvier and Schneider, "California's population growth 1990-2002."
4. "America's poverty capital," *Daily News* of Los Angeles, Aug. 29, 2004.
5. Texas Transportation Institute, Sept. 7, 2004.
6. Annette Haddad, "Least affordable rents in nation found in state," *Los Angeles Times*, Dec. 21, 2004.
7. Lee Baca and William J. Bratton, "Gang capital's police need reinforcements," *Los Angeles Times*, Oct. 29, 2004.
8. Heather MacDonald, "The illegal-alien crime wave," *City Journal*, Winter 2004.
9. Duke Helfand, "Nearly half of blacks, Latinos drop out, school study shows," *Los Angeles Times*, March 24, 2005.
10. Valerie Richardson, "Immigration fuels school-building frenzy," *The Washington Times*, April 25, 2004.
11. Hector Becerra, "Schools beef up patrols after fights," *Los Angeles Times*, Dec. 3, 2004.
12. Jia-Rui Chong, "Getting to ERs takes more time," *Los Angeles Times*, Nov. 2, 2004.
13. Howard Sutherland, "Citizen Hamdi: The case against birthright citizenship," *The American Conservative*, Sept. 27, 2004.
14. Rachel Uranga, "Illiteracy shockingly high in L.A.," *Daily News* of Los Angeles, Sept. 8, 2004.

15. Geoffrey Mohan and Ann M. Simmons, "Diversity spoken in 39 languages," *Los Angeles Times*, June 16, 2004.
16. Tim Sheehan, "Rangers ask help with pot gardens," *The Fresno Bee*, Oct. 12, 2003.
17. Teresa Watanabe, "Hundreds rally on behalf of immigrants," *Los Angeles Times*, Sept. 21, 2003.
18. Immigrant Workers Freedom Ride Coalition, available at http://www.iwfr.org/default.asp.

Chapter 2: Wake Up, America; Time Is Running Out

1. Conference titled "Preserving a nation: The battle to secure America's borders," sponsored by the American Cause, McLean, Virginia, Dec. 4, 2004.
2. Robert Justich and Betty Ng, "The underground labor force is rising to the surface," Bear Stearns report, Jan. 3, 2005.
3. Mary Curtius, "House vote on immigration may signal party battle," *Los Angeles Times*, Feb. 11, 2005.
4. Rep. Elton Gallegly, "State's biggest threat is illegal immigration," *Daily News* of Los Angeles, July 5, 2004.
5. Ricardo Alonso-Zaldivar, "U.S. to bolster Arizona border security," *Los Angeles Times*, March 30, 2005.
6. White House press conference, Dec. 20, 2004.
7. "Jobs crisis in America," AFL-CIO, 2005, available at http://www.aflcio.org/yourjobeconomy/jobs/jobcrisis.cfm.
8. White House press conference, Dec. 20, 2004.
9. Dean Reynolds, "Women upset by intrusive airport frisking," ABC News, Nov. 23, 2004.
10. Rich Connell and Robert J. Lopez, "Gang sweeps result in 103 arrests," *Los Angeles Times*, March 15, 2005.
11. Shelly Feuer Domash, "America's most dangerous gang," *Police Magazine*, March 18, 2005.
12. Shelly Feuer Domash, "America's most dangerous gang," *Police Magazine*, March 18, 2005.

13. Domash, "America's most dangerous gang."

14. Seper, Jerry, "Al Qaeda seeks tie to local gangs," *The Washington Times*, Sept. 28, 2004.

15. Rep. Elton Gallegly, "Remember, we're still a nation of laws," *Daily News* of Los Angeles, April 7, 2004.

16. Hattie Kauffman, CBS News, May 25, 2004, available at http://www.cbsnews.com/stories/2004/05/25/earlyshow/living.

17. Todd J. Gillman, "Local taxpayers stuck with bill to jail immigrants," *The Denton Record-Chronicle*, April 1, 2005.

18. Justin Ellis, "Baldacci order bars questions by state on immigration status," *Portland Press Herald*, April 10, 2004.

19. Carl F. Horowitz, "Housing 'shortages': The immigration dimension," www.Vdare.com, Dec. 21, 2004.

20. Andrew D. Smith, "Illegal immigrants inundate hospitals," *Trenton Times*, Jan. 9, 2005.

21. "L.A. emergency rooms full of illegal immigrants," Fox News, March 18, 2005.

22. Roneet Lev, "Emergency rooms are on life support," *San Diego Union-Tribune*, Oct. 26, 2004.

23. Jia-Rui Chong, "Getting to ERs takes more time," *Los Angeles Times*, Nov. 2, 2004.

24. Madeleine Pelner Cosman, "Illegal aliens and American medicine," *Journal of American Physicians and Surgeons*, Volume 10, Number 1, Spring 2005.

25. Cosman, "Illegal aliens and American medicine."

26. Rep. Elton Gallegly, "TB: A manifestation of failed enforcement," *Santa Barbara News-Press*, April 30, 2004.

27. Cosman, "Illegal aliens and American medicine."

28. "Tuberculosis halts Hmong immigration," KSTP-TV, Jan. 28, 2005, available at www.kstp.com/article/Pstories/S5908.html.

29. "Breaking the piggy bank: How illegal immigration is sending schools into the red," Federation for American Immigration Reform report, August 2003.

30. Hector Becerra, "Schools beef up patrols after fights," *Los Angeles Times*, Dec. 3, 2004.

31. William Lee, "Gang brawl breaks out at SE Side high school," *Daily Southtown*, Jan. 12, 2005.

32. Russell Rian, "Brawl's effects still felt," *The Dallas Morning News*, Feb. 5, 2005.

33. Geralda Miller, "Hug works to solve racial tensions," *Reno Gazette-Journal*, Oct. 15, 2004.

34. Michael O'Boyle, "Migrants changing Nebraska town," *El Universal*, Feb. 14, 2005.

35. "Undocumented immigrants buying homes with fake IDs," ABC7 Denver, Feb. 23, 2005, available at www.thedenverchannel.com/news/4224901/detail.html.

36. "Governor to review disaster request," *Idaho Press-Tribune*, Jan. 24, 2005.

37. "Three decades of mass immigration: The legacy of the 1965 Immigration Act," Center for Immigration Studies report, September 1995, and Synopses of Modern Immigration Laws, Federation for American Immigration Reform.

38. "Three decades of mass immigration," and Synopses of Modern Immigration Laws.

39. "Three decades of mass immigration."

40. Craig L. Hymowitz, "The birth of a nation: At the Ford Foundation ethnicity is always job 1," available at www.americanpatrol.com/REFERENCE/MALDEF-LA_RAZA-Hymowitz.html.

41. William F. Jasper, "Attorney General thanks La Raza militants," *The New American*, March 22, 2005.

42. Hymowitz, "The birth of a nation: At the Ford Foundation ethnicity is always job 1."

43. Synopses of Modern Immigration Laws, Federation for American Immigration Reform.

44. Full list of immigration quotations, Federation for American Immigration Reform.

45. "Correcting the record about President Bush's immigration proposal," press release, Federation for American Immigration Reform, Jan. 14, 2004.

46. "Home Depot forms hiring pact with Latinos," *The Business Journal of Phoenix*, Feb. 16, 2005.

47. "Home Depot names Tom Ridge to board," Associated Press, Feb. 24, 2005.

48. "Correcting the record about President Bush's immigration proposal," Federation for American Immigration Reform.

49. Synopses of Modern Immigration Laws, Federation for American Immigration Reform.

50. U.S. amnesties for illegal aliens, www.NumbersUSA. com, http://www.numbersusa.com/interests/amnesty. html.

51. U.S. amnesties for illegal aliens, www.NumbersUSA. com.

52. "Correcting the record about President Bush's immigration proposal," Federation for American Immigration Reform.

53. "Correcting the record about President Bush's immigration proposal," Federation for American Immigration Reform.

54. Donald L. Barlett and James B. Steele, "Who left the door open?" *Time* magazine, Sept. 20, 2004.

55. "Immigrant's stock share of U.S. population growth: 1970–2004," Federation for American Immigration Reform, February 2005.

56. Negative Population Growth, available at www.npg.org/ facts/us_pop_projections.htm.

57. Jerry Seper, "Border Patrol hails new ID system," *The Washington Times*, Dec. 21, 2004.

58. Chuck Henry, "Terrorists at the border?" NBC4 Los Angeles, Nov. 8, 2004, available at www.nbc4.tv/ newslinks/3901282/detail.html.

59. Rep. Tom Tancredo, "Proposal is 'wrongheaded,'" *USA Today*, March 23, 2005.

60. Henry, "Terrorists at the border?"

61. "Police: Man caught smuggling illegals via underwater tunnel," Associated Press, Jan. 18, 2005.

62. "32 stowaways found on ship," *Los Angeles Times*, Jan. 16, 2005.

63. Larry Altman, "29 Chinese arrested after traveling in cargo containers," *Los Angeles Daily Breeze*, April 5, 2005.

64. Brenda Walker, "Mexico is rich," www.limitstogrowth.org.

65. Enrique Andrade González, "The proposed U.S.-Mexico immigration accord," Mexidata.info, Dec. 6, 2004.

66. Edwin S. Rubenstein, "March employment data shows dramatic displacement of American workers," www.Vdare.com, April 2, 2005.

67. Rob Sanchez, "Mass Immigration: The economy and jobs," *Common Sense on Mass Immigration*, 2004.

68. Nathaniel Hernandez, "Mexican President Fox begins Chicago visits," Associated Press, June 16, 2004.

69. Marti Dinerstein, "IDs for illegals: The 'Matricula Consular' advances Mexico immigration agenda," Center for Immigration Studies, January 2003.

70. Yeh Ling-Ling, "Mexican Immigration and its potential impact on the political future of the United States," *The Journal of Social, Political and Economic Studies*, Volume 29, Number 4, Winter 2004.

71. "The Takeover of America," California Coalition for Immigration Reform audiocassette and booklet, 1997.

72. Valerie Richardson, "Denver school will replace Mexican flags," *The Washington Times*, Aug. 19, 2004.

73. "Celebrating Mexican Independence Day," *Yuma Sun*, Sept. 17, 2004.

74. Miller, "Hug works to solve racial tensions."

75. D.A. King, "Americans vs. illegals in 'Georgiafornia' – DHS AWOL," Vdare.com, Sept. 21, 2004.

76. Jessica Yadegaran, "Call sign KSJO rides its stairway to heaven," *Contra Costa Times*, Oct. 30, 2004.

77. "KLOL goes from rock to Latino format," KHOU-TV, Nov. 12, 2004.

78. "Clear Channel to grow in Spanish," *Los Angeles Times*, Sept. 17, 2004.

79. California radio stations, available at www.shgresources.com/ca/radio/.

80. Tim Porter, "Dismantling the language barrier," *American Journalism* Review, October/November 2003.

81. "L.A. now in Mexico?" www.WorldNetDaily.com, April 25, 2005.

82. Parker Ames, "Spanish radio station reveals plan to give driver's licenses to illegals," www.ChronWatch.com, March 27, 2004.

83. Stephanie Stassel, "Students seek training for Spanish-language media," *Los Angeles Times*, Nov. 12, 2003.

84. Bryanna Bevens, "That 'Guide for the Mexican migrant,': How about 'no'????" Vdare.com, Jan. 3, 2005.

85. Terry Graham, "Bill Owens' guide for illegal aliens: Cash in on Colorado!" www.Vdare.com, Jan. 29, 2005.

86. "Mexico threatens Arizona over anti-illegals measure," www.WorldNetDaily.com, Jan. 28, 2005.

87. Jerry Seper, "Snipers target border agents," *The Washington Times*, Feb. 3, 2005.

88. Public opinion surveys, http://numbersusa.com/interests/publicop.html.

89. Michelle Malkin, "Bloomberg to illegals: Make yourselves at home," www.Vdare.com, Sept. 22, 2003.

90. *Ken Minyard Show*, KABC Radio, Aug. 26, 2003, available at www.brattonmustgo.com/.

91. "US Rep. Pelosi says Wal-Mart arrests 'terrorizing,'" Reuters, Oct. 24, 2003.

92. Rudy Miller, "Morganelli fumes after judge frees, compliments illegal immigrants," *The Express-Times*, Nov. 4, 2004.

93. S.A. Miller, "Are the suburban counties inviting terrorists?" *The Washington Times*, April 12, 2004.

94. "Hutchinson's remarks indicate cheap labor bias of Administration," Federation for American Immigration Reform press release, Sept. 10, 2004.

95. Brian DeBose, "Hunter agrees to back measure," *The Washington Times*, Dec. 7, 2004.

96. Congressman Virgil Goode Web site, available at www. house.gov/goode/20050216.shtml.

97. White House press conference, Dec. 20, 2004.

98. "Senate gives Gonzales free hand on border," American Patrol Report, available at www.americanpatrol. com/05-FEATURES/050205-GONZO-RED-HERRING/050205_Feature.html.

99. William F. Jasper, "Attorney General thanks La Raza militants."

100. William F. Jasper, "'The nation-state is finished,'" *The New American*, Feb. 23, 2004.

101. Rep. Elton Gallegly, "Remember, we're still a nation of laws."

Chapter 3: The Real Victims of Mass Immigration

1. Transcript of debate between Bush and Kerry, with domestic policy the topic, *New York Times*, Oct. 13, 2004.

2. Donald L. Barlett and James B. Steele, "Who left the door open?" *Time* magazine, Sept. 20, 2004.

3. Joe Guzzardi, "The putrefaction of the press: A case study," www.Vdare.com, Feb. 20, 2004.

4. 2004 Eugene Katz Award For Excellence in the Coverage of Immigration, Center for Immigration Studies, June 10, 2004.

5. The O'Reilly Factor Flash, March 22, 2005, available at www.billoreilly.com/show?action=viewTVShow&showI D=189.

6. Valerie Richardson, "Radio hosts line up 'sacrifices,'" *The Washington Times*, Sept. 13, 2004.
7. Valerie Richardson, "Dreier targeted on immigration," *The Washington Times*, Oct. 31, 2004.
8. San Bernardino County's Election Results November 2nd, 2004 Presidential General Election, Nov. 29, 2004, available at www.co.san-bernardino.ca.us/rov/past_elections/archive/110204/results.aspx.
9. Joe Guzzardi, "For immigration realists, an OK old year – a happier new year," www.Vdare.com, Jan. 1, 2005.
10. Ben Bagdikian, *The New Media Monopoly*, Beacon Press, 2004.
11. Jennifer Mena, "'Dream Act' offers hope for immigrant students," *Los Angeles Times*, Sept. 19, 2004.
12. Jenalia Moreno, "Immigrants flee disastrous economies," *Houston Chronicle*, Oct. 18, 2003.
13. Heath Foster, "Immigrants' safety net unravels," *Seattle Post-Intelligencer Reporter*, Oct. 13, 2003.

Chapter 4: Glenn Spencer

1. "ABP brings 'WMD' across border fence," American Border Patrol video, July 20, 2004; and Ignacio Ibarra, "Border group claims 'WMD' test," *Arizona Daily Star*, July 22, 2004.
2. Bill Hess, "Governor critical of Mexican manual," *Sierra Vista Herald*, Jan. 12, 2005.
3. "ABP 'smuggles' second 'WMD' into U.S.," American Border Patrol video, July 27, 2004.
4. *Scarborough Country*, MSNBC, July 23, 2004.
5. Treaty of Guadalupe Hidalgo, Library of Congress, available at www.loc.gov/exhibits/ghtreaty/.
6. "Anchor babies: The children of illegal aliens," Federation for American Immigration Reform, June 2004.
7. Madeleine Pelner Cosman, "Illegal aliens and American medicine," *Journal of American Physicians and Surgeons*, Volume 10, Number 1, Spring 2005.

8. http://www.americanpatrol.com/FEATURES/020125-RIORDAN-RECONQUISTA/SpencertoRiordan1994.html.

9. http://www.americanpatrol.com/DUALCITIZENSHIP/VCTADGASP052498.html.

10. http://www.americanpatrol.com/NEXTWAR/OPINIONLETTERS/SPENDAILYBRUIN092297.html.

11. Jordan Rau, "Democrat's reject Gov.'s nominee," *Los Angeles Times*, Jan. 13, 2005.

12. Dorothy Korber, "Recall of Davis vowed," *Long Beach Press-Telegram*, Oct. 21, 1999.

13. "The American Border Patrol Story," video documentary, American Border Patrol.

14. Noam N. Levey and Jessica Garrison, "Villaraigosa's victory tour is marred by violence at school," *Los Angeles Times*, May 19, 2005.

15. *Sierra Vista Herald*, Sept. 30, 2002.

16. Duke Helfand, "Nearly half of blacks, Latinos drop out, school study shows," *Los Angeles Times*, March 24, 2005.

17. Ignacio Ibarra, "Pilotless aircraft on patrol," *Arizona Daily Star*, June 25, 2004.

18. Jennifer Loven, "Bush vows to ease rigid border checks for certain Mexicans," Associated Press, March 7, 2004.

19. Dennis Durband, "America's focus on Arizona's PAN initiative," *The Arizona Conservative*, www.azconservative.org, June 5, 2004.

20. "The costs of illegal immigration to Arizonans," Federation for American Immigration Reform report, June 4, 2004.

21. "It's official! Prop. 200 will be on the Arizona ballot in November," Federation for American Immigration Reform press release, September 2004.

22. Amanda J. Crawford, Elvia Diaz and Yvonne Wingett, "Prop 200: Migrant issue wins, may head to court," *The Arizona Republic*, Nov. 3, 2004.

23. Mark Krikorian, "Between the lines," *National Review*, Nov. 5, 2004.

24. "MALDEF Files Suit Against Proposition 200 'Pan' Initiative," Mexican American Legal Defense and Educational Fund press release, Nov. 30, 2004.

25. "MALDEF vows to continue case against Prop. 200," MALDEF press release, Dec. 22, 2004.

Chapter 5: Terry Anderson

1. Q&A about President's Bush's immigration proposal, Federation for American Immigration Reform, February 2004.

2. Michael Easterbrook, "Immigration must slow, activists says," *News & Observer*, Oct. 20, 2003.

3. Mark Havnes, "Residents form group to deal with illegal immigration," *The Salt Lake Tribune*, Oct. 28, 2004.

4. Phyllis Sears, "It's up to the citizenry to help fight illegal immigration," *The Spectrum*, Nov. 2, 2004.

5. Patrick Buchanan, "To live and die in L.A.," *The American Cause*, May 17, 2002.

6. Testimony of Terry Anderson, U.S House of Representatives, Judiciary Subcommittee on Immigration, June 10, 1999.

7. "The Takeover of America," California Coalition for Immigration Reform audiocassette and booklet, 1997.

8. Testimony of Vernon Briggs, Jr., U.S House of Representatives, Judiciary Subcommittee on Immigration, Border Security and Claims, Oct. 30, 2003.

9. Testimony of Terry Anderson, U.S House of Representatives, Judiciary Subcommittee on Immigration, Border Security and Claims, Oct. 30, 2003.

10. American Patriot Rally videotape, California Coalition for Immigration Reform and Save Our State, Nov. 1, 2003.

11. David Finkel, "The hard road to a paycheck," *The Washington Post*, Nov. 4, 2003.

12. Ricardo Alonso-Zaldivar, "Latinos now top minority," *Los Angeles Times*, June 19, 2003.
13. Alonso-Zaldivar, "Latinos now top minority."
14. Stephen Goode, "The 'greatest voice in radio and TV,'" *Insight* magazine, Sept. 2, 2002.

Chapter 6: Roy Beck

1. "Endorsement for Sierra Club elections," ProjectUSA, March 5, 2004.
2. Kenneth R. Weiss, "The man behind the land," *Los Angeles Times*, Oct. 27, 2004.
3. Comparisons of 20th century U.S. population growth by decade, www.NumbersUSA.com.
4. The voice of labor – Samuel Gompers, www.NumbersUSA.com.
5. "Three decades of mass immigration: The legacy of the 1965 Immigration Act," Center for Immigration Studies report, September 1995.
6. Paul Craig Roberts, "Job drought continues," *Chronicles* magazine, April 12, 2005.
7. David Finkel, "The hard road to a paycheck," *The Washington Post*, Nov. 4, 2003.
8. U.S. amnesties for illegal aliens, www.NumbersUSA.com.
9. U.S. amnesties for illegal aliens, www.NumbersUSA.com.
10. Madeleine Pelner Cosman, "Illegal aliens and American medicine," *Journal of American Physicians and Surgeons*, Volume 10, Number 1, Spring 2005.
11. Michelle Malkin, "Deadly diversity, dumb program," www.Townhall.com, July 10, 2002.
12. Joe Guzzardi, "Immigration: The line holds in Congress," www.Vdare.com, July 30, 2004.
13. Guzzardi, "Immigration: The line holds in Congress."
14. Congressman Bob Goodlatte press release, Sept. 15, 2004.

Chapter 7: Barbara Coe

1. Ricardo Alonso-Zaldivar, "Immigration laws might have stopped Sept. 11 plot," *Los Angeles Times*, Aug. 23, 2004.
2. Tina Borgatta, "Fight erupts at anti-immigration protest," *Los Angeles Times*, Dec. 9, 2001, and interviews with author.
3. "California Coalition for Immigration Reform and aggrieved individuals file federal civil rights lawsuit against city of Anaheim, mayor of Anaheim, Anaheim City Council members, Anaheim Police Department, and police chief," Judicial Watch press release, May 9, 2002.
4. Judicial Watch press release, May 9, 2002, and interviews with author.
5. Judicial Watch press release, May 9, 2002.
6. Judicial Watch press release, May 9, 2002.
7. Interview with author. Photos of graffiti.
8. Shelly Feuer Domash, "America's most dangerous gang," *Police Magazine*, March 18, 2005.
9. Rep. Elton Gallegly, "Remember, we're still a nation of laws," *Daily News* of Los Angeles, April 7, 2004.
10. Hattie Kauffman, CBS News, May 25, 2004, available at www.cbsnews.com/stories/2004/05/25/earlyshow/living.
11. Heather MacDonald, "The illegal-alien crime wave," *City Journal*, Winter 2004.
12. Susana Enriquez and Richard Winton, "Officers back new vision of sanctuary," *Los Angeles Times*, April 9, 2005.
13. Dick J. Reavis, "Big city, huge problem," *Los Angeles Times Magazine*, March 14, 2004.
14. Robert Rector, "A retirement home for immigrants," *The Wall Street Journal*, Feb. 20, 1996.
15. MacDonald, "The illegal-alien crime wave."
16. Dan Walters, "The politics of budget numbers prolong state's agony," *Sacramento Bee*, April 10, 2005.

17. Interview with author; and Debra J. Saunders, "Pete Wilson's vindication Proposition 187 has painted Democrats into a corner," *The Weekly Standard*, Oct. 20, 2003.
18. Interview with author.
19. William J. Eaton, "Latino panel calls for hiring-sanction 'hit list' politics," *Los Angeles Times*, April 23, 1990.
20. Eaton, "Latino panel calls for hiring-sanction 'hit list' politics."
21. Save Our State, Frequently Asked Questions, available at www.angelfire.com/in4/save187/FAQ.html.
22. Testimony of Rep. Dana Rohrabacher, Committee on the Judiciary, Subcommittee on the Constitution, U.S. House of Representatives, Oct. 19, 1995.
23. Ruth Larson, "Immigration reformer threatened by Justice," *The Washington Times*, Nov. 17, 1996.
24. Larson, "Immigration reformer threatened by Justice."
25. Letters to and from the FBI, October 2003.
26. "Rohrabacher receives death threat over immigrant bill," www.NewsMax.com, Jan. 28, 2004.
27. Ashleigh Collins, "ERs to stay out of immigration checks," *Los Angeles Times*, May 19, 2004.
28. Treaty of Guadalupe Hidalgo, Library of Congress, available at www.loc.gov/exhibits/ghtreaty/.
29. Bert Corona, American Patrol Report, available at www.americanpatrol.com/RECONQUISTA/HERMANCORONATIMES52482.html.
30. MEChA Web pages, www.azteca.net/aztec/mecha/index.shtml.
31. El Plan de Aztlan, University of Oregon, available at http://gladstone.uoregon.edu/~mecha/plan.html.
32. "The Takeover of America," California Coalition for Immigration Reform, available at www.ccir.net.
33. "Rabid Mexican Reconquista Antonio Villaraigosa," California Coalition for Immigration Reform, available at http://ccir.net/MECHA-MAN/MEChAMan-040227.html.

34. David Reyes, "Billboard draws fire from Latino leaders," *Los Angeles Times*, June 11, 1998.

35. Reyes, "Billboard draws fire from Latino leaders."

36. Mario Obledo, American Patrol Report, available at www.americanpatrol.com/REFERENCE/ obledospanicstate990610.html.

37. Mike Soraghan, "Anti-immigration groups to host Tancredo; Event's planners accused of hate," *Denver Post*, Oct. 30, 2003.

38. Joe Guzzardi, "Treason in Colorado: Tom Tancredo vs. the *Denver Post*," www.Vdare.com, Oct. 8, 2002.

39. Save Our State, Frequently Asked Questions, available at www.angelfire.com/in4/save187/FAQ.html.

40. Save Our State, Frequently Asked Questions, available at www.angelfire.com/in4/save187/FAQ.html.

41. "Adios to a mean initiative," *Los Angeles Times*, May 1, 2004.

42. "Save our license initiative will stop government from giving benefits to illegal aliens," www.saveourlicense. com, Aug. 4, 2004.

43. "Save our license initiative," www.saveourlicense.com.

44. "Save our license initiative," www.saveourlicense.com.

45. "Save our license initiative," www.saveourlicense.com.

Chapter 8: Joe Guzzardi

1. Joe Guzzardi, "The education of Joe Guzzardi," www. Vdare.com, Feb. 8, 2002.
2. "Ten good reasons to recall Gray Davis," *Human Events*, Sept. 29, 2003.
3. John Gizzi, "Californians start movement to recall Davis," *Human Events*, Feb. 28, 2003.
4. "Effort to recall California Gov. Davis now considered likely to make ballot," Associated Press, June 16, 2003.
5. "California governor to face recall vote," www.CNN. com, July 25, 2003.
6. "California governor to face recall vote," www.CNN. com.
7. Joe Guzzardi, "Recalling Davis—and ending immigration?" www.Vdare.com, June 27, 2003.
8. Guzzardi, "Recalling Davis—and ending immigration?"
9. Joe Guzzardi, "I voted for Proposition 187—and I would vote for it again today," www.CalNews.com, Aug. 20, 2003.
10. "California governor to face recall vote," www.CNN. com.
11. Joe Guzzardi, "If you want change, vote for me," www. CalNews.com, Aug. 8, 2003.
12. Joe Guzzardi, "Establishment to California: Shut up about immigration in this election!" www.Vdare.com, Aug. 8, 2003.
13. Joe Guzzardi, "Joe Guzzardi returns from the campaign trail!" www.Vdare.com, Oct. 7, 2003.
14. Save Our License Web site, Nov. 25, 2003.
15. Leon Bouvier, Ph.D., and Dick Schneider, "California's population growth 1990-2002: Virtually all from immigration," Californians for Population Stabilization report, June 2003.
16. Bouvier and Schneider, "California's population growth 1990-2002."

17. Joe Guzzardi, "View from Lodi, CA: Immigration-driven sprawl continues to appall," www.Vdare.com, July 18, 2003.
18. Joe Guzzardi, "Joe Guzzardi replies to Eric Stern," www.Vdare.com, Oct. 24, 2003.
19. Joe Guzzardi, "More not so savory stuff about Lt. Gov. Cruz Bustamante," www.CalNews.com, Sept. 6, 2003.
20. Results of the 2003 California recall, Wikipedia, The free encyclopedia, http://en.wikipedia.org/wiki/Results_of_the_2003_California_recall.
21. Joe Guzzardi, "Why I won," www.Vdare.com, Oct. 10, 2003.

Chapter 9: Tom Tancredo

1. Jerry Seper, "Bush's 'open door' slammed," *The Washington Times*, April 19, 2002.
2. Holly Bailey and Daren Briscoe, "Crossing over: Bush's other battle," *Newsweek*, Feb. 7, 2005.
3. Betsy Rothstein, "Tancredo to fight over immigration," *The Hill*, Aug. 30, 2004.
4. Steve Quayle, "Border troops sought to halt illegal aliens," *The Washington Times*, June 19, 2002.
5. Quayle, "Border troops sought to halt illegal aliens."
6. "Tancredo describes GOP platform on immigration as weak, Clintonesque," press release, Aug. 25, 2004.
7. www.tennesseansfortancredo.com/.
8. Chad Groening, Agape Press, Aug. 25, 2004.
9. "Tancredo considers White House bid," www.WorldNetDaily.com, March 28, 2005.
10. American Patriot Rally videotape, California Coalition for Immigration Reform and Save Our State, Nov. 1, 2003.
11. American Patriot Rally videotape, California Coalition for Immigration Reform and Save Our State.
12. Steve Brown, Tancredo interview, FrontPageMagazine.com, Dec. 22, 2003.

13. K.C. McAlpin, "Common Sense on Mass Immigration," The Social Contract Press, 2004.

14. Julia Malone, "Immigration critic stirs controversy, sees gains," Cox, June 21, 2002.

15. Linda Gorman and Robert Drake, "Compassion vs. Compulsion," Independence Institute, May 1, 1995, available at http://i2i.org/article.aspx?ID=880.

16. Special Order Speech, Feb. 24, 2004.

17. American Patriot Rally videotape, California Coalition for Immigration Reform and Save Our State.

18. Special Order Speech, May 15, 2003.

19. Special Order Speech, May 15, 2003.

20. President Bush Proposes New Temporary Worker Program, White House, Jan. 7, 2004.

21. "Special interests big winners in White House immigration plan," Federation for American Immigration Reform press release, Jan. 7, 2004.

22. Jerry Seper, "Border council calls Bush plan 'slap in the face,'" The Washington Times, Jan. 12, 2004.

23. Ricardo Alonso-Zaldivar, "Bush would open U.S. to guest workers," Los Angeles Times, Jan. 8, 2004.

24. Lawrence Auster, "Letter to Bush," www. ViewFromTheRight.com, Jan. 12, 2004.

25. "Savage: Impeach Bush over immigration plan," www. WorldNetDaily.com, Jan. 12, 2004.

26. "Bush amnesty backlash may signal turning point," www.ProjectUSA.org, Jan. 14, 2004.

27. "Tancredo calls president's immigration proposals 'dangerous and unworkable,'" press release, Jan. 7, 2004.

28. "Tancredo calls president's immigration proposals 'dangerous and unworkable,'" press release.

29. U.S. amnesties for illegal aliens, www.NumbersUSA. com.

30. Public opinion, www.NumbersUSA.com.

31. Alonso-Zaldivar, "Bush would open U.S. to guest workers."

32. Alonso-Zaldivar, "Bush would open U.S. to guest workers."
33. Alonso-Zaldivar, "Bush would open U.S. to guest workers."
34. Alonso-Zaldivar, "Bush would open U.S. to guest workers."
35. Valerie Richardson, "Republicans warn Bush on immigration proposal," *The Washington Times*, Jan. 28, 2004.
36. Richardson, "Republicans warn Bush on immigration proposal."
37. Amy Fagan, "Democrats offer plan on aliens," *The Washington Times*, Jan. 29, 2004.
38. "Democrats declare war on working men & women in the United States," Tancredo press release, Jan. 30, 2004.
39. Ralph Z. Hallow and James G. Lakely, "GOP slams Bush policies at retreat," *The Washington Times*, Feb. 6, 2004.
40. Stephen Dinan, "Bush 'amnesty' blamed for rise in illegals," *The Washington Times*, April 16, 2004.
41. Dinan, "Bush 'amnesty' blamed for rise in illegals."
42. Mark Krikorian, "Amnesties beget more illegal immigration," *National Review*, Oct. 16, 2000.
43. Juan Mann, "Amnesty betrayals past and present—A handy reference guide," www.Vdare.com, Aug. 30, 2004.
44. Craig Nelsen, "Divided USA, divided GOP, divided Bush-Cheney website," ProjectUSA, Sept. 2, 2004.
45. Malone, "Immigration critic stirs controversy, sees gains."
46. "Rohrabacher receives death threat over immigrant bill," www.NewsMax.com, Jan. 28, 2004.
47. "Congressman wants to 'stop amnesty' at GOP convention," Tancredo press release, Aug. 23, 2004.
48. From the Web site of Congressman Virgil Goode, available at www.house.gov/goode/20050216.shtml.

49. Mark Krirkorian, "Splintered plank: The White House spins and misses on immigration," *National Review*, Aug. 26, 2004.

50. Sergio Bustos, "GOP delegates divided over party's immigration position," *USA Today*, Aug. 27, 2004.

51. Ralph Z. Hallow, "GOP to finesse immigration issue," *The Washington Times*, Aug. 23, 2004.

52. Froma Harrop, "Border splits the GOP," *The Providence Journal*, Sept. 2, 2004.

53. "Some family, survivors say GOP exploits 9/11 terror attacks," NY1 News, Aug. 30, 2004.

54. Joe Guzzardi, "Treason in Colorado: Tom Tancredo vs. the *Denver Post*," www.Vdare.com, Oct. 8, 2002.

55. Cindy Rodriguez, "Newcomer takes aim at Tancredo," *Denver Post*, March 3, 2004.

56. Craig Nelsen, "Columnist embarrasses *Denver Post*, raises ethical questions," March 8, 2004, ProjectUSA.

57. "A platform for immigrants," *New York Times*, Aug. 29, 2004.

58. Public Opinion, www.NumbersUSA.com.

59. "First Data/Western Union and Latino Advocacy Organizations Call for Action on Immigration Reform," HispanicBusiness.com, Feb. 27, 2004.

60. Joe Guzzardi, "Western disunion: CEO Charlie Fote betrays America," www.Vdare.com, July 28, 2004.

61. Campaign election results, CBSNews.com, available at http://election.cbsnews.com/election2004/state/state_co.shtml.

62. American Patriot Rally videotape, California Coalition for Immigration Reform and Save Our State.

Chapter 10: The Minuteman Project

1. James Gilchrist, "Update: The Minuteman Project," e-mail, Oct. 20, 2004.

2. Steve Lopez, "Posse is headed for the wrong roundup," *Los Angeles Times*, April 1, 2005.

3. Chris Richard, "Minuteman border project challenged by activists," *The Press-Enterprise*, March 19, 2005.

4. "The Takeover of America," California Coalition for Immigration Reform, www.ccir.net.

5. "Remarks with Mexican Foreign Secretary Ernesto Derbez," http://www.state.gov/secretary/rm/2005/43229.htm, March 10, 2005.

6. Wesley Pruden, "Mr. Fox's elephant at the summit," *The Washington Times*, March 22, 2005.

7. "President meets with President Fox and Prime Minister Martin," www.WhiteHouse.gov, March 23, 2005.

8. "Vigilantes," *The Washington Times*, March 25, 2005.

9. "ACLU, advocacy groups fear anti-immigration violence," American Civil Liberties Union press release, March 30, 2005.

10. Jerry Seper, "ACLU to keep tabs on protest," *The Washington Times*, March 21, 2005.

11. Seper, "ACLU to keep tabs on protest."

12. "Minuteman Project causes concern in Mexico," KVOA-TV, March 30, 2005.

13. "Showdown at border," www.WorldNetDaily.com, March 7, 2005

14. Rich Connell and Robert J. Lopez, "Gang sweeps result in 103 arrests," *Los Angeles Times*, March 15, 2005.

15. "Aztecs confront minutemen," www.AmericanPatrol.com, April 2, 2005.

16. "Excerpts from Congressman Tom Tancredo's speech to the Minutemen rally," teamamericapac.org, April 2005.

17. Margaret Talev, "Minutemen gather near Mexico border," *Star Tribune*, April 2, 2005.

18. "Minutemen send message to president," 9*1*1, California Coalition for Immigration Reform newsletter, April 2004.

19. Letter from Rep. Tancredo to James Gilchrist and Chris Simcox, April 11, 2005.

20. Letter from Rep. Tancredo to James Gilchrist and Chris Simcox.

21. Minuteman Project press release, April 18, 2005.
22. "Comments from CIRC Members on Minutemen," Tancredo news release, April 27, 2005.
23. Author interview with Gianluca Zanna, Jan. 30, 2006.
24. Author interview with Chris Simcox, Jan. 27, 2006.
25. *Lou Dobbs Tonight*, CNN, July 18, 2005.
26. Keyonna Summers, "Hispanic group challenges Minuteman initiative," *The Washington Times*, Oct. 22, 2005.
27. Judy Gibbs, "Group to focus on illegal workers," *The Oklahoman*, Dec. 23, 2005.
28. Summers, "Hispanic group challenges Minuteman initiative."
29. Brynn Grimley, "Minutemen surveillance," *Herndon Connection*, Dec. 15, 2005.
30. Oscar Avila, "2 sides clash over immigration," *Chicago Tribune*, Oct. 16, 2005; and Chicago Public Radio report, Oct. 15, 2005.
31. Avila, "2 sides clash over immigration."
32. Matt Weiser, "Immigration clash at capitol," *Sacramento Bee*, Oct. 30, 2005.
33. Arthur H. Rotstein, "Group opposing illegal immigration gains national foothold," Associated Press, Dec. 17, 2005.
34. Author interview with Chris Simcox, Jan. 27, 2006.
35. "Minuteman co-founder to run for Congress?" www.worldnetdaily.com, Aug. 10, 2005.
36. "Jim Gilchrist to run for Congress!" www.jimgilchrist.com, Aug. 19, 2005,
37. Dena Bunis, "A new focus on immigration," *Orange County Register*, Aug. 20, 2005.
38. Bunis, "A new focus on immigration."
39. "Transcript: Jim Gilchrist on the *John and Ken Show*," www.jimgilchrist.com, Aug. 31, 2005.
40. Tim Chapman, "Interview with CA state Senator John Campbell," www.townhall.com, Sept. 29, 2005.
41. www.leginfo.ca.gov.

42. www.leginfo.ca.gov.

43. Frank Mickadeit, "Campbell says a border wall might do the job," *Orange County Register*, Aug. 19, 2005.

44. "Republican Congressman Tom Tancredo breaks party ranks to endorse Gilchrist," Jim Gilchrist campaign news release, Sept. 27, 2005.

45. *National Journal*, September 2005.

46. Jean O. Pasco, "Minuteman a wild card in O.C. race," *Los Angeles Times*, Oct. 6, 2006.

47. Pasco, "Minuteman a wild card in O.C. race."

48. "Congressman Tom Tancredo, Minuteman leader Chris Simcox join Jim Gilchrist for Monday campaign events," Gilchrist press release, Nov. 19, 2005.

49. Dena Bunis and Martin Wisckol, "John Campbell: O.C.'s newest congressman," *Orange County Register*, Dec. 7, 2005.

50. Bunis and Wisckol, "John Campbell: O.C.'s newest congressman."

51. "Gilchrist labels Campbell 'suspect' on border security and illegal immigration," Gilchrist press release, Dec. 1, 2005.

52. Dan Balz, "GOP official urges caution on immigrants," *Washington Post*, Dec. 2, 2005.

53. "GOP national chairman Mehlman is the one on the 'wrong side of history,' says Minuteman Jim Gilchrist," Gilchrist press release, Dec. 2, 2005.

54. www.smartvoter.org.

55. Author interview with Jim Gilchrist, February 2006.

56. Minuteman Civil Defense Corps e-mail, Dec. 24, 2005.

57. Joe Guzzardi, "Candidate Gilchrist: 'Rocky Balboa never won a fight in the first round.' Grinch Guzzardi: 'Too bad!'" www.Vdare.com, Dec. 16, 2005.

Chapter 11: Thousands of Patriots Across America

1. "Home Depot forms hiring pact with Latinos," *The Business Journal of Phoenix*, Feb. 16, 2005.
2. Joe Turner's summary of protest, www.saveourstate.org.
3. Phyllis Sears, "It's up to the citizenry to help fight illegal immigration," *The Spectrum/Daily News*, Nov. 2, 2004.
4. Valerie Richardson, "Utahans target businesses to fight illegal immigration," *The Washington Times*, Dec. 13, 2004.
5. Sears, "It's up to the citizenry to help fight illegal immigration."
6. Henri Brickey, "Hiring pledge getting notice," *The Press-Enterprise*, Sept. 9, 2004.
7. Interview with author, November 2004.
8. www.hispanics4secureborders.org.
9. Interview with author, April 2004.
10. Interview with author, December 2003.
11. www.theamericanresistance.com.
12. Michael Easterbrook, "Immigration must slow, activists say," *The News & Observer*, Oct. 20, 2003.
13. www.mayor4u.com.
14. Interview with author, November 2003.
15. Interview with Linda Purdue, formerly of NumbersUSA, for the author, November 2004.
16. www.projectusa.org.
17. Defend Colorado Now news release, Jan. 3, 2006.

Chapter 12: Bush and Other Elites Merging the U.S., Mexico, and Canada

1. James Perloff, *The Shadows of Power*, Western Islands, 2005.
2. "Remarks with Mexican Foreign Secretary Ernesto Derbez," U.S. Department of State Web site, March 10, 2005.

3. "Preserving a nation: The battle to secure America's borders," conference sponsored by the American Cause, McLean, Virginia, Dec. 4, 2004.

4. Wesley Pruden, "Mr. Fox's elephant at the summit," *The Washington Times*, March 22, 2005.

5. Robert Justich and Betty Ng, "The underground labor force is rising to the surface," Bear Stearns report, Jan. 3, 2005.

6. Paul Blustein and Mike Allen, "Trade pact approved by House," *The Washington Post*, July 28, 2005.

7. Blustein and Allen, "Trade pact approved by House."

8. "CAFTA blamed for layoffs at Edenton textile plant," Associated Press, Dec. 3, 2005.

9. Dan Stein, "FAIR's statement regarding proposed CAFTA treaty," Federation for American Immigration Reform, July 5, 2005.

10. Tom Tancredo, "CAFTA undermines immigration laws," *North County Times*, July 17, 2005.

11. William F. Jasper, "Council for revolution," *The New American*, Oct. 3, 2005.

12. "North American officials outline common security, prosperity plans," U.S. Department of State, June 28, 2005.

13. "*The Phyllis Schlafly Report*," July 2005.

14. Joseph Farah, "Merger with Mexico," www.worldnetdaily.com, July 20, 2005.

15. Patrick J. Buchanan, "A national emergency," www.worldnetdaily.com, Aug. 29, 2005.

16. Joseph Farah, "Impeach Bush," www.worldnetdaily.com, Aug. 31, 2005.

17. Ron Strom, "Tancredo won't initiate Bush impeachment," www.worldnetdaily.com, Sept. 2, 2005.

18. Steven A. Camarota, "Immigrants at mid-decade," Center for Immigration Studies, December 2005.

19. "President Discusses Border Security and Immigration Reform in Arizona," White House transcript, Nov. 28, 2005.

Epilogue: My 'Vacation' with the FBI

1. Stewart Stogel, "Author: Al-Qaida has nuclear weapons inside U.S.," www.NewsMax.com, July 14, 2004.
2. "ABP brings 'WMD' across border fence," American Border Patrol video, July 20, 2004; and Ignacio Ibarra, "Border group claims 'WMD' test," *Arizona Daily Star*, July 22, 2004.
3. Audrey Hudson, "Syrians flew with expired visas," *The Washington Times*, July 27, 2004.
4. Bill Gertz, "Chechen terrorists probed," *The Washington Times*, Oct. 13, 2004.
5. "Preserving a nation: The battle to secure America's borders," conference sponsored by the American Cause, McLean, Virginia, Dec. 4, 2004.
6. "Comments from CIRC members on Minutemen," Congressman Tom Tancredo press release, April 27, 2005.

Index

W

Y

Z

Photo by Gary Kious

About the Author

Daniel Sheehy's communications career has spanned broadcast and print journalism, corporate communications, and public speaking. He first worked as an assistant news producer and writer for WBAL-TV in Baltimore while completing his studies at Towson University in Maryland, where he received a bachelor's degree in mass communications. Afterward, he worked as a business reporter at *Aviation Daily* in Washington, D.C. Later, Sheehy worked as a corporate communications manager, writer, and editor for United Airlines, TRW Space & Electronics, and other companies. He has been a guest on numerous radio talk shows and spoken to scores of organizations about immigration and plans for a North American Union. He lives in Southern California.